# A More Perfect Union

# A More Perfect Union

DOCUMENTS IN U.S. HISTORY

FIFTH EDITION

## Volume 1: To 1877

**Paul F. Boller, Jr.**

*Professor Emeritus, Texas Christian University*

**Ronald Story**

*University of Massachusetts, Amherst*

HOUGHTON MIFFLIN COMPANY

Boston    New York

*To Martin and Eliza*

Sponsoring Editor: Colleen Kyle
Associate Editor: Leah Strauss
Senior Project Editor: Christina M. Horn
Senior Production/Design Coordinator: Carol Merrigan
Assistant Manufacturing Coordinator: Andrea Wagner
Senior Cover Design Coordinator: Deborah Azerrad Savona
Senior Marketing Manager: Sandra McGuire


Cover Design: Wing Ngan/Stoltze Design
Cover Image: © Everett C. Johnson/© FOLIO, Inc.

Printed in the U.S.A.

Library of Congress Catalog Card Number: 99-72019

ISBN: 0-395-95958-6

23456789-CS-03 02 01 00

# CONTENTS

CHAPTER FOUR
★————————————————

# The Age of Reform

CHAPTER FIVE

★————————————

# Rebels, Yankees, and Freedmen

# PREFACE

Our two-volume reader, *A More Perfect Union: Documents in U.S. History*, presents students with the original words of speeches and testimony, political and legal writings, and literature that have reflected, precipitated, and implemented pivotal events of the past four centuries. The readings in Volume I cover the era from Columbus's voyage of discovery to Reconstruction. Volume II begins with the post–Civil War period and concludes with selections that relate to recent history. We are pleased with the reception that *A More Perfect Union* has received, and we have worked toward refining the contents of this new edition.

Nearly a third of the material is new to this edition. New selections in Volume I include, for example, the rules and regulations of seventeenth-century Harvard, a description of the Great Awakening by Jonathan Edwards, addresses by labor organizer Ely Moore and Transcendentalist poet and essayist Ralph Waldo Emerson, and a freshly edited version of Roger B. Taney's *Dred Scott* decision of 1857. Among the new selections in Volume II are a suffragist Declaration of Principles and statements by Theodore Roosevelt on taxation, George C. Marshall on rebuilding postwar Europe, and Representative Barbara Jordan on the impeachment of Richard Nixon.

The readings in these volumes represent a blend of social and political history, along with some cultural and economic trends, suitable for introductory courses in American history. We made our selections with three thoughts in mind. First, we looked for famous documents with a lustrous place in the American tradition—or the Gettysburg Address, for example, or Franklin D. Roosevelt's First Inaugural Address. These we chose for their great mythic quality, as expressions of fundamental sentiments with which students should be familiar. Second, we looked for writings that caused something to happen or had an impact when they appeared. Examples include the Virginia slave statutes, Thomas Paine's *The Crisis*, the Emancipation Proclamation, and Earl Warren's opinion in *Brown v. Board of Education of Topeka*—all of them influential pieces, some of them famous as well. Third, we looked for documents that seem to reflect important attitudes or developments. Into this group fall the writings of Upton Sinclair on industrial Chicago and of Martin Luther King, Jr., on Vietnam. In this category, where the need for careful selection from a wide field was most apparent, we looked especially for thoughtful pieces with a measure of fame and influence. Horace Mann's statement on schools reflected common attitudes; it also caused something to happen and is a well-known reform statement. We have also tried to mix a few unusual items into the stew, as with the "Report of the Joint Committee on Reconstruction" and a letter from a Catholic nun in early Colorado.

We have edited severely in places, mostly when the document is long or contains extraneous material or obscure references. We have also, in some cases, modernized spelling and punctuation.

Each document has a lengthy headnote that summarizes the relevant trends of the era, provides a specific setting for the document, and sketches the life of the author. In addition, "Questions to Consider" guide students through the prose and suggest ways of thinking about the selections.

We would like to thank the following people who reviewed the fifth edition manuscript for one or both volumes: Kurk Dorsey, University of New Hampshire; Paul G. Faler, University of Massachusetts at Boston; Richard H. Peterson, San Diego State University.

We would also like to thank the following people who reviewed the manuscript in prior editions: John K. Alexander, University of Cincinnati; June G. Alexander, University of Cincinnati; Judith L. Demark, Northern Michigan University; Harvey Green, Northeastern University; Ben Rader, University of Nebraska at Lincoln; C. Elizabeth Raymond, University of Nevada–Reno; Thomas Templeton Taylor, Wittenberg University; and John Scott Wilson, University of South Carolina.

We owe a debt of gratitude to Laura Ricard, our editorial assistant for this edition. We also wish to express our appreciation to the editorial staff of Houghton Mifflin Company for their hard and conscientious work in producing these volumes.

P. F. B.
R. S.

# A More Perfect Union

**An Indian village in the early Virginia region.** This engraving from a watercolor by the Englishman John White shows an Algonquian community with quonset-style huts, scenes of family and religious life, and plantings of corn on the right and tobacco on the left. A hunting party is at the top. White hoped to spur colonization by persuading European readers that the North Americans were settled and civilized rather than nomadic savages. (Miriam and Ira D. Wallah Division of Art, Prints and Photographs, The New York Public Library. Astor, Lenox and Tilden Foundations.)

# CHAPTER ONE

# Planters and Puritans

# CONTACT

According to Icelandic saga, the Scandinavian adventurer Leif Ericsson set foot in the New World in the eleventh century. Even if the tales are true, and even if the discoveries had become widely known during that time, Europeans were not yet ready for expansion. The economically feeble and politically fragmented European society would have had little interest in daring and costly colonization schemes.

By the late fifteenth century Europe had changed dramatically. Its population was increasing, more people demanded the goods and services that a new merchant class was eager to provide, and trade and commerce grew accordingly. As new markets emerged, and improvements in shipbuilding and navigation made seafaring less hazardous, incentives for expanding trade multiplied. Impatient to advance the economic growth of their infant nation-states, powerful new rulers began to think about subsidizing exploratory voyages. Europe was poised to produce a man like Christopher Columbus.

The Italian seaman Columbus proposed to reach the riches of the Orient by sailing west. Unable to convince the Portuguese to bankroll his scheme, he appealed to Ferdinand and Isabella, the sovereigns of Spain. Ambitious and visionary, they financed the 1492 voyage in which Columbus "discovered" the New World, an achievement the eighteenth-century economist Adam Smith heralded as perhaps the "greatest and most important event recorded in the history of mankind."

Columbus kept an extraordinarily detailed record of his voyage. Columbus addressed this journal to his patrons, Ferdinand and Isabella, but given his hunger for personal glory, he no doubt made his entries for the eyes of future generations as well. Although the journal was lost some forty years after the voyage, Bartolomé, de Las Casas, a fierce critic of Spanish treatment of American Indians, preserved and edited it from a version recorded by a scribe. Thus the *Diario de Colón* (Spanish) or the *Journal of the First Voyage* (English) is really a close "translation" of the original.

Las Casas observed that Columbus "was called Christopher, that is to say *Christum ferens,* which means carrier or bearer of Christ."

There is plenty of evidence to suggest that Columbus was driven as much by God as he was by "gold and glory," but the millions who followed him to the shores of the New World seemed to dream mostly of gold. "Gold is most excellent [and] whoever has it may do what he wishes in the world," Columbus wrote, and indeed, partly as a result of his voyages, Europe accumulated unprecedented wealth and power. But Europe's astonishing transformation came at enormous cost to the New World's native peoples.

Columbus made several voyages to the New World. During his second voyage he founded Isabela, the first European city in the New World, and during his third voyage he reached the South American mainland. He undertook his fourth and last voyage in direct violation of royal orders. It was on these later voyages that Columbus and his men began enslaving native people.

Suffering from disease and plagued by persistent hallucinations, in 1506 Columbus left this world as he had entered it in 1451—in obscurity. Except that he spent most of his youth at sea, little is known about his family or his early years, and even his birthplace has been disputed. He was buried in Valladolid, Spain, but his body was exhumed several times, and it was not until 1898 that Columbus was interred in his final resting place in Seville.

**Questions to Consider.** What were Columbus's primary objectives in the New World? How did he treat the natives at this first encounter? Were he and his men intolerant? To what extent was he alert to the new landscape? What evidence suggests that he was a religious man? What evidence is there that his religion and that of Imperial Spain had an intolerant dimension?

# Journal of the First Voyage (1492)

CHRISTOPHER COLUMBUS

PROLOGUE

*In the Name of Our Lord Jesus Christ*
Most Christian and most exalted and most excellent and most mighty princes, King and Queen of the Spains and of the islands of the sea, our Sovereigns:

Forasmuch as, in this present year of 1492, after that your Highnesses had made an end of the war with the Moors who reigned in Europe, and

From Cecil Jane, trans., *The Journal of Christopher Columbus* (London, 1968), 3–6, 39–52.

**Columbus at the court of King Ferdinand and Queen Isabella.** Ferdinand and Isabella extended Castilian monarchical authority across all of Spain at about the same time that the Tudor and Valois monarchies were consolidating their power in England and France. Columbus found himself seeking Spanish rather than Italian help in part because Italy had no single central government that could tax the wealth of the entire country to finance costly voyages into unknown regions. Spain now did. (Brown Brothers)

had brought that war to a conclusion in the very great city of Granada, where, in this same year, on the second day of the month of January, I saw the royal banners of your Highnesses placed by force of arms on the towers of the Alhambra, which is the citadel of the city, and I saw the Moorish king come out of the gates of the city and kiss the royal hands of your Highnesses and of the Prince, My Lord, and afterwards in that same month, on the ground of information which I had given to your Highnesses concerning the lands of India, and concerning a prince who is called "Grand Khan," which is to say in our Romance tongue "King of Kings," how many times he and his ancestors had sent to Rome to beg for men learned in our holy faith, in order that they might instruct him therein, and how the Holy Father had never made provision in this matter, and how so many nations had been lost, falling into idolatries and taking to themselves doctrines of perdition, and Your Highnesses, as Catholic Christians and as princes devoted to the holy Christian faith and propagators thereof, and enemies of the sect of Mahomet and of all idolatries and heresies, took thought to send me, Christopher Columbus, to the said parts of India, to see those princes and peoples and lands and the character of them and of all else, and the manner which should be used to bring about their conversion to our holy faith, and ordained that I should not go by land to the eastward, by which way it was the custom to go, but by way of the west, by which down to this day we do not know certainly that anyone has passed; therefore, after having driven out all the Jews from your realms and lordships, in the same month of January, your Highnesses commanded me that, with a sufficient fleet, I should go to the said parts of India and for this accorded to me great rewards and ennobled me so that from that time henceforward I might style myself "don" and be high admiral of the Ocean Sea and viceroy and perpetual governor of the islands and continent which I should discover and gain and which from now henceforward might be discovered and gained in the Ocean Sea, and that my eldest son should succeed to the same position, and so on from generation to generation. And I departed from the city of Granada on the twelfth day of the month of May in the same year of 1492, on a Saturday, and came to the town of Palos, which is a port of the sea, where I made ready three ships, very suited for such an undertaking, and I set out from that port, well furnished with very many supplies and with many seamen, on the third day of the month of August of the same year, on a Friday, half an hour before the rising of the sun.

"Sunday, October 21st/ At ten o'clock I arrived here at this *Cape del Isleo* [northwest point of Crooked Island] and anchored, as did the caravels. . . . The inhabitants, when they saw us, all fled and left their houses and hid their clothing and whatever they had in the undergrowth. I did not allow anything to be taken, even the value of a pin. Afterwards, some of the men among them came towards us and one came quite close. I gave him some hawks' bells and some little glass beads, and he was well content and very joyful. And that this friendly feeling might grow stronger and to make some request of them, I asked him for water; and, after I had returned to the ship, they came presently to the beach with their gourds full, and were delighted to give it to us, and I commanded that another string of small glass beads should be given to them, and they said that they would come here tomorrow. I was anxious to fill all the ships' casks with water here; accordingly, if the weather permit, I shall presently set out to go round the island, until I have had speech with this king and have seen whether I can obtain from him the gold which I hear that he wears. After that I wish to leave for another very large island, which I believe must be Cipangu [Japan], according to the signs which these Indians whom I have with me make; they call it "Colba" [Cuba]. They say that there are ships and many very good sailors there. Beyond this island, there is another which they call "Bofio" [Santo Domingo], which they say is also very large. The others, which lie between them, we shall see in passing, and according to whether I shall find a quantity of gold or spices, I shall decide what is to be done. But I am still determined to proceed to the mainland and to give the letters of Your Highnesses to the Grand Khan, and to request a reply and return with it."

"Monday, October 22nd/ All this night and today I have been here, waiting to see if the king of this place or other personages would bring gold or anything else of importance. There did come many of these people, who were like the others in the other islands, just as naked and just as painted, some white, some red, some black, and so in various ways. They brought spears and some skeins of cotton to exchange, and they bartered these with some sailors for bits of glass from broken cups and for bits of earthenware. Some of them wore some pieces of gold, hanging from the nose, and they gladly gave these for a hawks' bell, of the kind made for the foot of a sparrow hawk, and for glass beads, but the amount is so small that it is nothing. It is true that whatever little thing might be given to them, they still regarded our coming as a great wonder, and they believed that we had come from heaven."

"Tuesday, October 23rd/ I wished today to set out for the island of Cuba, which I believe must be Cipangu, according to the indications which these people give me concerning its size and riches. I did not delay longer here. . . . I say that it is not right to delay, but to go on our way and to discover much land, until a very profitable land is reached. My impression, however, is that this is very rich in spices, but I have no knowledge of these matters, which causes me the greatest sorrow in the world, for I see a thousand kind of trees, each one of which bears fruit after its kind and is as green now as in Spain in the months of May and June, and a thousand kind of herbs, also in bloom." . . .

Sunday, October 28/ He went from there in search of the nearest point in the island of Cuba to the south-southwest, and he entered a very lovely river, very free from danger of shoals or of other obstacles, and the water all along the coast, where he went, was very deep and clear up to the shore. . . . He says that the island is the most lovely that eyes have ever seen; it is full of good harbors and deep rivers, and it seems that the sea can never be stormy, for the vegetation on the shore runs down almost to the water, which it does not generally do where the sea is rough. Up to that time, he had not experienced a high sea among all those islands. He says that the island is full of very beautiful mountains, although there are no very long ranges, but they are lofty, and all the rest of the land is high like Sicily. It is full of many waters, as he was able to gather from the Indians whom he carried with him and whom he had taken in the island of Guanahani; they

told him by signs that there are ten large rivers, and that they cannot go
round it in their canoes in twenty days. When he went near the shore with
the ships, two boats or canoes came out, and as they saw that the sailors entered the boat and rowed about in order to see the depth of the river, to
know where they should anchor, the canoes fled. The Indians said that in
that island there are gold mines and pearls; the admiral saw that the place
was suited for them, and that there were mussels, which are an indication of
them. And the admiral understood that the ships of the Grand Khan come
there, and that they are large; and that from there to the mainland it is ten
days' journey. . . .

Tuesday, October 30th/ He went from the Rio de Mares to the northwest
and saw a cape full of palms, and he named it "Cape de Palmas" [Punta
Urero]. After having gone fifteen leagues, the Indians who were in the car-
avel *Pinta* said that behind that cape there was a river, and that from the
river to Cuba it was four days' journey. The captain of the *Pinta* said he understood that this Cuba was a city, and that land was a very extensive mainland which stretched far to the north, and that the king of that land was at
war with the Grand Khan, whom they called "cami," and his land or city
they called "Saba" and by many other names. The admiral resolved to go to
that river and send a present to the king of the land, and send him the letter
of the sovereigns. For this purpose he had a sailor who had gone to Guinea
[West Africa] in the same way, and certain Indians from Guanahani who
were ready to go with him, on condition that afterwards they might return
to their own land. He says that he must attempt to go to the Grand Khan,
for he thought that he was in that neighborhood, or to the city of Cathay,
which belongs to the Grand Khan, which, as he says, is very large, as he was
told before he set out from Spain. He says that all this land is low-lying and
lovely, and the sea deep.

Thursday, November 1st/ At sunrise, the admiral sent the boats to land,
to the houses which were there, and they found that all the people had fled,
and after some time a man appeared, and the admiral ordered that he
should be allowed to become reassured, and the boats returned to the ships.
After eating, he proceeded to send ashore one of the Indians whom he carried with him and who, from a distance, called out to them, saying that they
should not be afraid, because these were good people and did harm to no
one, and were not from the Grand Khan, but in many islands to which they
had been, had given of what they possessed. And the Indian threw himself
into the water and swam ashore, and two of those who were there took him
by the arms and brought him to a house, where they questioned him. And
when they were certain that no harm would be done to them, they were reassured, and presently there came to the ships more than sixteen boats or canoes, with spun cotton and their other trifles, of which the admiral
commanded that nothing should be taken, in order that they might know

that the admiral sought nothing except gold, which they call "nucay." So all day they were going and coming from the land to the ships, and they went to and fro from the Christians to the shore with great confidence. The admiral did not see any gold among them. But the admiral says that he saw on one of them a piece of worked silver, hanging from the nose, which he took to be an indication that there was silver in that land. They said by signs that within three days many merchants would come from the interior to buy the things which the Christians brought there, and that they would give news of the king of that land, who, as far as he could understand from the signs which they made, was four days' journey from there, because they had sent many men through the whole land to tell of the admiral.

Friday, November 2nd/ The admiral decided to send two men, Spaniards: one was called Rodrigo de Jerez, who lived in Ayamonte, and the other was a certain Luis de Torres, who had lived with the *adelantado* [civil and military governor] of Murcia and who had been a Jew, and who, as he says, understood Hebrew and Chaldee and even some Arabic. With these, he sent two Indians: one from among those whom he brought with him from Guanahani, and the other from those houses which were situated on the river. He gave them strings of beads with which to buy food, if they were in need of it, and appointed six days as the time within which they must return. He gave them specimens of spices to see if they found any, and instructed them how they were to ask for the king of that land, and what they were to say on behalf of the sovereigns of Castile, how they had sent the admiral to present letters on their behalf and a gift. They were also to learn of his estate, establish friendship with him, and favor him in whatever he might need from them, etc.; and they should gain knowledge of certain provinces and harbors and rivers, of which the admiral had information, and learn how far they were from this place, etc. He still affirms that this is the mainland.

Saturday, November 3rd/ In the morning, the admiral entered the boat, and as the river at its mouth forms a great lake, which makes a very remarkable harbor, very deep and free from rocks, with an excellent beach on which to careen ships and with much wood, he went up the river until he came to fresh water, which was a distance of some two leagues. And he ascended an eminence, in order to see something of the land, and he could see nothing, owing to the large groves, luxuriant and odorous, on which account he did not doubt that there were aromatic plants. He says that everything he saw was so lovely that his eyes could not weary of beholding such beauty, nor could he weary of the songs of birds, large and small. That day there came many boats or canoes to the ships, to barter articles of spun cotton and the nets in which they sleep, which are hammocks.

# 2

# CONFLICT

Englishmen came to Virginia in 1607 with one overriding purpose: to find gold and find it quickly. If possible, they would achieve this goal by raiding Spanish treasure galleons; more likely, they would force the so-called Indians to mine it for them, as the Spaniards had in Mexico and Peru. "Our gilded refiners with their golden promises made all men their slaves in hope of recompense," complained Captain John Smith, the settlement's military leader and chronicler. "There was no talk, no hope, but dig gold, wash gold, refine gold, load gold."

Unfortunately for the English, the Chesapeake Bay region proved not only too distant from the Spanish Main for raiding but also barren of precious metal. The Virginia Company, which was organized militarily, was short of provisions and top-heavy with "gentlemen adventurers" and luxury craftsmen without the skill or will to grow crops. The company lost half its men within two years, and without help from the Native American population, the remainder would also have perished.

The Chesapeake region was inhabited mostly by Powhatans, a confederacy of ten thousand people in one hundred and thirty villages. Their shrewd leader, Chief Powhatan, bore the tribal name. Powhatan might easily have refused to help the hapless English. European-born diseases had afflicted the tribal population even before these English arrived. European raiders, English and Spanish, had attacked and burned Powhatan villages. But there were also reasons to offer help. The Powhatans, reared in a collective, uncompetitive ethos, were generous—both among themselves and with nonthreatening neighbors, as the tiny English band probably appeared at first. Chief Powhatan was looking for allies in a territorial dispute with nonconfederacy tribes. The English, who carried edged metal weapons and primitive firearms, appeared likely recruits.

Reduced to eating "dogs, cats, rats, and mice" (and eventually cadavers and one another), the English should have received Powhatan's gifts of corn and meat with gratitude. But Captain Smith was an aggressive mercenary soldier who had once been enslaved by "infidel" Turks and was deeply suspicious of "infidel Indians," particularly given the defenseless state of the English settlement. He tended to see even acts of generosity as the mere treachery of "wild cruel Pagans."

Smith preferred to take by force what he needed rather than to receive it by gift. While engaged in raiding forays, he sometimes found himself trapped by Powhatan's forces. On one such occasion, Powhatan sought to demonstrate his authority by arranging a mock execution of Smith. He had Pocahantas, his young daughter, halt the proceedings by throwing herself upon the prisoner in a symbolic adoption gesture. Smith, perhaps understandably, misinterpreted the gesture as an expression of love for the English, thus supplying one of the earliest Anglo-American fables.

Powhatan delivered the address reprinted below during an encounter with Smith in the winter of 1608, when the English were again desperate for provisions. The speech first appeared in Smith's *A Map of Virginia, with a Description of the Countrey, the Commodities, People, Government, and Religion,* published in London in 1612. Transcribed into Elizabethan English by men barely familiar with Native American ways and language, the passage nevertheless seems a clear and straightforward rendering of Powhatan's concerns and hopes.

The chief, whom Smith estimated to be about sixty years old in 1607, was himself the son of a chief from south of the Chesapeake, possibly from Spanish Florida. When Powhatan saw the English continually raiding villages despite his overtures to John Smith, this accomplished statesman and stern ruler determined to starve the English into submission through intermittent war. His policy was partially successful. English weakness and the marriage of Pocahantas to settler John Rolfe in 1614 brought an uneasy truce that lasted until Powhatan's death in 1618. However, his successor, Opechankanough, saw the English as competitors for land rather than as raiders for food. In 1622 he launched an attack that killed a third of the settlers. The bankruptcy of the Virginia Company, the conversion of Virginia to a royal colony, and a rapid increase in European settlement soon followed. By 1669, when the first Virginia census was taken, the Powhatans themselves numbered barely 2,000.

**Questions to Consider.** Do Powhatan's opening remarks contain anything to substantiate his reputation for shrewd statecraft? According to Powhatan, why had his people refused to give corn to the English? What arguments did Powhatan use in trying to persuade the English not to wage war against him? What did he mean by the word that the English translated as *love?* Was Powhatan aware that Captain Smith was a much younger man? Why did Powhatan want John Smith and his men to come unarmed for talks? Why did the English fail to respond to so promising and open-handed an appeal?

**Pocahontas saving the life of John Smith.** Smith, an aggressive mercenary soldier, had escaped death at the hands of the Turks and others many times before, but probably not in so melodramatic a fashion as shown here. (Culver Pictures)

# Address to John Smith  (1608)

### POWHATAN

Captain Smith, some doubt I have of your coming hither, that makes me not so kindly seek to relieve you as I would; for many do inform me, your coming is not for trade, but to invade my people and possess my Country, who dare not come to bring you corn, seeing you thus armed with your men. To cheer [relieve] us of this fear, leave aboard your weapons, for here they are needless, we being all friends and forever Powhatans. . . .

Captain Smith, you may understand that I, having seen the death of all my people thrice, and not one living of those three generations but myself, I know the difference of peace and war better than any in my Country. But now I am old, and ere long must die. My brethren, namely Opichapam,

From Edward Arber, ed., *Travels and Works of Captain John Smith* (Edinburgh, 1910), I: 132–136.

Opechankanough, and Kekataugh, [and] my two sisters, and their two daughters, are distinctly each others' successors. I wish their experiences no less than mine, and your love to them, no less than mine to you: but this brute [noise] from Nansamund, that you are come to destroy my Country, so much affrighteth all my people, as they dare not visit you. What will it avail you to take that which perforce, you may quietly have with love, or to destroy them that provide you food? What can you get by war, when we can hide our provision and flee to the woods, whereby you must famish, by wronging us your friends? And why are you thus jealous of our love, seeing us unarmed, and both do, and are willing still to feed you with what you cannot get but by our labors?

Think you I am so simple not to know it is better to eat good meat, lie well, and sleep quietly with my women and children, laugh, and be merry with you, have copper, hatchets, or what I want being your friend; than be forced to flee from all, to lie cold in the woods, feed upon acorns, roots and such trash, and be so hunted by you that I can neither rest, eat nor sleep, but my tired men must watch, and if a twig but break, everyone cry, there comes Captain Smith: then must I flee I know not wither, and thus with miserable fear end my miserable life, leaving my pleasures to such youths as you, which through your rash unadvisedness, may quickly as miserably end, for want of that you never know how to find? Let this therefore assure you of our loves, and every year our friendly trade shall furnish you with corn; and now also, if you would come in friendly manner to see us, and not thus with your guns and swords as to invade your foes.

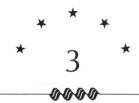

# 3

# FIRST PRIVILEGES

The first representative body in the New World was the Virginia Assembly, or House of Burgesses. This development came about when the directors of the Virginia Company, a joint-stock corporation of British investors, decided to allow more freedom in order to attract more colonists. The directors scrapped the colony's military and communal organization when the little settlement at Jamestown, established in 1607, failed to produce a profit and came close to collapsing due to disease and starvation. The company directors distributed land to the settlers, arranged to transport craftsmen and servants, as well as women, to the colony, and authorized the election of a general assembly to help govern the colony. On July 30, 1619, twenty-two burgesses, chosen by the settlers, met for the first time with the governor and the council, appointed by the company.

The document authorizing the House of Burgesses has been lost, but an "ordinance" of 1621 (reproduced below) is believed to reproduce the provisions of 1619. Largely the work of Sir Edwin Sandys, one of the leading directors of the Virginia Company, the ordinance provided for a Council of State, appointed by the company, as well as for an assembly elected by the people. The Virginia Assembly had the power to "make, ordain, and enact such general Laws and Orders, for the Behoof of the said Colony, and the good Government thereof, as shall, from time to time, appear necessary or requisite," subject to the company's approval. The new governmental arrangements, together with the discovery that tobacco could be a lucrative crop, soon made Virginia a thriving enterprise, and these arrangements were continued after Virginia became a royal colony in 1624.

**Questions to Consider.** In examining the ordinance's description of the two councils for governing Virginia, it is helpful to consider the following questions: How large was the Council of State? How was it chosen? What responsibilities did it possess? How did the responsibilities of the General Assembly compare in importance with those of the Council of State? Who possessed the ultimate authority in Virginia?

1 chosen in England
2 chosen locally

————————★ ★ 🌀🌀🌀🌀 ★ ★————————

# The Virginia Ordinance of 1619

An ordinance and Constitution of the Treasurer, Council, and Company in England, for a Council of State and General Assembly. . . .

To all People, to whom these Presents shall come, be seen, or heard the Treasurer, Council, and Company of Adventurers and Planters for the city of *London* for the first colony of *Virginia*, send Greeting. . . .

We . . . the said Treasurer, Council, and Company, by Authority directed to us from his Majesty under the Great Seal, upon mature Deliberation, do hereby order and declare, that, from henceforward, there shall be TWO SUPREME COUNCILS in *Virginia*, for the better Government of the said Colony aforesaid.

The one of which Councils, to be called THE COUNCIL OF STATE (and whose Office shall chiefly be assisting, with their Care, Advise, and Circumspection, to the said Governor) shall be chosen, nominated, placed and displaced, from time to time, by Us, the said Treasurer, Council, and Company, and our Successors: Which Council of State shall consist, for the present, only of these Persons, as are here inserted, *viz.* Sir *Francis Wyat,* Governor of *Virginia,* Captain *Francis West,* Sir *George Yeardley,* Knight, Sir *William Neuce,* Night Marshal of *Virginia,* Mr. *George Sandys,* Treasurer, Mr. *George Thorpe,* Deputy of the College, Captain *Thomas Neuce,* Deputy for the Company, Mr. *Pawlet,* Mr. *Leech,* Captain *Nathaniel Powel,* Mr. *Harwood,* Mr. *Samuel Macock,* Mr. *Christopher Davison,* Secretary, *Doctor Pots,* Physician to the Company, Mr. *Roger Smith,* Mr. *John Berkley,* Mr. *John Rolfe,* Mr. *Ralph Hamer,* Mr. *John Pountis,* Mr. *Michael Lapworth.* Which said Counsellors and Council we earnestly pray and desire, and in his Majesty's Name strictly charge and command, that (all Factions, Partialities, and sinister Respect laid aside) they bend their Care and Endeavors to assist the said Governor; first and principally in the Advancement of the Honour and Service of God, and the Enlargement of his Kingdom amongst the Heathen People; and next, in erecting of the said Colony in due obedience to his Majesty, and all lawful Authority from his Majesty's Directions; and lastly, in maintaining the said People in Justice and *Christian* Conversation amongst themselves, and in Strength and Ability to withstand their Enemies. And this Council, to be always, or for the most Part, residing about or near the Governor.

The other Council, more generally to be called by the Governor, once yearly, and no oftener, but for very extraordinary and important occasions, shall consist, for the present, of the said Council of State, and of two Burgesses out of every Town, Hundred, or other particular Plantation, to be

From F. N. Thorpe, ed., *The Federal and State Constitutions* (7 v., Government Printing Office, Washington, D.C., 1909), VII: 3810–3812.

respectively chosen by the Inhabitants; Which Council shall be called THE GENERAL ASSEMBLY, wherein (as also in the said Council of State) all Matter shall be decided, determined, and ordered, by the greater Part of the Voices then present; reserving to the Governor always a Negative Voice. And this General Assembly shall have free Power to treat, consult, and conclude, as well of all emergent Occasions concerning the Public Weal of the said Colony and every Part thereof, as also to make, ordain, and enact such general Laws and Orders, for the Behoof of the said Colony, and the good Government thereof, as shall, from time to time, appear necessary or requisite. . . .

Whereas in all other Things, we require the said General Assembly, as also the said Council of State, to imitate and follow the Policy of the Form of Government—Laws, Customs, and Manner of Trial, and other administration of Justice, used in the Realm of *England,* as near as may be, even as ourselves, by his Majesty's Letters Patent, are required.

Provided, that no Law or Ordinance, made in the said General Assembly, shall be or continue in Force or Validity, unless the same shall be solemnly ratified and confirmed, in a General Quarter Court of the said Company here in England and so ratified, be returned to them under our Seal; It being our Intent to afford the like Measure also unto the said Colony, that after the Government of the said Colony shall once have been well framed, and settled accordingly, which is to be done by Us, as by Authority derived from his Majesty, and the same shall have been so by Us declared, no Orders of Court afterwards shall bind the said Colony, unless they be ratified in like Manner in the General Assemblies. IN WITNESS whereof we have here unto set our Common Seal, the 24th of *July* 1621, and in the Year of the Reign of our Sovereign Lord, JAMES, King of *England,* &c.

# 4

# THE PURITAN VISION

In 1630 the Great Migration of Puritans to America began. That summer, under the direction of John Winthrop, a fleet of seventeen ships carrying about one thousand men and women crossed the Atlantic to Massachusetts Bay. A few months later, the settlers founded a colony on the site of the present city of Boston. Within a few years Massachusetts Bay Colony was the largest of all the English colonies on the American mainland.

John Winthrop, a college-educated squire from Groton Manor, Suffolk, had been elected governor of the new colony even before the settlers left England. Though not a clergyman, he was a devout Puritan. During the passage he delivered a lecture called "A Model of Christian Charity" to his coreligionists on the flagship *Arbella*. In it he reminded them of their Puritan ideals and outlined the religious and social purposes by which he expected them to organize their settlement in the New World. He wanted Massachusetts Bay Colony to be a model "Christian commonwealth," that is, a kind of "city upon a hill" for the rest of the world to admire and perhaps imitate. The settlers, he said, had a special commission from God to establish such a community in the New World. The new colony was to be dedicated to the glory of God rather than to worldly success. The "care of the public," he declared, "must oversway all private respects," and the settlers must strive at all times "to do justly, to love mercy, to walk humbly with our God."

For almost two decades Winthrop dominated Massachusetts Bay Colony. John Cotton, Boston's leading clergyman, called him "a brother . . . who has been to us a mother," but he was a father as well. He was convinced he was destined to rule and was an exacting parent. Born to wealth in Suffolk in 1588, he was educated at Trinity College, Cambridge, became prominent in the legal profession, and served as justice of the peace and lord of Groton Manor before heading the expedition to America. A strong leader who opposed both religious dissent and popular rule in Massachusetts, Winthrop served as governor for twelve years; when not governor he served as deputy governor and member of the governing council. He regarded democracy as "the meanest and worst form of government," and most people agreed with him in those days. When criticized for highhandedness, he managed to convince his critics that "liberty" meant not the right to do as one pleased but, rather, emancipation from selfish desires and obedience to the moral law. A journal he kept from the inception of the colony until his death in 1649 is a rich source for the early history of Massachusetts Bay Colony.

**Questions to Consider.** In his lecture to the settlers, Winthrop spoke of the "law of the Gospel." In what ways did he make the Bible the basis of his plans for Massachusetts Bay Colony? How close were relations between church and state to be in the new settlement? Which was to come first: the individual or the community? What principles of behavior did he consider essential to the success of the enterprise? What did he mean by his statement that the Puritans were operating under a "special overruling providence"? What did he think would be the fate of the colonists if they failed to carry out the high purposes he had outlined for them?

# A Model of Christian Charity (1630)

JOHN WINTHROP

This law of the Gospel propounds likewise a difference of seasons and occasions. There is a time when a Christian must sell all and give to the poor as they did in the apostles' times; there is a time also when a Christian, though they give not all yet, must give beyond their ability, as they of Macedonia (II Cor. 8). Likewise, community of perils calls for extraordinary liberality, and so doth community in some special service for the church. Lastly, when there is no other means whereby our Christian brother may be relieved in this distress, we must help him beyond our ability, rather than tempt God in putting him upon help by miraculous or extraordinary means.

1. For the persons, we are a company professing ourselves fellow members of Christ, in which respect only, though we were absent from each other many miles, and had our employments as far distant, yet we ought to account ourselves knit together by this bond of love, and live in the exercise of it, if we would have comfort of our being in Christ.

From *The Winthrop Papers* (5 v., Massachusetts Historical Society, Boston, 1931), II: 282–295. Courtesy Massachusetts Historical Society.

**John Winthrop, second governor of Massachusetts Bay Company.** This undated engraving shows Winthrop in the prime of life. He was forty-two and living in England when he became governor in 1629. In 1630 he sailed to America on the *Arbella* with a fleet of seventeen ships carrying close to one thousand men and women. The colony's freemen elected Winthrop to ten one-year terms as governor. Puritans believed in humility and simplicity, but on important occasions the colony's prominent men, unless they were ministers, still wore the elaborate cuffs and throat ruffs depicted in this portrait. (Courtesy, American Antiquarian Society)

2. For the work we have in hand, it is by mutual consent, through a special overruling providence and a more than an ordinary approbation of the churches of Christ, to seek out a place of cohabitation and consortship, under a due form of government both civil and ecclesiastical. In such cases as this, the care of the public must oversway all private respects by which not only conscience but mere civil policy doth bind us; for it is a true rule that particular estates cannot subsist in the ruin of the public.

3. The end is to improve our lives to do more service to the Lord, the comfort and increase of the body of Christ whereof we are members, that

ourselves and posterity may be the better preserved from the common corruptions of this evil world, to serve the Lord and work out our salvation under the power and purity of His holy ordinances.

4. For the means whereby this must be effected, they are twofold: a conformity with the work and the end we aim at; these we seek are extraordinary, therefore we must not content ourselves with usual ordinary means. Whatsoever we did or ought to have done when we lived in England, the same must we do, and more also where we go. That which the most in their churches maintain as a truth in profession only, we must bring into familiar and constant practice: as in this duty of love we must love brotherly without dissimulation; we must love one another with a pure heart fervently, we must bear one another's burdens, we must not look only on our own things but also on the things of our brethren. Neither must we think that the Lord will bear with such failings at our hands as He doth from those among whom we have lived. . . .

Thus stands the cause between God and us; we are entered into covenant with Him for this work; we have taken out a commission, the Lord hath given us leave to draw our own articles. We have professed to enterprise these actions upon these and these ends; we have hereupon besought Him of favor and blessing. Now if the Lord shall please to hear us and bring us in peace to the place we desire, then hath He ratified this covenant and sealed our Commission, [and] will expect a strict performance of the articles contained in it. But if we shall neglect the observation of these articles which are the ends we have propounded, and dissembling with our God, shall fall to embrace this present world and prosecute our carnal intentions, seeking great things for ourselves and our posterity, the Lord will surely break out in wrath against us, be revenged of such a perjured people, and make us know the price of the breach of such a covenant.

Now the only way to avoid this shipwreck and to provide for our posterity is to follow the counsel of Micah: to do justly, to love mercy, to walk humbly with our God. For this end, we must be knit together in this work as one man. We must entertain each other in brotherly affection; we must be willing to abridge ourselves of our superfluities for the supply of others' necessities; we must uphold a familiar commerce together in all meekness, gentleness, patience and liberality. We must delight in each other, make others' condition our own, rejoice together, mourn together, labor and suffer together: always having before our eyes our commission and community in the work, our community as members of the same body. So shall we keep the unity of the spirit in the bond of peace, the Lord will be our God and delight to dwell among us, as His own people, and will command a blessing upon us in all our ways, so that we shall see much more of His wisdom, power, goodness, and truth than formerly we have been acquainted with. We shall find that the God of Israel is among us, when ten of us shall be able to resist a thousand of our enemies, when He shall make us a praise and glory, that men shall say of succeeding plantations: "The Lord make it like that of New England." For we must consider that we shall be as a city upon a hill, the eyes of all people are upon us. So that if we shall deal falsely with our God in this work we have undertaken, and so cause Him to withdraw His present help from us, we shall be made a story and a by-word through the world: we shall open the mouths of enemies to speak evil of the ways of God and all professors for God's sake; we shall shame the faces of many of God's worthy servants, and cause their prayers to be turned into curses upon us, till we be consumed out of the good land whither we are going.

And to shut up this discourse with that exhortation of Moses, that faithful servant of the Lord, in his last farewell to Israel (Deut. 30): Beloved, there is now set before us life and good, death and evil, in that we are commanded this day to love the Lord our God, and to love one another, to walk in His ways and to keep His commandments and His ordinance and His laws and the articles of our covenant with Him, that we may live and be multiplied, and that the Lord our God may bless us in the land whither we go to possess it: but if our hearts shall turn away so that we will not obey, but shall be seduced and worship . . . other gods, our pleasures and profits, and serve them, it is propounded unto us this day, we shall surely perish out of the good land whither we pass over this vast sea to possess it.

> *Therefore, let us choose life,*
> *that we, and our seed,*
> *may live; by obeying His*
> *voice and cleaving to Him,*
> *for He is our life and*
> *our prosperity.*

# 5

# THE UNDERSIDE OF PRIVILEGE

In 1619 a Dutch trader brought twenty "Negars" from Africa and sold them in Jamestown. For a long time, however, black slavery, though common in Spanish and Portuguese colonies in the New World, was not important in Virginia. For many years white indentured servants from England performed most of the labor in the colony; after three decades there were still only about three hundred blacks in the English colonies. By the end of the seventeenth century, however, transporting Africans to America had become a profitable business for English and American merchants, and the slave trade had grown to enormous proportions.

In Virginia the planters used Africans as cheap labor on their plantations and also employed them as household servants, coachmen, porters, and skilled workers. Their status was indeterminate at first, and they may have been treated somewhat like indentured servants for some time. As tobacco became important, however, and the number of blacks working on plantations soared, the position of blacks declined rapidly. The Virginia Assembly began enacting laws governing their behavior and regulating their relations with whites. The statutes, some of which are reproduced here, do not show whether racial prejudice and discrimination preceded slavery, followed it, or, more likely, accompanied it. But they do dramatize the fact that in Virginia, as elsewhere, the expansion of freedom and self-government for European Americans could go hand in hand with the exploitation and oppression of African-Americans.

**Questions to Consider.** How strictly did the Virginia lawmakers attempt to control the behavior of Africans in the colony? How severe were the punishments provided for offenders against the law? What penalties were provided for the "casual killing" of slaves? What appeared to be the greatest fear of the Virginia lawmakers?

———— ★ ★ 🐚🐚🐚🐚 ★ ★ ————

# Virginia Slavery Legislation (1630–1691)

[1630]   Hugh David to be soundly whipped, before an assembly of Negroes and others for abusing himself to the dishonor of God and shame of Christians, by defiling his body in lying with a negro; which fault he is to acknowledge next Sabbath day.

[1640]   Robert Sweet to do penance in church according to laws of England, for getting a negro woman with child and the woman whipt.

[1661]   *Be it enacted* That in case any English servant shall run away in company with any negroes who are incapable of making satisfaction by addition of time, *Be it enacted* that the English so running away in company with them shall serve for the time of the said negroes absence as they are to do for their own by a former act.

[1668]   Whereas some doubts, have arisen whether negro women set free were still to be accompted tithable according to a former act, *It is declared by this grand assembly* that negro women, though permitted to enjoy their Freedom yet ought not in all respects to be admitted to a full fruition of the exemptions and impunities of England, and are still liable to payment of taxes.

[1669]   Whereas the only law in force for the punishment of refractory servants resisting their master, mistress or overseer cannot be inflicted upon negroes, nor the obstinancy of many of them by other than violent means supprest, *Be it enacted and declared by this grand assembly*, if any slave resist his master (or other by his master's order correcting him) and by the extremity of the correction should chance to die, that his death shall not be accompted Felony, but the master (or that other person appointed by the master to punish him) be acquit from molestation, since it cannot be presumed that prepensed malice (which alone makes murder Felony) should induce any man to destroy his own estate.

[1680]   *It is hereby enacted by the authority aforesaid,* that from and after the publication of this law, it shall not be lawful for any negro or other slave to carry or arm himself with any club, staff, gun, sword, or any other weapon of defence or offence, nor to go to depart from his master's ground without a certificate from his master, mistress or overseer, and such permission not to be granted but upon particular and necessary occasions; and every negro or slave so offending not having a certificate as aforesaid shall be sent to the next constable, who is hereby enjoined and required to give the said negro twenty lashes on his bare back well laid on, and so sent home to his said master, mistress or overseer. *And it is further enacted by the authority aforesaid*

From William Hening, ed., *The Laws of Virginia, 1619–1792* (13 v., Samuel Pleasants, Richmond, 1809–1823).

that if any negro or other slave shall presume to lift up his hand in opposition against any christian, shall for every such offense, upon due proof made thereof by the oath of the party before a magistrate, have and receive thirty lashes on his bare back well laid on.

[1691]   *It is hereby enacted,* that in all such cases upon intelligence of any such negroes, mulattoes, or other slaves lying out, two of their majesties' justices of the peace of that county, whereof one to be of the quorum, where such negroes, mulattoes or other slave shall be, shall be impowered and commanded, and are hereby impowered and commanded, to issue out their warrants directed to the sheriff of the same county to apprehend such negroes, mulattoes, and other slaves, which said sheriff is hereby likewise required upon all such occasions to raise such and so many forces from time to time as he shall think convenient and necessary for the effectual apprehending such negroes, mulattoes and other slaves, and in case any negroes, mulattoes or other slave or slaves lying out as aforesaid shall resist, run away, or refuse to deliver and surrender him or themselves to any person or persons that shall be by lawful authority employed to apprehend and take such negroes, mulattoes or other slaves that in such cases it shall and may be lawful for such person and persons to kill and destroy such negroes, mulattoes, and other slave or slaves by gun or any other ways whatsoever.

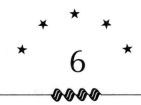

# 6

# FAITH AND DISSENT

Although John Winthrop's "Christian commonwealth" flourished for several decades, it did not do so without difficulty. Location (near a forest that enticed settlers westward and an ocean that tugged them back east) was one problem, enemies (Spaniards and Native Americans) another. But the colony also had internal troubles. Some of these stemmed from the fact that many tradesmen, sailors, and other inhabitants were not professing Congregationalists. Other troubles can be traced to stress within the Puritan community itself. As early as 1635, for example, colonial leaders, including Winthrop, banished a popular young minister named Roger Williams for spreading two "dangerous opinions." Williams believed that Englishmen should not settle North America unless the "Indians" gave their permission. Even worse, in the eyes of his judges, he taught that church and state should be totally separate lest the one corrupt the other and both corrupt the individual's striving for true faith. Other dissidents faced excommunication, fines, imprisonment, and sometimes death.

In this community, there was no more zealous Puritan than Anne Hutchinson. The daughter of a learned English clergyman, Hutchinson had migrated to Boston with her husband in 1634, following a favorite Puritan minister. Taking seriously the rule that saints (or members of the true Church), should study God's word, she invited people into her home to discuss scripture and sermons. Hutchinson extended her invitations to women she met in her work as midwife as well as to ministers and prominent merchants. Among the sermons they discussed were those of ministers whom she criticized for preaching salvation through "works" (good behavior) rather than "grace" (faith). This doctrine implied that people could save themselves through good deeds rather than by relying on God's will. It seemed to imply that God is not all-powerful and to encourage the sin of human pride, positions that were anathema to most good Puritans.

Hutchinson's activities unsettled not only the ministers she criticized but John Winthrop and other political leaders. They brought her to trial in 1637 for "traducing the ministers." The magistrates disliked criticism of the ministry, a pillar of the Massachusetts establishment.

Moreover, to urge "grace" over "works" *too* hotly was to imply that God considered polite behavior, including obedience to the law, unimportant—a position the magistrates considered dangerous to society. Indeed, as the following excerpts from the record of Hutchinson's interrogation make clear, to urge "grace" too hotly was to claim divine inspiration. Such a claim constituted a heresy that struck at the very heart of congregational Puritanism and the Christian commonwealth—at least as understood by the leadership of Massachusetts Bay. Moreover, Hutchinson was female in a patriarchal world, which clearly disturbed her accusers and underscored her guilt.

In 1638 the Massachusetts General Court found Anne Hutchinson guilty and banished her from the colony; a short time later her church excommunicated her as well. She and her family, including most of her fifteen children, then moved to an island off the coast of Rhode Island. Following the death of her husband in 1642, Hutchinson moved her family to Long Island in the New Netherlands (later New York). In 1643, she and several of her children perished in an Indian raid.

**Questions to Consider.** When John Winthrop accused Anne Hutchinson of holding opinions that "troubled the peace of the commonwealth and the churches," to what opinions was he referring? What was it about Hutchinson's meetings at her home that upset Winthrop? Why was Deputy Governor Dudley distressed that Hutchinson might have accused Puritan ministers of preaching a "covenant of works"? Why did he compare her to a "Jesuit"? When Governor Winthrop ("the Court") exclaimed "Very well, very well" after the exchanges concerning Hutchinson's criticism of the ministers, had she won the point, or had he? Hutchinson delivered a long statement to demonstrate her innocence, but it clearly agitated the magistrates, particularly when she referred to "immediate revelation." What did they think she was claiming? Why did they think this was dangerous to society? Did Anne Hutchinson's beliefs, her practices, or her manner most aggravate her examiners?

# The Examination of Anne Hutchinson (1637)

*Mr. Winthrop, governor.* Mrs. Hutchinson, you are called here as one of those that have troubled the peace of the commonwealth and the churches here; you are known to be a woman that hath had a great share in the promoting

From Thomas Hutchinson, *History of the Colony and Province of Massachusetts Bay* (Boston, 1767).

**Anne Hutchinson.** In this engraving Anne Hutchinson is standing before the magistrates of Massachusetts Bay, on trial for heresy. She was found guilty and expelled from the colony in 1638. (Culver Pictures)

and divulging of those opinions that are causes of this trouble, and to be nearly joined not only in affinity and affection with some of those the court had taken notice of and passed censure upon. But you have spoken divers things as we have been informed very prejudicial to the honour of the churches and ministers thereof, and you have maintained a meeting and an assembly in your house that hath been condemned by the general assembly as a thing not tolerable nor comely in the sight of God nor fitting for your sex; and notwithstanding that was cried down, you have continued the same. Therefore we have thought good to send for you to understand how things are. . . .

*Mrs. Hutchinson.* I am called here to answer before you but I hear no things laid to my charge.

*Gov.* I have told you some already and more I can tell you. *(Mrs. H.)* Name one Sir.

*Gov.* Have I not named some already?

*Mrs. H.* What have I said or done?

*Gov.* Why for your doings, this you did harbour and countenance those that are parties in this faction that you have heard of. *(Mrs. H.)* That's matter of conscience, Sir.

*Gov.* Your conscience you must keep, or it must be kept for you. . . .

*Gov.* Why do you keep such a meeting at your house as you do every week upon a set day?

*Mrs. H.* It is lawful for me so to do, as it is all your practices; and can you find a warrant for yourself and condemn me for the same thing? The ground of my taking it up was, when I first came to this land, because I did not go to such meetings as those were, it was presently reported that I did not allow of such meetings but held them unlawful, and therefore in that regard they said I was proud and did despise all ordinances. Upon that, a friend came unto me and told me of it and I to prevent such aspersions took it up, but it was in practice before I came; therefore I was not the first.

*Gov.* For this, that you appeal to our practice you need no confutation. If your meeting had answered to the former it had not been offensive, but I will say that there was no meeting of women alone. But your meeting is of another sort, for there are sometimes men among you.

*Mrs. H.* There was never any man with us.

*Gov.* Well, admit there was no man at your meeting and that you was sorry for it, there is no warrant for your doings; and by what warrant do you continue such a course?

*Mrs. H.* I conceive there is a clear rule in Titus, that the elder women should instruct the younger; and then I must have a time wherein I must do it.

*Gov.* All this I grant you, I grant you a time for it; but what is this to the purpose that you, Mrs. Hutchinson, must call a company together from their callings to come to be taught of you?

*Mrs. H.* Will it please you to answer me this and to give me a rule, for then I will willingly submit to any truth? If any come to my house to be instructed in the ways of God, what rule have I to put them away?

*Gov.* But suppose that a hundred men come unto you to be instructed, will you forbear to instruct them?

*Mrs. H.* As far as I conceive I cross a rule in it.

*Gov.* Very well and do you not so here?

*Mrs. H.* No Sir, for my ground is they are men.

*Gov.* Men and women all is one for that, but suppose that a man should come and say, "Mrs. Hutchinson, I hear that you are a woman that God hath given his grace unto and you have knowledge in the word of God. I pray instruct me a little." Ought you not to instruct this man?

*Mrs. H.* I think I may.—Do you think it not lawful for me to teach women, and why do you call me to teach the court?

*Gov.* We do not call you to teach the court but to lay open yourself.

*Mr. Dudley, dep. gov.* Here hath been much spoken concerning Mrs. Hutchinson's meetings and among other answers she saith that men come not there. I would ask you this one question then, whether never any man was at your meeting?

*Gov.* There are two meetings kept at their house.

*Dep. Gov.* How; is there two meetings?

*Mrs. H.* Ey Sir, I shall not equivocate, there is a meeting of men and women, and there is a meeting only for women.

*Dep. Gov.* Are they both constant?

*Mrs. H.* No, but upon occasions they are deferred.

*Mr. Endicot.* Who teaches in the men's meetings, none but men? Do not women sometimes?

*Mrs. H.* Never as I heard, not one. . . .

*Dep. Gov.* Now it appears by this woman's meeting that Mrs. Hutchinson hath so forestalled the minds of many by their resort to her meeting that now she hath a potent party in the country. Now if all these things have endangered us as from that foundation, and if she in particular hath disparaged all our ministers in the land that they have preached a covenant of works, . . . why this is not to be suffered. And therefore being driven to the foundation, and it being found that Mrs. Hutchinson is she that hath depraved all the ministers and hath been the cause of what is fallen out, why we must take away the foundation and the building will fall.

*Mrs. H.* I pray, Sir, prove it that I said they preached nothing but a covenant of works.

*Dep. Gov.* Nothing but a covenant of works? Why, a Jesuit may preach truth sometimes.

*Mrs. H.* Did I ever say they preached a covenant of works, then?

*Dep. Gov.* If they do not preach a covenant of grace clearly, then they preach a covenant of works.

*Mrs. H.* No Sir, one may preach a covenant of grace more clearly than another, so I said.

*Dep. Gov.* We are not upon that now, but upon position.

*Mrs. H.* Prove this then, Sir, that you say I said.

*Dep. Gov.* When they do preach a covenant of works, do they preach truth?

*Mrs. H.* Yes Sir, but when they preach a covenant of works for salvation, that is not truth.

*Dep. Gov.* I do but ask you this: when the ministers do preach a covenant of works, do they preach a way of salvation?

*Mrs. H.* I did not come hither to answer to questions of that sort.

*Dep. Gov.* Because you will deny the thing.

*Mrs. H.* Ey, but that is to be proved first.

*Dep. Gov.* I will make it plain that you did say that the ministers did preach a covenant of works.

*Mrs. H.* I deny that.

*Dep. Gov.* And that you said they were not able ministers of the new testament. . . .

*Mrs. H.* If ever I spake that, I proved it by God's word.

*Court.* Very well, very well. . . .

*Mrs. H.* If you please to give me leave, I shall give you the ground of what I know to be true. Being much troubled to see the falseness of the constitution of the church of England, I had like to have turned separatist; whereupon I kept a day of solemn humiliation and pondering of the thing; this scripture was brought unto me—he that denies Jesus Christ to be come in the flesh is antichrist—This I considered of, and in considering found that the papists did not deny him to be come in the flesh, nor we did not deny him—who then was antichrist? Was the Turk antichrist only? The Lord knows that I could not open scripture; he must by his prophetical office open it unto me. So after that, being unsatisfied in the thing, the Lord was pleased to bring this scripture out of the Hebrews. He that denies the testament denies the testator, and in this did open unto me and give me to see that those which did not teach the new covenant had the spirit of antichrist, and upon this he did discover the ministry unto me and ever since. I bless the Lord, he hath let me see which was the clear ministry and which the wrong. Since that time I confess I have been more choice, and he hath let me to distinguish between the voice of my beloved and the voice of Moses, the voice of John Baptist and the voice of antichrist, for all those voices are spoken of in scripture. Now if you do condemn me for speaking what in my conscience I know to be truth, I must commit myself unto the Lord.

*Mr. Nowell.* How do you know that that was the spirit?

*Mrs. H.* How did Abraham know that it was God that bid him offer his son, being a breach of the sixth commandment?

*Dep. Gov.* By an immediate voice.

*Mrs. H.* So to me by an immediate revelation.

*Dep. Gov.* How! an immediate revelation.

*Mrs. H.* By the voice of his own spirit to my soul. I will give you another scripture, Jer. 46. 27,28—out of which the Lord shewed me what he would do for me and the rest of his servants.—But after he was pleased to reveal himself to me, I did presently like Abraham run to Hagar. And after that, he did let me see the atheism of my own heart, for which I begged of the Lord that it might not remain in my heart; and being thus, he did shew me this (a twelvemonth after) which I told you of before. Ever since that time I have been confident of what he hath revealed unto me. . . . You see this scripture fulfilled this day, and therefore I desire you that as you tender the Lord and the church and commonwealth to consider and look what you do. You have power over my body, but the Lord Jesus hath power over my body and soul; and assure yourselves thus much, you do as much as in you lies to put the Lord Jesus Christ from you; and if you go on in this course you begin, you will bring a curse upon you and your posterity, and the mouth of the Lord hath spoken it.

*Dep. Gov.* What is the scripture she brings?

*Mr. Stoughton.* Behold I turn away from you.

*Mrs. H.* But now having seen him which is invisible, I fear not what man can do unto me.

*Gov.* Daniel was delivered by miracle. Do you think to be deliver'd so too?

*Mrs. H.* I do here speak it before the court. I look that the Lord should deliver me by his providence.

*Mr. Harlakenden.* I may read scripture and the most glorious hypocrite may read them and yet go down to hell.

*Mrs. H.* It may be so. . . .

*Mr. Endicot.* I would have a word or two with leave of that which hath thus far been revealed to the court. I have heard of many revelations of Mr. Hutchinson's, but they were reports, but Mrs. Hutchinson I see doth maintain some by this discourse; and I think it is a special providence of God to hear what she hath said. Now there is a revelation you see which she doth expect as a miracle. She saith she now suffers, and let us do what we will she shall be delivered by a miracle. I hope the court takes notice of the vanity of it and heat of her spirit.

# 7

## PIETY AND KNOWLEDGE

Of all the people of early England, the Puritans were the most concerned with proper education. In seventeenth-century Massachusetts, one male in every forty families had graduated from Oxford, Cambridge, or Dublin, giving the Bay Colony an exceptional intellectual energy. Civic and religious leaders were almost always well educated. Pastors showed enormous regard for their parishioners by preaching on challenging subjects and teaching scripture in a way that even a Biblical scholar might find daunting.

Contrary to the stereotype, however, Puritan educators felt it was as important to study history, languages, science, poetry, and "pagan" texts as it was to study the scriptures and theology. They believed that all knowledge came from God. The reason to study was ultimately to glorify Him. But they also felt a duty to explore science and other areas of thought, even if those subjects seemed to contradict biblical precept and faith. As the Reverend Increase Mather exhorted a group of students, "You who are wont to philosophize in a liberal spirit are pledged to the words of no particular master, yet I would have you hold fast to that one truly golden saying of Aristotle: *Above all find a friend in Truth.*"

Ministers, since they were responsible for the salvation of human souls, felt especially keenly the need to search for "Truth." And so great was the Puritan dread of an uneducated ministry that in 1636, only six years after the colony's founding, the Massachusetts General Court voted money "towards a schoale or colledge." Named after the Reverend John Harvard, a private benefactor, Harvard College opened its doors in 1638 in a house in a cattle yard donated by the town of Cambridge, and in 1642 graduated the first class of nine men. In 1650 the legislature granted Harvard an official charter, decreeing that the college's purpose was the "education of youth in all manner of good literature Artes and sciences."

Built squarely on the edifice of classical learning established during the medieval era, Puritan education met the highest humanistic standards. Students at Harvard studied grammar, rhetoric, logic (the *trivium*); ethics, natural science, metaphysics (the three philosophies);

and arithmetic, geometry, and astronomy (the *quadrivium*, with music omitted). They also mastered Latin, Greek, and (in order to interpret the Old Testament) Hebrew. And in the spirit of the Renaissance, they read history.

Such a demanding course of study required intensive preparation. In the earliest years of settlement, children were taught at home. But alarmed by possible lapses in home education, and wishing to prevent "that old deluder, Satan" from keeping men "from the knowledge of the Scriptures," in 1647 Massachusetts legislators passed a School Law ordering every town to appoint a teacher. Grammar schools would meanwhile teach boys Latin, Greek, and the classics, including Cicero, Virgil, and Hesiod.

After seven years of study, a boy was ready to enter Harvard. There he lived in a dormitory room with a roommate, ate his meals with tutors, and after four years of lectures and recitations, having defended a thesis in Latin, graduated with a bachelor's degree. Theology received no greater emphasis than any other subject. Prospective ministers, who constituted the majority of Harvard's graduates, had to study theology an additional three years in order to graduate with a master's degree. But the Congregational Church seldom interfered in the curriculum or training at Harvard or the grammar schools.

Harvard students, many of whose families paid their educational bills with farm produce and cattle, were not totally consumed by their studies. They consumed much "beef, bread, and beer," and fathers frequently conferred with their sons about why the bill for broken windows was so high. Masters, too, sometimes went awry. One early instructor fought with his charges, served them contaminated food, and embezzled virtually the whole college treasury! Yet the institution flourished, served its purpose, and became a model for American higher learning.

**Questions to Consider.** Why didn't the Puritans build a college as soon as they arrived in New England? What feature of the new Harvard was the author of the document most proud of? Why was it considered so important to study ancient Greek and Latin writers even though they were not Christian? Was a Harvard education "practical" given conditions in early New England? Should it have been more practical? Why wasn't it?

# New England's First Fruits—Harvard College (1643)

1. After God had carried us safe to New England, and we had builded our houses, provided necessaries for our livelihood, reared convenient

places for God's worship, and settled the civil government, one of the next things we longed for and looked after was to advance learning and perpetuate it to posterity; dreading to leave an illiterate ministry to the churches, when our present ministers shall lie in the dust. And as we were thinking and consulting how to effect this great work, it pleased God to stir up the heart of one Mr. Harvard (a godly gentleman, and a lover of learning, there living amongst us) to give the one half of his estate (it being in all about £1700) towards the erecting of a college, and all his library: after him, another gave £300, others after them cast in more, and the public hand of the state added the rest. The college was, by common consent, appointed to be at Cambridge (a place very pleasant and accommodate) and is called (according to the name of the first founder) Harvard College.

The edifice is very fair and comely within and without, having in it a spacious hall (where they daily meet at commons, lectures, exercises), and a large library with some books to it, the gifts of divers of our friends, their chambers and studies also fitted for, and possessed by the students, and all other rooms of office necessary and convenient, with all needful offices thereto belonging. And by the side of the College, a fair grammar school, for the training up of young scholars, and fitting of them for academical learning, that still as they are judged ripe, they may be received into the College of this school. Master Corlet is the master, who hath very well approved himself for his abilities, dexterity, and painfulness in teaching and education of the youth under him.

Over the College is Master Dunster placed, as president, a learned, conscionable, and industrious man, who hath so trained up his pupils in the tongues and arts, and so seasoned them with the principles of divinity and Christianity, that we have to our great comfort (and in truth, beyond our hopes) beheld their progress in learning and godliness also; the former of these hath appeared in their public declamations in Latin and Greek, and disputations logical and philosophical, which they have been wonted (besides their ordinary exercises in the College hall), in the audience of the magistrates, ministers, and other scholars, for the probation of their growth in learning, upon set days, constantly once every month, to make and uphold. The latter hath been manifested in sundry of them, by the savory breathings of their spirits in their godly conversation, insomuch that we are confident, if these early blossoms may be cherished and warmed with the influence of the friends of learning, and lovers of this pious work, they will, by the help of God, come to happy maturity in a short time.

Over the College are twelve overseers chosen by the General Court: six

From *New England's First Fruits* (London, 1643), in Samuel Eliot Morison, *The Founding of Harvard College* (Cambridge, Mass., 1935), 16–18. Copyright © 1935, 1963 by Samuel Eliot Morison. Reprinted by permission of Harvard University Press.

**A view of Harvard College about seventy-five years after its establishment.** Located in Cambridge, near Boston, the college's buildings included a student dormitory, classrooms, a dining commons, and quarters for instructors. The decision to erect these costly public buildings (Harvard became a private institution only in the nineteenth century) exemplified New England's commitment to higher learning. (Massachusetts Historical Society)

of them are of the magistrates, the other six of the ministers, who are to promote the best good of it, and (having a power of influence into all persons in it) are to see that everyone be diligent and proficient in his proper place.

*2. Rules, and Precepts that are Observed in the College.*

1. When any scholar is able to understand Tully or such like classical author *extempore*, and make and speak true Latin in verse and prose, *suo ut aiunt marte*, and decline perfectly the paradigms of nouns and verbs in the Greek tongue: let him then, and not before, be capable of admission into the College.

2. Let every student be plainly instructed and earnestly pressed to consider well, the main end of his life and studies is, "to know God and Jesus

Christ which is eternal life," John 17:3, and therefore to lay Christ in the bottom, as the only foundation of all sound knowledge and learning.

And seeing the Lord only giveth wisdom, let everyone seriously set himself by prayer in secret to seek it of Him, Prov. 2:3.

3. Everyone shall so exercise himself in reading the scriptures twice a day, that he shall be ready to give such an account of his proficiency therein, both in theoretical observations of the language, and logic, and in practical and spiritual truths, as his tutor shall require, according to his ability; seeing "the entrance of the Word giveth light, it giveth understanding to the simple," Psalm 119:130.

4. That they, eschewing all profanation of God's name, attributes, word, ordinances, and times of worship, do study with good conscience, carefully to retain God, and the love of His truth in their minds. Else, let them know, that (notwithstanding their learning) God may give them up "to strong delusions," and in the end "to a reprobate mind," 2 Thes. 2:11, 12, Rom. 1:28.

5. That they studiously redeem the time; observe the general hours appointed for all the students, and the special hours for their own classes; and then diligently attend the lectures, without any disturbance by word or gesture. And if in anything they doubt, they shall inquire, as of their fellows, so (in case of "non-satisfaction"), modestly of their tutors.

6. None shall, under any pretense whatsoever, frequent the company and society of such men as lead an unfit and dissolute life.

Nor shall any without his tutor's leave, or (in his absence) the call of parents or guardians, go abroad to other towns.

7. Every scholar shall be present in his tutor's chamber at the seventh hour in the morning, immediately after the sound of the bell, at his opening the scripture and prayer; so also at the fifth hour at night, and then give account of his own private reading, as aforesaid in particular the third, and constantly attend lectures in the hall at the hours appointed. But if any (without necessary impediment) shall absent himself from prayer or lectures, he shall be liable to admonition, if he offend above once a week.

8. If any scholar shall be found to transgress any of the laws of God, or the school, after twice admonition, he shall be liable, if not *adultus*, to correction; if *adultus*, his name shall be given up to the overseers of the College, that he may be admonished at the public monthly act.

## 3. The Times and Order of Their Studies, unless Experience Shall Shew Cause to Alter.

The second and third day of the week, read lectures, as followeth:

To the first year, at eight of the clock in the morning, logic the first three quarters, physics the last quarter.

To the second year, at the ninth hour, ethics and politics, at convenient distances of time.

To the third year, at the tenth, arithmetic and geometry the first three quarters, astronomy the last.

*Afternoon:*

The first year disputes at the second hour.
The second year at the third hour.
The third year at the fourth, everyone in his art.

The fourth day, reads Greek:
To the first year, the etymology and syntax at the eighth hour. To the second, at the ninth hour, *prosodia* and *dialects.*

*Afternoon:*

The first year, at second hour, practice the precepts of grammar in such authors as have variety of words.

The second year, at third hour, practice in poesy. . . .

The third year, perfect their theory before noon, and exercise style, composition, imitation, epitome, both in prose and verse, afternoon.

The fifth day, reads Hebrew and the Eastern tongues:
Grammar to the first year, hour the eighth.
To the second, Chaldee at the ninth hour.
To the third, Syriac at the tenth hour.

*Afternoon:*

The first year, practice in the Bible at the second hour.
The second, in Ezra and Daniel at the third hour.
The third, at the fourth hour in Trostius' New Testament.

The sixth day, reads rhetoric to all at the eighth hour:
Declamations at the ninth. So ordered that every scholar may declaim once a month. The rest of the day, vacat *rhetoricis studiis.*

The seventh day, reads divinity catechetical at the eighth hour; commonplaces at the ninth hour.

*Afternoon:*

The first hour, reads history in the winter, the nature of plants in the summer.

The sum of every lecture shall be examined, before the new lecture be read.

Every scholar, that on proof is found able to read the originals of the Old and New Testament into the Latin tongue, and to resolve them logically, withal being of godly life and conversation, and at any public act hath the approbation of the overseers and master of the College, is fit to be dignified with his first degree.

# 8

# THE HAND OF EMPIRE

The Navigation Acts, passed by the British Parliament over the span of a century, reflected the goals of mercantilism: to advance the interests of English merchants, shippers, shipbuilders, and producers and to make England, not other parts of the empire, wealthy. In this system the colonies would produce raw materials. England would ship, process, and market those materials and then sell manufactured goods back to the colonies.

There were, to be sure, some benefits for Americans. The English government paid bounties to producers of naval stores and indigo in America, for example, and saw to it that American tobacco had a preferential position in England. The British navy, moreover, protected the colonies as well as the mother country, and Britain clearly had a long-term interest in making the entire British Empire prosperous. Inevitably, however, given the realities of British political power, the system usually promoted the interests of businesses in Britain, not the colonies. Even among the British colonies, it was usually India and the Caribbean sugar islands, where profits were incredibly high, that got favored treatment, and not the North American mainland.

The first Act (1660) became the foundation for the entire trade and navigation system. As cracks appeared and the American economy changed, many other acts followed. Thus the Staple Act (1663) decreed that European products should pass through English ports before being shipped to the American colonies. When New England shippers defied this rule by smuggling goods into more profitable European ports, Parliament responded with the Act of 1672 to plug the illicit trade. The important Act of 1696 tried to reassert control by establishing a fully developed customs system in America (giving customs officers enormous powers to search and punish) and by declaring colonial laws contrary to the Act "illegal and void."

The 1733 "Sugar" (or Molasses) Act was ineffectual largely because Americans quickly elevated bribery and smuggling to an art form. Other measures tried to keep Americans from making beaver hats, a lucrative business, or starting their own banks. The 1764 Act tightened sugar controls and restricted the manufacture of iron products, thereby further injuring American industry. By now, moreover, Britain was carrying a huge war debt from its conquest of France in the Seven Years' ("French and Indian") War. It seemed only fair that the Americans, who benefitted from the English victory, should pay their share of the costs by means of customs duties.

But the Americans resisted. They refused, in the name of liberty, to submit to any authority not of their own making. Parliament claimed the right to regulate trade and raise revenue. Americans evaded, challenged, and defied, arguing that with Parliament free to tax trade, there could be "no Liberty, no Happiness, no Security." The 1764 Act seemed the culmination of a mercantile system designed to coerce the colonies. The Navigation Acts looked like a "conspiracy" to "tyrannize" them. A habit and a vocabulary of opposition arose in America that set Parliament and the colonists on a collision course.

**Questions to Consider.**  To what extent did the changing provisions of the Navigation Acts reflect changes in the colonial economies? What British economic interests did the different Acts appear to be protecting? How important were the sheer difficulties of enforcement in prompting the various Acts? What caused the Navigation Acts, which were imperial regulatory measures, to become a hot political issue?

# The Navigation Acts (1660–1764)

## 1660

For the increase of Shipping and encouragement of the Navigation of this Nation, wherein under the good providence and protection of God the Wealth, Safety and Strength of this Kingdom is so much concerned, Be it Enacted . . . That . . . from thence forward no Goods or Commodities whatsoever shall be Imported into or Exported out of any Lands, Islands, Plantations or Territories to his Majesty belonging or in his possession or which may hereafter belong unto or be in the possession of His Majesty His Heirs and Successors in Asia, Africa, or America in any other Ship or Ships, Vessel or Vessels whatsoever but in such Ships or Vessels as do truly and without fraud belong only to the people of England or Ireland, . . . or are of the built of, and belonging to any of the said Lands, Islands, Plantations or Territories as the Proprietors and right Owners thereof and whereof the

From Danby Pickering, *The Statutes at Large from the Magna Carta to the End of the Eleventh Parliament* (J. Bentham, Cambridge, 1806).

Master and three fourths of the Mariners at least are English under the penalty of the Forfeiture and Loss of all the Goods and Commodities which shall be Imported into, or Exported out of, any the aforesaid places in any other Ship or Vessel, as also of the Ship or Vessel with all its Guns, Furniture, Tackle, Ammunition and Apparel.

## 1663

Be it enacted . . . That . . . no Commodity of the Growth, Production or Manufacture of Europe shall be imported into any Land, Island, Plantation, Colony, Territory or Place to His Majesty belonging, (or) . . . in the Possession of His Majesty . . . in Asia, Africa, or America (Tangier only excepted) but what shall be bona fide and without fraud laden and shipped in England . . . and in English built Shipping, or which were bona fide bought before . . . 1662 . . . and whereof the Master and three Fourths of the Mariners at least are English, and which shall be carried directly thence to the said Lands, Islands, Plantations, Colonies, Territories or Places, and from no other place or places whatsoever, Any Law Statute or Usage to the contrary notwithstanding, under the Penalty of the loss of all such Commodities of the Growth, Production or Manufacture of Europe as shall be imported into any of them from any other Place whatsoever by Land or Water, and if by Water, of the Ship, or Vessel also in which they were imported with all her Guns, Tackle, Furniture, Ammunition and Apparel.

## 1672

[W]hereas by . . . [the Navigation Act of 1660] . . . , and by several other Laws passed since that time it is permitted to ship, carry, convey and transport Sugar, Tobacco, Cotton-wool, Indigo, Ginger, Fustic and all other Dyeing wood of the Growth, Production and Manufacture of any of your Majesties Plantations in America, Asia or Africa from the places of their Growth, Production and Manufacture to any other of your Majesties Plantations in those Parts (Tangier only excepted) and that without paying of Customs for the same either at lading or unlading of the said Commodities by means whereof the Trade and Navigation in those Commodities from one Plantation to another is greatly increased, and the Inhabitants of diverse of those Colonies not contenting themselves with being supplied with those Commodities for their own use free from all Customs (while the Subjects of this your Kingdom of England have paid great Customs and Impositions for what of them has been spent here) but contrary to the express Letter of the aforesaid Laws have brought into diverse parts of Europe great quantities thereof, and do also daily vend great quantities thereof to the shipping of other Nations who bring them into diverse parts of Europe to the great hurt and diminution of your Majesties Customs and of the Trade and Navigation of this your Kingdom; For the prevention thereof . . . be it enacted . . . That

... If any Ship or Vessel which by Law may trade in any of your Majesties Plantations shall come to any of them to ship and take on board any of the aforesaid Commodities, and that Bond shall not be first given with one sufficient Surety to bring the same to England or Wales ... and to no other place, and there to unload and put the same on shore (the danger of the Seas only excepted) that there shall be ... paid to your Majesty ... for so much of the said Commodities as shall be laded and put on board such Ship or Vessel these following Rates and Duties. ...

## 1696

[F]or the more effectual preventing of Frauds and regulating Abuses in the Plantation Trade in America Be it further enacted ... That all Ships coming into or going out of any of the said Plantations and lading or unlading any Goods or Commodities whether the same be His Majesties Ships of War or Merchants Ships and the Masters and Commanders thereof and their Ladings shall be subject and liable to the same Rules, Visitations, Searches, Penalties, and Forfeitures as to the entering, lading or discharging their respective Ships and Ladings as Ships and their Ladings and the Commanders and Masters of Ships are subject and liable unto in this Kingdom ... And that the Officers for collecting and managing His Majesties Revenue and inspecting the Plantation Trade in any of the said Plantations shall have the same Powers and Authorities for visiting and searching of Ships and taking their Entries and for seizing and securing or bringing on Shore any of the Goods prohibited to be imported or exported into or out of any of the said Plantations or for which any Duties are payable or ought to have been paid by any of the before mentioned Acts as are provided for the Officers of the Customs in England ... and also to enter Houses or Warehouses to search for and seize any such Goods ...

And ... That all laws, by-laws, usages or customs, at this time, or which hereafter shall be in practice ... in any of the said Plantations, which are in any wise repugnant to the before mentioned laws, or any of them, so far as they do relate to the said Plantations, ... or which are any ways repugnant to this present Act, or to any other law hereafter to be made in this Kingdom, so far as such law shall relate to and mention the said Plantations, are illegal, null and void. ...

## 1733

WHEREAS the welfare and prosperity of your Majesty's sugar colonies in America are of the greatest consequence and importance to the trade, navigation and strength of this kingdom: and whereas the planters of the said sugar colonies have of late years fallen under such great discouragements, that they are unable to improve or carry on the sugar trade upon an equal footing with the foreign sugar colonies, without some advantage and relief be given to them from Great Britain: . . . be it enacted . . ., That . . . there shall be raised, levied, collected and paid, unto and for the use of his Majesty . . ., upon all rum or spirits of the produce or manufacture of any of the colonies or plantations in America, not in the possession or under the dominion of his Majesty . . ., which at any time or times within or during the continuance of this act, shall be imported or brought into any of the colonies or plantations in America, which now are or hereafter may be in the possession or under the dominion of his Majesty . . ., the sum of nine pence, money of Great Britain, . . . for every gallon thereof, and after that rate for any greater or lesser quantity: and upon all molasses or syrups of such foreign produce or manufacture as aforesaid, which shall be imported or brought into any of the said colonies or plantations . . ., the sum of six pence of like money for every gallon thereof . . .; and upon all sugars and paneles of such foreign growth, produce or manufacture as aforesaid, which shall be imported into any of the said colonies or plantations . . ., a duty after the rate of five shillings of like money, for every hundred weight. . . .

## 1764

WHEREAS it is expedient that new provisions and regulations should be established for improving the revenue of this Kingdom, and for extending and securing the navigation and commerce between Great Britain and your Majesty's dominions in America, which, by the peace, have been so happily enlarged: and whereas it is just and necessary, that a revenue be raised, in your Majesty's said dominions in America, for defraying the expenses of defending, protecting and securing the same; . . . be it enacted . . ., That there shall be raised, levied, collected, and paid, unto his Majesty . . ., for and upon all white or clayed sugars of the produce or manufacture of any colony or plantation in America, not under the dominion of his Majesty . . .; for and upon indigo, and coffee of foreign produce or manufacture; for and upon all wines (except French wine;) for and upon all wrought silks, bengals, and stuffs, mixed with silk or herba, of the manufacture of Persia, China, or East India, and all calico painted, dyed, printed, or stained there; and for and upon all foreign linen cloth called Cambrick and French Lawns, which shall be imported or brought into any colony or plantation in America, which now is, or hereafter may be, under the dominion of his Majesty . . ., the several rates and duties following; . . .

. . . And be it further enacted . . ., That . . . no rum or spirits of the produce or manufacture of any of the colonies or plantations in America, not in the possession or under the dominion of his Majesty . . ., shall be imported or brought into any of the colonies or plantations in America which now are, or hereafter may be, in the possession or under the dominion of his Majesty . . ., upon forfeiture of all such rum or spirits, together with the ship or vessel in which the same shall be imported, with the tackle, apparel, and furniture thereof. . . .

. . . And it is hereby further enacted . . ., That . . . no iron, nor any sort of wood, commonly called Lumber, as specified in an act passed in the eighth year of the reign of King George the First, entitled, An act for giving further encouragement for the importation of naval stores, and for other purposes therein mentioned, of the growth, production, or manufacture, of any British colony or plantation in America, shall be there loaded on board any ship or vessel to be carried from thence, until sufficient bond shall be given, with one surety besides the master of the vessel, to the collector or other principal officer of the customs at the loading port, in a penalty of double the value of the goods, with condition, that the said goods shall not be landed in any part of Europe except Great Britain.

**A liberty pole.** A liberty pole is raised in celebration of the Declaration of Independence. (Kennedy Galleries)

CHAPTER TWO

# Strides Toward Freedom

# 9

## DIVERSITY AND ABUNDANCE

Driven out of Scotland by the wars of British succession, the Ulster Scots were initially lured to northern Ireland by James I's promises of good land. But the Ulstermen, as they came to call themselves, became victims of severe political and economic oppression at the hands of both Crown and Parliament—the great poet John Milton referred to them as "blockish Presbyterians" from a "barbarous nook of Ireland," and they soon fled Ireland in search of economic opportunity and freedom in America. Unwelcome in seventeenth-century Puritan towns, when the Scotch-Irish (as Americans called them) learned that Pennsylvania would accommodate them, they poured into the backcountry in great waves in the 1700s.

By the time of the American Revolution, the Scotch-Irish numbered more than a quarter of a million, and Pennsylvania had become the most cosmopolitan colony. To the distress of politicians who feared that "if they continue to come, they will make themselves proprietors of the province," the Scotch-Irish flouted all rules of settlement, squatting on virtually any "spot of vacant ground." Contemptuous even of legal requirements to show title, they asserted that it was "against the laws of God and nature that so much land should lie idle while so many Christians wanted it to labor on and raise their bread." They used virtually the same reasoning the Puritans had when they took over Indian lands in the fertile Connecticut Valley.

Like the Puritans, the Scotch-Irish were Calvinists, but while the Puritans migrated to New England to create a "holy commonwealth," the Scotch-Irish came to Pennsylvania because its rich farmland provided a way to make a living, and a good one. The Scotch-Irish looked at life through a markedly different lens, one that reflected expanding opportunities, as in this anonymous Pennsylvania poem of 1730:

*Stretched on the bank of Delaware's rapid stream*
*Stands Philadelphia, not unknown to fame.*
*Here the tall vessels safe at anchor ride,*
*And Europe's wealth flows in with every tide.*

The Scotch-Irish viewpoint was utilitarian and practical. The earliest Puritans labored for the glory of God. The Scotch-Irish labored for themselves and their families.

In the beginning of the eighteenth century, settlers in search of economic prospects ventured inland, away from the tidewater and the reassuring smell of the sea; as the frontier moved gradually westward, they were exposed to new vistas. The Scotch-Irish also carried religious convictions into the Pennsylvania frontier, but as the following document suggests, things of the spirit were somehow less newsworthy than the soil and its "extraordinary increase."

Robert Parke arrived in Pennsylvania from northern Ireland about 1723 when good land was still cheap, and he and his family were fortunate to have funds sufficient to see them through the first difficult year of their arrival. Enough money remained to allow them to acquire a sizable and fruitful piece of property. Parke wrote the following letter to his sister back in Ireland.

**Questions to Consider.**  To what extent is this a strictly practical document? How did Parke relate to his children? How would you describe his feelings for the land? Is there evidence that Parke had a personality suited for life in a demanding environment? Was he a religious man?

# Letter from Pennsylvania (1725)

ROBERT PARKE

Thee writes in thy letter that there was a talk went back to Ireland that we were not satisfied in coming here, which was utterly false. Now, let this suffice to convince you. In the first place he that carried back this story was an idle fellow, and one of our shipmates, but not thinking this country suitable to his idleness, went back with [Captain] Cowman again. He is sort of a lawyer, or rather a liar, as I may term him; therefore, I would not have you give credit to such false reports for the future, for there is not one of the family but what likes the country very well and would, if we were in Ireland again, come here directly, it being the best country for working folk and tradesmen of any in the world. But for drunkards and idlers, they cannot live well anywhere. . . . Land is of all prices, even from ten pounds to one hundred pounds a hundred [acres], according to the goodness or else the situation thereof, and grows dearer every year by reason of vast quantities of

From Charles A. Hanna, *The Scotch-Irish* (New York and London, 1902), II: 64–67.

people that come here yearly from several parts of the world. Therefore, thee and thy family or any that I wish well, I would desire to make what speed you can to come here, the sooner the better.

We have traveled over a pretty deal of this country to seek land and though we met with many fine tracts of land here and there in the country, yet my father being curious and somewhat hard to please did not buy any land until the second day of tenth month last, and then he bought a tract of land consisting of five hundred acres for which he gave 350 pounds. It is excellent good land but none cleared, except about twenty acres, with a small log house and orchard planted. We are going to clear some of it directly, for our next summer's fallow. We might have bought land much cheaper but not so much to our satisfaction. We stayed in Chester three months and then we rented a place one mile from Chester with a good brick house and 200 acres of land for———pounds a year, where we continue till next May. We have sowed about 200 acres of wheat and seven acres of rye this season. We sowed but a bushel on an acre. . . .

I am grown an experienced plowman and my brother Abell is learning. Jonathan and thy son John drives for us. He is grown a lusty fellow since thou saw him. We have the finest plows here that can be. We plowed up our summer's fallows in May and June with a yoke of oxen and two horses and they go with as much ease as double the number in Ireland. We sow our wheat with two horses. A boy of twelve or fourteen years old can hold plow here; a man commonly holds and drives himself. They plow an acre, nay, some plows two acres a day.

They sow wheat and rye in August and September. We have had a crop of oats, barley, and very good flax and hemp, Indian corn and buckwheat all of our own sowing and planting this last summer. We also planted a bushel of white potatoes which cost us five shillings and we had ten or twelve bushels' increase. This country yields extraordinary increase of all sorts of grain likewise. . . .

This country abounds in fruit, scarce an house but has an apple, peach, and cherry orchard. As for chestnuts, walnuts, and hazelnuts, strawberries, billberries, and mulberries, they grow wild in the woods and fields in vast quantities.

They also make great preparations against harvest. Both roast and boiled [meats], cakes and tarts and rum, stand at the land's end, so that they may eat and drink at pleasure. A reaper has two shillings and threepence a day, a mower has two shillings and sixpence and a pint of rum, besides meat and drink of the best, for no workman works without their victuals in the bargain throughout the country.

As to what thee writ about the governor's opening letters, it is utterly false and nothing but a lie, and anyone except bound servants[1] may go out

---

1. **Bound servants:** Indentured servants, who agreed to work without rights or wages for a specified number of years in exchange for having their passage paid from Europe to America. The right to their labor could be sold from one owner to another.—*Eds.*

of the country when they will and servants when they serve their time may come away if they please. But it is rare any are such fools to leave the country except men's business require it. They pay nine pounds for their passage (of this money) to go to Ireland.

There is two fairs yearly and two markets weekly in Philadelphia; also two fairs yearly in Chester and likewise in Newcastle, but they sell no cattle nor horses, no living creatures, but altogether merchants' goods, as hats, linen and woolen cloth, handerchiefs, knives, scissors, tapes and threads, buckles, ribbons, and all sorts of necessaries fit for our wooden country, and here all young men and women that wants wives or husbands may be supplied. Let this suffice for our fairs. As to [religious] meetings, they are so plenty one may ride to their choice. . . .

Dear sister, I desire thee may tell my old friend Samuel Thornton that he could give so much credit to my words and find no "ifs" nor "ands" in my letter, that in plain terms he could not do better than to come here, for both his and his wife's trade are very good here. The best way for him to do is to pay what money he can conveniently spare at that side and engage himself to pay the rest at this side, and when he comes here, if he can get no friend to lay down the money for him, when it comes to the worst, he may hire out two or three children.

# 10

## SELF-IMPROVEMENT

Benjamin Franklin was amazingly versatile. He was at various times printer, journalist, editor, educator, satirist, reformer, scientist, inventor, political activist, and diplomat. He was also a successful businessman. His printing business did so well that he was able to retire from active work while in his forties and devote the rest of his life to public service, humanitarian causes, and science and invention. His most famous and rewarding publication was Poor Richard's Almanac, which he published annually from 1733 to 1758. In addition to weather and astronomical information, Franklin's Almanac also printed mottoes and proverbs touting the virtues of diligence, temperance, moderation, and thrift. "Keep thy shop and thy shop will keep thee," advised Franklin. "Early to bed, and early to rise, makes a man healthy, wealthy, and wise." God, after all, "helps them that help themselves."

Franklin filled his *Almanac* with self-help proverbs because they were popular. But he also believed they worked. He himself had risen from the obscurity of working-class Boston to become a notable Pennsylvanian through self-discipline and improvement—by training himself to think clearly, speak correctly, and write elegantly and to labor diligently in his print shop.

Franklin believed the self-help maxims would work for communities as well as for individuals. He was the quintessential community organizer and was responsible for the establishment of Philadelphia's first public library and its first fire company. Among his other accomplishments were an academy that became the University of Pennsylvania and the first scientific society and the first hospital in British North America.

Perhaps Franklin's earliest civic initiative was an improvement society, the "Junto," whose members met each Friday to discuss some point of morals, politics, or science. The society's members, mostly young craftsmen, discussed each of the following twenty-four "standing queries" at every Junto meeting, with "a pause between each while one might fill and drink a glass of wine." Discussion must have been sober enough, however. From the Junto came numerous spin-off improvement societies, the library and other public projects, and, eventually, much of the civic leadership of eighteenth-century Pennsylvania.

Born in Boston in 1706, the son of a candlemaker, Benjamin Franklin was apprenticed at the age of twelve to his brother, a printer. At seventeen, having mastered the trade, Franklin ran away to Philadelphia and soon established a thriving printing establishment of his own. Not only did he become famous as a writer and publisher, he also represented the colonies in England from 1757 to 1775 and served as minister to France during the war for independence. For his pioneering work in the field of electricity, he was as famous in Europe as in America. In his *Autobiography,* which he wrote for his son in 1777, he dwelt on his early years, to make it, he said, "of more general use to young readers, as exemplifying strongly the effects of prudent and imprudent conduct in the commencement of a life of business." He remained active until his death in 1790, becoming president of the executive council of Pennsylvania at the age of seventy-nine and representing his state in the Constitutional Convention, which met in Philadelphia in 1787.

**Questions to Consider.** Why might young male workers who enjoyed a good time want to discuss "queries" of this kind at their meetings? Do the twenty-four queries seem to have been drawn up in any particular order? Which query strikes you as most interesting, surprising, or absurd? Do organizations like the Junto exist today? Would the queries have to be amended to be useful today? What sort of society were the Junto members hoping to create? Was this a good way to create it?

# The Junto Queries (1729)

### BENJAMIN FRANKLIN

Have you read over these queries this morning, in order to consider what you might have to offer the Junto[1] touching any one of them viz:?

1. Have you met with anything in the author you last read, remarkable, or suitable to be communicated to the Junto, particularly in history, morality, poetry, physic, travels, mechanic arts, or other parts of knowledge?

2. What new story have you lately heard agreeable for telling in conversation?

---

1. **Junto:** A group of persons joined for a common purpose.

From John Bigelow, ed., *The Complete Works o]f Benjamin Franklin* (G.P. Putnam & Sons, New York and London, 1887), I: 319–322.

FRANKLIN'S YOUTHFUL, INDUSTRIOUS HABITS,
' I was called home to assist my father in his occupation, which was that
of a Soap boiler and Tallow-chandler "

**Benjamin Franklin as an apprentice craftsman.** Franklin's father, a Boston artisan, walked with young Ben through the town's working-class districts so that the boy could decide which trade, such as candlemaking or leatherworking, to learn. Ben ended up as an apprentice to a printer, in which business he eventually made his fortune. This picture, from an early edition of Franklin's autobiography, shows Ben as an adolescent apprentice carrying a bucket of molten lead for making metal letters and a frame in which to arrange the finished type. Other members of the Junto would have gone through similar apprenticeships. (Historical Society of Pennsylvania)

3. Hath any citizen in your knowledge failed in his business lately, and what have you heard of the cause?

4. Have you lately heard of any citizen's thriving well, and by what means?

5. Have you lately heard how any present rich man, here or elsewhere, got his estate?

6. Do you know of a fellow-citizen, who has lately done a worthy action, deserving praise and imitation; or who has lately committed an error, proper for us to be warned against and avoid?

7. What unhappy effects of intemperance have you lately observed or heard; of imprudence, of passion, or of any other vice or folly?

8. What happy effects of temperance, prudence, of moderation, or of any other virtue?

9. Have you or any of your acquaintance been lately sick or wounded? if so, what remedies were used, and what were their effects?

10. Whom do you know that are shortly going on voyages or journeys, if one should have occasion to send by them?

11. Do you think of anything at present, in which the Junto may be serviceable to *mankind,* to their country, to their friends, or to themselves?

12. Hath any deserving stranger arrived in town since last meeting, that you have heard of?; and what have you heard or observed of his character or merits?; and whether, think you, it lies in the power of the Junto to oblige him, or encourage him as he deserves?

13. Do you know of any deserving young beginner lately set up, whom it lies in the power of the Junto anyway to encourage?

14. Have you lately observed any defect in the laws of your *country,* of which it would be proper to move the legislature for an amendment?; or do you know of any beneficial law that is wanting?

15. Have you lately observed any encroachment on the just liberties of the people?

16. Hath anybody attacked your reputation lately?; and what can the Junto do towards securing it?

17. Is there any man whose friendship you want, and which the Junto, or any of them, can procure for you?

18. Have you lately heard any member's character attacked, and how have you defended it?

19. Hath any man injured you, from whom it is in the power of the Junto to procure redress?

20. In what manner can the Junto or any of them, assist you in any of your honorable designs?

21. Have you any weighty affair on hand in which you think the advice of the Junto may be of service?

22. What benefits have you lately received from any man not present?

23. Is there any difficulty in matters of opinion, of justice, and injustice, which you would gladly have discussed at this time?

24. Do you see anything amiss in the present customs or proceedings of the Junto, which might be amended?

# 11

# A Right to Criticize

In 1735 came the first great battle over freedom of the press in America. Two years earlier, John Peter Zenger, publisher of the outspoken New-York Weekly Journal, began printing articles satirizing corruption and highhandedness in the administration of William Cosby, the new royal governor of New York, and he also distributed song sheets praising those who would "boldly despise the haughty knaves who keep us in awe." In 1734 Cosby arranged for Zenger to be arrested, charged with seditious libel, and thrown in prison. He also ordered copies of the New-York Weekly Journal burned in public. When Zenger's case came before the court in 1735, Andrew Hamilton, a prominent Philadelphian who was the most skillful lawyer in America, agreed to defend him. According to English law, a printed attack on a public official, even if true, was considered libelous; and the judge ruled that the fact that Zenger had criticized the New York governor was enough to convict him. But Hamilton argued that no one should be punished for telling the truth; Zenger, he pointed out, had told the truth and should not be convicted of libel. In "a free government," he insisted, the rulers should "not be able to stop the people's mouths when they feel themselves oppressed." Liberty, he added, is the "only bulwark against lawless power." Hamilton was so eloquent in his plea that in the end the jury voted "not guilty" and spectators in the courtroom cheered the verdict.

After his release, Zenger printed a complete account of the trial in his paper (some of which appears below) and also arranged to have it printed separately as a pamphlet. The report of the trial aroused great interest in Britain as well as in America and went through many editions. Hamilton's plea to the jury on behalf of "speaking and writing the truth" was one of the landmarks in the struggle for a free press in America. Though other royal judges did not accept the principle enunciated by Hamilton, the decision in the Zenger case did set an important precedent against judicial tyranny in libel suits. Gouverneur Morris, a statesman and diplomat from New York, called it "the morning star of that liberty which subsequently revolutionized America."

Zenger did not speak on his own behalf during the trial. But he had planned, if found guilty, to make a speech reminding the jurors that he and his parents had "fled from a country where oppression, tyranny, and arbitrary power had ruined almost all the people." Zenger, who was born in Germany in 1697, came to America, along with many other German immigrants, when he was twelve years old and was indentured to William Bradford, "the pioneer printer of the middle colonies." In 1726 he set up a printing shop of his own, publishing tracts and pamphlets mainly of a religious nature, and in 1730 he published the first arithmetic text in New York. A few years after his famous trial he became public printer for the colony of New York and a little later for New Jersey as well. He died in 1746. Andrew Hamilton was a well-known and successful Philadelphia lawyer, trained in Britain and hired by a disgruntled New York political faction to take Zenger's case.

**Questions to Consider.** In the following exchange between the prosecuting attorney and Hamilton, Zenger's lawyer, why did Hamilton place such emphasis on the word *false?* What complaint did he make about his effort to present evidence to the court on behalf of his client? What did he mean by saying that "the suppression of evidence ought always to be taken for the strongest evidence"? Why did he think Zenger's case was so important? Do you consider his final appeal to the jury a convincing one?

# John Peter Zenger's Libel Trial (1735)

*Mr. Attorney.* . . . The case before the court is whether Mr. Zenger is guilty of libeling His Excellency the Governor of New York, and indeed the whole administration of the government. Mr. Hamilton has confessed the printing and publishing, and I think nothing is plainer than that the words in the information [indictment] are scandalous, and tend to sedition, and to disquiet the minds of the people of this province. And if such papers are not libels, I think it may be said there can be no such thing as a libel.

*Mr. Hamilton.* May it please Your Honor, I cannot agree with Mr. Attorney. For though I freely acknowledge that there are such things as libels, yet I must insist, at the same time, that what my client is charged with is not a libel. And I observed just now that Mr. Attorney, in defining a libel, made use of the words "scandalous, seditious, and tend to disquiet the people." But (whether with design or not I will not say) he omitted the word "false."

From J. P. Zenger, *The Tryal of J. P. Z. of New York* (London, 1738), 10–17.

**The trial of John Peter Zenger.** This tapestry depicts the New York courtroom in August 1735, when a jury acquitted the printer of a charge of libel. Crown officers and attorneys wore white-powdered wigs, as officials did in England, to emphasize their authority. Since imperial bureaucrats such as these not only were distant geographically from the real center of British power in London but also had to deal with obstreperous colonials such as Zenger, they may have taken even more care than their counterparts at home to keep their wigs white and imposing as symbols of British authority. (The Metropolitan Museum of Art, A Bicentennial Gift to America from a Grateful Armenian-American People, 1978)

*Mr. Attorney.* I think I did not omit the word "false." But it has been said already that it may be a libel, notwithstanding it may be true.

*Mr. Hamilton.* In this I must still differ with Mr. Attorney; for I depend upon it, we are to be tried upon this information now before the court and jury, and to which we have pleaded not guilty, and by it we are charged with printing and publishing a certain false, malicious, seditious, and scandalous libel. This word "false" must have some meaning, or else how came it there? . . .

*Mr. Chief Justice.* You cannot be admitted, Mr. Hamilton, to give the truth of a libel in evidence. A libel is not to be justified; for it is nevertheless a libel that it is true. . . .

*Mr. Hamilton.* I thank Your Honor. Then, gentlemen of the jury, it is to you we must now appeal, for witnesses, to the truth of the facts we have offered, and are denied the liberty to prove. And let it not seem strange that I apply myself to you in this manner. I am warranted so to do both by law and reason.

The law supposes you to be summoned out of the neighborhood where the fact [crime] is alleged to be committed; and the reason of your being taken out of the neighborhood is because you are supposed to have the best knowledge of the fact that is to be tried. And were you to find a verdict against my client, you must take upon you to say the papers referred to in the information, and which we acknowledge we printed and published, are false, scandalous, and seditious. But of this I can have no apprehension. You are citizens of New York; you are really what the law supposes you to be, honest and lawful men. And, according to my brief, the facts which we offer to prove were not committed in a corner; they are notoriously known to be true; and therefore in your justice lies our safety. And as we are denied the liberty of giving evidence to prove the truth of what we have published, I will beg leave to lay it down, as a standing rule in such cases, that the suppressing of evidence ought always to be taken for the strongest evidence; and I hope it will have weight with you. . . .

I hope to be pardoned, sir, for my zeal upon this occasion. It is an old and wise caution that when our neighbor's house is on fire, we ought to take care of our own. For though, blessed be God, I live in a government [Pennsylvania] where liberty is well understood, and freely enjoyed, yet experience has shown us all (I'm sure it has to me) that a bad precedent in one government is soon set up for an authority in another. And therefore I cannot but think it mine, and every honest man's duty, that (while we pay all due obedience to men in authority) we ought at the same time to be upon our guard against power, wherever we apprehend that it may affect ourselves or our fellow subjects.

I am truly very unequal to such an undertaking on many accounts. And you see I labor under the weight of many years, and am borne down with great infirmities of body. Yet old and weak as I am, I should think it my duty, if required, to go to the utmost part of the land, where my service could be

of any use, in assist—to quench the flame of prosecutions upon informa-
tions, set on foot by the government, to deprive a people of the right of re-
monstrating (and complaining too) of the arbitrary attempts of men in
power. Men who injure and oppress the people under their administration
provoke them to cry out and complain; and then make that very complaint
the foundation for new oppressions and prosecutions. I wish I could say
there were no instances of this kind.

But to conclude. The question before the court and you, gentlemen of the
jury, is not of small nor private concern. It is not the cause of a poor printer,
nor of New York alone, which you are now trying. No! It may, in its consequence, affect every freeman that lives under a British government on the
main[land] of America. It is the best cause. It is the cause of liberty. And I
make no doubt but your upright conduct, this day, will not only entitle you
to the love and esteem of your fellow citizens; but every man who prefers
freedom to a life of slavery will bless and honor you, as men who have baf-
fled the attempt of tyranny, and, by an impartial and uncorrupt verdict,
have laid a noble foundation for securing to ourselves, our posterity, and
our neighbors, that to which nature and the laws of our country have given
us a right—the liberty both of exposing and opposing arbitrary power (in
these parts of the world, at least) by speaking and writing truth. . . .

# ★ 12 ★

~~~

# THE GREAT AWAKENING

Jonathan Edwards was upset by the "extraordinary dullness in religion" he observed around him. During the first part of the eighteenth century, as the population of the colonies increased and Americans developed a thriving trade with other parts of the world, they became increasingly worldly in their outlook. It wasn't that they abandoned religion; what they abandoned was the stern religion that Edwards considered essential to salvation. Edwards, like John Winthrop, was a devout Puritan. He believed human beings were incorrigible sinners, filled with greed, pride, and lust, and that a just God had condemned them to eternal damnation for their transgressions. But God was merciful as well as just. Because Jesus had atoned for man's sins by dying on the cross, God agreed to shed his grace on some men and women and elect them for salvation. The individual who was chosen for salvation experienced God's grace while being converted. For Edwards the conversion experience was the greatest event in a person's life. After conversion, the individual dedicated himself to the glory of God and possessed a new strength to resist temptation.

In his sermons, Edwards, pastor of the Congregational church in Northampton, Massachusetts, tried to impress on people the awful fate that awaited them unless they acknowledged their sinfulness and threw themselves upon the mercy of God. During the last part of 1734 Edwards delivered a series of sermons that moved his congregation deeply. He gave such vivid descriptions of human depravity and the torments awaiting the unredeemed in the next world that people in the congregation wept, groaned, and begged for mercy. Edward's sermons produced scores of conversions. During the winter and spring over three hundred people were converted and admitted to full membership in the church. "This town," wrote Edwards joyfully, "never was so full of Love, nor so full of Joy, nor so full of distress as it has lately been." The religious revival that Edwards led in Northampton was only one of many revivals sweeping America at this time—in New England, in the Middle Colonies, and in the South. The Great Awakening, as the revivalist movement was called, affected the Presbyterians as well as the Congregationalists, and also swept through other denominations, keeping the churches in turmoil from about 1734 to 1756. The Great Awakening did produce a renewed interest in religion, but not always in Edwards's austere Puritanism. Edwards led revivals only in New England. George Whitefield, an English associate of John Wesley, the founder of Methodism, came to America, toured the colonies, and led revivals wherever he went. He helped make the Great Awakening an intercolonial movement. It was the first movement in which all the colonies participated before the American Revolution.

Jonathan Edwards's mind was so exceptional that even those who disagreed with him had to respect the clarity and originality of his theology. He was probably the only American of his day who understood the implications of modern physics and psychology for religious faith. But he also needed to defend the Great Awakening from its detractors. In many places in the colonies the revival flamed out of control, producing hysterical behavior (fainting, wild dancing, screaming "fits"). Edwards knew he had to account for all this, or opponents would question the revival's methods and divine inspiration. He wrote "Revival of Religion in New England," excerpted below, mainly to diagnose the irrational behavior of the newly converted. But the treatise is also valuable for describing the changes that came over New Englanders as a result of the revival.

Edwards, who was born in East Windsor, Connecticut, in 1703, was a precocious lad. He wrote a treatise on spiders at age twelve and entered Yale College at age thirteen. The son of a Congregational minister, he experienced conversion as a young man, dedicated his life to the church, and pursued theological studies at Yale after graduation. In 1726 he became associate pastor of the Congregational church in Northampton, and in 1729 he was appointed pastor. For twenty-one years he labored hard in Northampton, studying, writing, and preaching; he also launched his ambitious plan for publishing treatises on all of the great Puritan doctrines. In 1750 he took his family to Stockbridge, Massachusetts. There he spent the rest of his life, preaching and serving as missionary to the Native Americans. In 1758 he was appointed president of the College of New Jersey (Princeton), but he died of smallpox before beginning his duties there.

**Questions to Consider.** Why was Jonathan Edwards so concerned to justify the "imprudence" and "irregularities" of the revival? What did he see as its chief benefits? Did he think the revival benefitted society as a whole or only individuals? Why did he use the word "love" so frequently in his account? What particular groups especially concerned him? Was he being realistic in his criticism and expectations of his community? In what ways might the Great Awakening, as Edwards described it, have fostered antiestablishment, anti-imperial attitudes among the colonists?

# The Revival of Religion in New England (1742)

### JONATHAN EDWARDS

Whatever imprudences there have been, and whatever sinful irregularities; whatever vehemence of the passions and heats of the imagination, transports and ecstasies; and whatever error in judgment, and indiscreet zeal; and whatever outcries, and faintings, and agitations of body; yet it is manifest and notorious, that there has been of late a very uncommon influence upon the minds of a very great part of the inhabitants of New England, from one end of the land to the other, that has been attended with the following effects: a great increase of a spirit of seriousness, and sober consideration of the things of the eternal world; a disposition to hearken to anything that is said of things of this nature, with attention and affection; a disposition to treat matters of religion with solemnity, and as matters of great importance; a disposition to make these things the subject of conversation; and a great disposition to hear the Word of God preached, and to take all opportunities in order to it; and to attend on the public worship of God, and all external duties of religion in a more solemn and decent manner; so that there is a remarkable and general alteration in the face of New England in these respects.

Multitudes in all parts of the land, of vain, thoughtless, regardless persons are quite changed, and become serious and considerate: there is a vast increase of concern for the salvation of the precious soul, and of that inquiry, "What shall I do to be saved?" [Acts 16:30]. The hearts of multitudes have been greatly taken off from the things of the world, its profits, pleasures and honors; and there has been a great increase of sensibleness and tenderness of conscience. Multitudes in all parts have had their consciences awakened, and have been made sensible of the pernicious nature and consequences of sin, and what a dreadful thing it is to lie under guilt and the displeasure of God, and to live without peace and reconciliation with him: they have also been awakened to a sense of the shortness and uncertainty of life, and the reality of another world and future judgment, and of the necessity of an interest in Christ: they are more afraid of sin, more careful and inquisitive that they may know what is contrary to the mind and will of God, that they may avoid it, and what he requires of them, that they may do it; more careful to guard against temptations, more watchful over their own hearts, earnestly

From *The Works of Jonathan Edwards* (London, 1848), I: 374–375.

desirous of being informed what are the means that God has directed them to, for their salvation, and diligent in the use of the means that God has appointed in his Word, in order to it. Many very stupid, senseless sinners, and persons of a vain mind, have been greatly awakened.

There is a strange alteration almost all over New England amongst young people: by a powerful, invisible influence on their minds, they have been brought to forsake those things in a general way, as it were at once, that they were extremely fond of, and greatly addicted to, and that they seemed to place the happiness of their lives in, and that nothing before could induce them to forsake; as their frolicking, vain company-keeping, nightwalking, their mirth and jollity, their impure language, and lewd songs. In vain did ministers preach against those things before, and in vain were laws made to restrain them, and in vain was all the vigilance of magistrates and civil officers; but now they have almost everywhere dropped them as it were of themselves.

And there is a great alteration amongst old and young as to drinking, tavern-haunting, profane speaking, and extravagance in apparel. Many notoriously vicious persons have been reformed, and become externally quite new creatures: some that are wealthy, and of a fashionable, gay education; some great beaus and fine ladies, that seemed to have their minds swallowed up with nothing but the vain shews and pleasures of the world, have been wonderfully altered, and have relinquished these vanities, and are become serious, mortified and humble in their conversation. 'Tis astonishing to see the alteration that is in some towns, where before was but little appearance of religion, or anything but vice and vanity: and so remote was all that was to be seen or heard amongst them from anything that savored of vital piety or serious religion, or that had any relation to it, that one would have thought, if they had judged only by what appeared in them, that they had been some other species from the serious and religious, which had no concern with another world, and whose natures were now made capable of those things that appertain to Christian experience, and pious conversation; especially was it thus among young persons. And now they are transformed into another sort of people; their former vain, worldly and vicious conversation and dispositions seem to be forsaken, and they are as it were, gone over to a new world: their thoughts, and their talk, and their concern, affections and inquiries are now about the favor of God, an interest in Christ, a renewed sanctified heart, and a spiritual blessedness, and acceptance and happiness in a future world. And through the greater part of New England, the Holy Bible is in much greater esteem and use than it used to be; the great things that are contained in it are much more regarded, as things of the greatest consequence, and are much more the subjects of meditation and conversation; and other books of piety that have long been of established reputation, as the most excellent, and most tending to promote true godliness, have been abundantly more in use. The Lord's day is more religiously and strictly observed: and abundance has been lately done at making up differences, and confessing faults one to another, and making restitution; probably more within these two years, than was done in thirty years before: it has been so undoubtedly in many places. And surprising has been the power of that Spirit that has been poured out on the land, in many instances, to destroy old grudges, and make up long continued breaches, and to bring those that seemed to be in a confirmed irreconcilable alienation, to embrace each other in a sincere and entire amity. . . .

Multitudes in New England have lately been brought to a new and great conviction of the truth and certainty of the things of the Gospel; to a firm persuasion that Christ Jesus is the Son of God, and the great and only Saviour of the world; and that the great doctrines of the Gospel touching reconciliation by his blood, and acceptance in his righteousness, and eternal life and salvation through him, are matters of undoubted truth; together with a most affecting sense of the excellency and sufficiency of this Saviour, and the glorious wisdom and grace of God shining in this way of salvation; and of the wonders of Christ's dying love, and the sincerity of Christ in the invitations of the Gospel, and a consequent affiance and sweet rest of soul in Christ, as a glorious Saviour, a strong rock and high tower, accompanied with an admiring and exalting apprehension of the glory of the divine perfections, God's majesty, holiness, sovereign grace, etc.; with a sensible, strong and sweet love to God, and delight in him, far surpassing all temporal delights, or earthly pleasures; and a rest of soul in him as a portion and the fountain of all good, attended with an abhorrence of sin, and self-loathing for it, and earnest longings of soul after more holiness and conformity to God, with a sense of the great need of God's help in order to holiness of life; together with a most dear love to all that are supposed to be the children of God, and a love to mankind in general, and a most sensible and tender compassion for the souls of sinners, and earnest desires of the advancement of Christ's kingdom in the world. And these things have appeared to be in many of them abiding now for many months, yea, more than a year and a half; with an abiding concern to live an holy life, and great complaints of remaining corruption, longing to be more free from the body of sin and death [cf. Rom. 6:6, 7:24, 8:2].

And not only do these effects appear in new converts, but great numbers of those that were formerly esteemed the most sober and pious people have, under the influence of this work, been greatly quickened, and their hearts renewed with greater degrees of light, renewed repentance and humiliation, and more lively exercises of faith, love and joy in the Lord. Many, as I am well knowing, have of late been remarkably engaged to watch, and strive, and fight against sin, and cast out every idol, and sell all for Christ, and give up themselves entirely to God, and make a sacrifice of every worldly and carnal thing to the welfare and prosperity of their souls. And there has of late appeared in some places an unusual disposition to bind themselves to it in a solemn covenant with God. And now instead of meetings at taverns and drinking houses, and meetings of young people in frolics and vain company, the country is full of meetings of all sorts and ages of persons, young and old, men, women and little children, to read and pray, and sing praises, and to converse of the things of God and another world. In very many places the main subject of the conversation in all companies turns on religion, and things of a spiritual nature. Instead of vain mirth amongst young people, there is now either mourning under a sense of the guilt of sin, or holy rejoicing in Christ Jesus; and instead of their lewd songs, are now to be heard from them songs of praise to God, and to the Lamb that was slain to redeem them by his blood [cf. Rev. 5:6, 9, and 12]. And there has been this alteration abiding on multitudes all over the land, for a year and a half, without any appearance of a disposition to return to former vice and vanity. . . .

I suppose there is scarcely a minister in this land, but from Sabbath to Sabbath used to pray that God would pour out his Spirit, and work a reformation and revival of religion in the country, and turn us from our intemperance, profaneness, uncleanness, worldliness and other sins; and we have kept from year to year days of public fasting and prayer to God, to acknowledge our backslidings, and humble ourselves for our sins, and to seek of God forgiveness and reformation: and now when so great and extensive a reformation is so suddenly and wonderfully accomplished, in those very things that we have sought to God for, shall we not acknowledge it? Or when we do, do it with great coldness, caution and reserve, and scarcely take any notice of it in our public prayers and praises, or mention it but slightly and cursorily, and in such a manner as carried an appearance as though we would contrive to say as little of it as ever we could, and were glad to pass from it? And that because (although indeed there be such a work attended with all these glorious effects, yet) the work is attended with a mixture of error, imprudences, darkness and sin; because some persons are carried away with impressions, and are indiscreet, and too censorious with their zeal; and because there are high transports of religious affection; and because of some effects on persons' bodies that we don't understand the reason of?

# 13

## A SHATTERED EMPIRE

On June 7, 1776, Richard Henry Lee, delegate from Virginia to the Second Continental Congress meeting in Philadelphia, proposed a resolution calling for independence from Great Britain. Three days later Congress appointed a committee of five to prepare a statement giving reasons for independence. The committee appointed a sub-committee, consisting of John Adams and Thomas Jefferson, to draft such a statement. The subcommittee met, according to Adams, and Jefferson suggested that Adams write up a statement. "I will not," said Adams emphatically. "You should do it," said Jefferson. "Oh, no," persisted Adams. "Why will you not?" asked Jefferson. "You ought to do it." "I will not," said Adams stubbornly. "Why?" cried Jefferson. "Reasons enough," said Adams. "What can be your reasons?" Jefferson wanted to know. Explained Adams: "Reason first—you are a Virginian, and a Virginian ought to appear at the head of this business. Reason second—I am obnoxious, suspected, and unpopular. You are very much otherwise. Reason third—you can write ten times better than I can." "Well," said Jefferson, "If you are decided, I will do as well as I can." In the end, Jefferson wrote the Great Declaration, minor changes being made by Adams and Franklin, and after the Continental Congress made some additional changes in it, the delegates voted to adopt it on July 4. Two days earlier Congress had accepted Lee's resolution for independence. But July 4, not July 2, soon became the great day for patriotic celebrations.

Jefferson's "peculiar felicity of expression," according to John Adams, made him the ideal choice for writing the Declaration. In simple, lucid, logical language, Jefferson explained to the world what he thought the American people were fighting for: to establish a government based, not on force and fraud, but on the freely given consent of the people and dedicated to safeguarding the basic rights of all citizens. Jefferson's Declaration made it clear that the American Revolution was more than a fight for independence. "Take away from the Declaration of Independence its self-evident truths," said Adams, "and you rob the North American Revolution of all its moral principles, and proclaim it a foul and unnatural rebellion." After the United States achieved its independence in 1783, the Declaration continued to inspire countless reformers seeking to make their country a better place in which to live: abolitionists, feminists, farmers, and working people. The Declaration also influenced reformers and revolutionaries in other parts of the world—Europe, Asia, and Africa—during the nineteenth and twentieth centuries.

Thomas Jefferson was born in 1743 on his father's Virginia tobacco plantation. After he graduated from William and Mary College in 1762, he studied law and entered politics, joining the Virginia House of Burgesses in 1769. In 1775 he became a delegate to the Continental Congress and was chosen to draft the Declaration of Independence. He served as governor of Virginia from 1779 to 1781 and as U.S. minister to France from 1785 to 1789. Insistent, in his correspondence with James Madison, on the necessity of adding a Bill of Rights to the Constitution, he became increasingly disturbed by the policies of Hamilton and Washington and saw his election as president as partial vindication of his own views on the importance of land, liberty, and localism in the new republic. His reputation as a scholar and architect flourished after his retirement from office in 1809, although his personal finances did not. He died, deeply revered as the Sage of Monticello but still an indebted slaveholder, at his Monticello estate on July 4, 1826, fifty years to the day after the adoption of his Declaration of Independence. On the same day John Adams died in Quincy, Massachusetts. Jefferson and Adams had been friends at the time of the American Revolution but became political enemies during the early years of the American republic. They became reconciled later in life and entered into a lively correspondence that has delighted generations of Americans. Just before he died Adams exclaimed: "Thomas Jefferson survives!"

**Questions to Consider.** In 1858, when Massachusetts lawyer Rufus Choate contemptuously dismissed the Declaration as a collection of "glittering generalities," Ralph Waldo Emerson exclaimed indignantly: "Glittering generalities! Say, rather, blazing ubiquities!" Do you agree with Choate or with Emerson? What are the main generalities set forth in the first two paragraphs of the Declaration? How valid do you think Jefferson's assertions are about equality, "unalienable Rights," and the right of the people to "alter or abolish" their governments? How much prudence do you think the Founding Fathers exercised in their decision to fight for independence? What were Jefferson's major charges against King George III? Do you think he was successful in his attempt to make a long list of abuses and usurpations by the king? Was he fair in blaming the king for all of these abuses and usurpations? Why did he attack the king and avoid any mention of Parliament? What did he say about the English people and why? Do you find any inconsistencies or omissions in the Declaration?

──────── ★ ★ 🌀🌀🌀🌀 ★ ★ ────────

*get attention of British crown*

# The Declaration of Independence (1776)

### THOMAS JEFFERSON

When in the Course of human events, it becomes necessary for one people to dissolve the political bands which have connected them with another, and to assume among the Powers of the earth, the separate and equal station to which the Laws of Nature and of Nature's God entitle them, a decent respect to the opinions of mankind requires that they should declare the causes which impel them to the separation.

We hold these truths to be self-evident, that all men are created equal, that they are endowed by their Creator with certain unalienable Rights, that among these are Life, Liberty and the pursuit of Happiness. That to secure these rights, Governments are instituted among Men, deriving their just powers from the consent of the governed. That whenever any Form of Government becomes destructive of these ends, it is the Right of the People to alter or to abolish it, and to institute new Government, laying its foundation on such principles and organizing its powers in such form, as to them shall seem most likely to effect their Safety and Happiness. Prudence, indeed, will dictate that Governments long established should not be changed for light and transient causes; and accordingly all experience hath shown, that mankind are more disposed to suffer, while evils are sufferable, than to right themselves by abolishing the forms to which they are accustomed. But when a long train of abuses and usurpations, pursuing invariably the same Object evinces a design to reduce them under absolute Despotism, it is their right, it is their duty, to throw off such Government, and to provide new Guards for their future security.—Such has been the patient sufferance of these Colonies; and such is now the necessity which constrains them to alter their former Systems of Government. The history of the present King of Great Britain is a history of repeated injuries and usurpations, all having in direct object the establishment of an absolute Tyranny over these States. To prove this, let Facts be submitted to a candid world.

He has refused his Assent to Laws, the most wholesome and necessary for the public good.

He has forbidden his Governors to pass Laws of immediate and pressing importance, unless suspended in their operation till his Assent should be obtained; and when so suspended, he has utterly neglected to attend to them.

He has refused to pass other Laws for the accommodation of large districts of people, unless those people would relinquish the rights of Repre-

From F. N. Thorpe, ed., *The Federal and State Constitutions* (7 v., Government Printing Office, Washington, D.C., 1909), I:3.

**A depiction from the 1780s of the drafting committee of the Declaration of Independence, with (left to right) John Adams of Massachusetts, Roger Sherman of Connecticut, Robert Livingston of New York, Thomas Jefferson of Virginia, and Benjamin Franklin of Pennsylvania.** The painter, John Trumbull, gives Jefferson, the document's main author, pride of place in his picture, although Adams, who contributed ideas as well as phrases, is prominent as well. (Yale University Art Gallery, Mabel Brady Garven Collection)

sentation in the Legislature, a right inestimable to them and formidable to tyrants only.

He has called together legislative bodies at places unusual, uncomfortable, and distant from the depository of their Public Records, for the sole purpose of fatiguing them into compliance with his measures.

He has dissolved Representative Houses repeatedly, for opposing with manly firmness his invasions on the rights of the people.

He has refused for a long time, after such dissolutions, to cause others to be elected; whereby the Legislative Powers, incapable of Annihilation, have returned to the People at large for their exercise; the State remaining in the mean time exposed to all the dangers of invasion from without, and convulsions within.

He has endeavoured to prevent the population of these States; for that purpose obstructing the Laws of Naturalization of Foreigners; refusing to pass others to encourage their migration hither, and raising the conditions of new Appropriations of Lands.

He has obstructed the Administration of Justice, by refusing his Assent to Laws for establishing Judiciary Powers.

He has made Judges dependent on his Will alone, for the tenure of their offices, and the amount and payment of their salaries.

He has erected a multitude of New Offices, and sent hither swarms of Officers to harass our People, and eat out their substance.

He has kept among us, in times of peace, Standing Armies without the Consent of our legislature.

He has affected to render the Military independent of and superior to the Civil Power.

He has combined with others to subject us to a jurisdiction foreign to our constitution, and unacknowledged by our laws; giving his Assent to their acts of pretended legislation:

For quartering large bodies of armed troops among us:

For protecting them, by a mock Trial, from Punishment for any Murders which they should commit on the Inhabitants of these States:

For cutting off our Trade with all parts of the world:

For imposing taxes on us without our Consent:

For depriving us in many cases, of the benefits of Trial by Jury:

For transporting us beyond Seas to be tried for pretended offences:

For abolishing the free System of English Laws in a neighbouring Province, establishing therein an Arbitrary government, and enlarging its Boundaries so as to render it at once an example and fit instrument for introducing the same absolute rule into these Colonies:

For taking away our Charters, abolishing our most valuable Laws, and altering fundamentally the Forms of our Governments:

For suspending our own Legislature, and declaring themselves invested with Power to legislate for us in all cases whatsoever.

He has abdicated Government here, by declaring us out of his Protection and waging War against us.

He has plundered our seas, ravaged our Coasts, burnt our towns, and destroyed the lives of our people.

He is at this time transporting large armies of foreign mercenaries to compleat the works of death, desolation and tyranny, already begun with circumstances of Cruelty & perfidy scarcely paralleled in the most barbarous ages, and totally unworthy the Head of a civilized nation.

He has constrained our fellow Citizens taken Captive on the high Seas to bear Arms against their Country, to become the executioners of their friends and Brethren, or to fall themselves by their Hands.

He has excited domestic insurrections amongst us, and has endeavoured to bring on the inhabitants of our frontiers, the merciless Indian Savages, whose known rule of warfare, is an undistinguished destruction of all ages, sexes and conditions.

In every state of these Oppressions We have Petitioned for Redress in the most humble terms: Our repeated Petitions have been answered only by repeated injury. A Prince, whose character is thus marked by every act which may define a Tyrant, is unfit to be the ruler of a free People.

Nor have We been wanting in attention to our British brethren. We have warned them from time to time of attempts by their legislature to extend an unwarrantable jurisdiction over us. We have reminded them of the circumstances of our emigration and settlement here. We have appealed to their native justice and magnanimity, and we have conjured them by the ties of our common kindred to disavow these usurpations, which, would inevitably interrupt our connections and correspondence. They too have been deaf to the voice of justice and of consanguinity. We must, therefore, acquiesce in the necessity, which denounces our Separation, and hold them, as we hold the rest of mankind, Enemies in War, in Peace Friends.

We, therefore, the Representatives of the united States of America, in General Congress, Assembled, appealing to the Supreme Judge of the world for the rectitude of our intentions, do, in the Name, and by Authority of the good People of these Colonies, solemnly publish and declare, That these United Colonies are, and of Right ought to be Free and Independent States; that they are Absolved from all Allegiance to the British Crown, and that all political connection between them and the State of Great Britain, is and ought to be totally dissolved; and that as Free and Independent States, they have full Power to levy War, conclude Peace, contract Alliances, establish Commerce, and to do all other Acts and Things which Independent States may of right do. And for the support of this Declaration, with a firm reliance on the Protection of Divine Providence, we mutually pledge to each other our Lives, our Fortunes and our sacred Honor.

# 14

## IDEOLOGY AND AGITATION

On December 18, 1776, George Washington wrote his brother discouragingly: "Between you and me, I think our affairs are in a very bad situation. . . . If every nerve is not strained up to the utmost to recruit the new army with all possible expedition, I think the game is up." A few days later Thomas Paine published the first number of *The Crisis*, a pamphlet calling attention to the heartbreaking difficulties the Americans faced in their struggle with Britain and appealing for renewed dedication to the Revolutionary cause. Paine said he wrote in "a passion of patriotism." His essay quickly "rallied and reanimated" the people, according to one observer, and before long "hope succeeded to despair, cheerfulness to gloom, and firmness to irresolution." In twelve more issues of *The Crisis* Paine continued his impassioned fight against apathy, indifference, and defeatism in American ranks. He wrote additional numbers about American problems after the Yorktown victory in 1781.

Paine, a British corset maker and excise officer, was an ardent supporter of the American cause from almost the beginning. Shortly after arriving in Philadelphia in November 1774, he became editor of the *Pennsylvania Magazine,* discovered he had great gifts as a journalist, and in January 1776 published a little pamphlet entitled *Common Sense,* urging Americans to convert their resistance to British oppression into a fight for national independence. Before long thousands of copies of his pamphlet were circulating in the colonies and Washington arranged to have passages from it read to his troops. The first bestseller in history, *Common Sense* persuaded many Americans who were wavering that separation from Britain was both possible and desirable.

Paine pioneered in a new kind of journalism. He avoided the elegant and ornate kind of writing fashionable in aristocratic circles and wrote simply, naturally, and forcefully. He used homely metaphors, introduced everyday words and phrases into his essays, translated foreign phrases for his readers, interspersed his logical arguments with lively anecdotes, and brought a sense of immediacy to his writings by including personal, on-the-spot reports. He was, in short, writing for the plain people from whom he himself had come. His influence on the thinking of countless people was enormous.

Paine, born in England of Quaker parents in 1737, lived in obscurity until he came to America in 1774. He became editor of the *Pennsylvania Magazine* and quickly identified himself with the American cause. After the American Revolution he went to France, supported the revolution that broke out there in 1789, and published *The Rights of Man* (1791–1792), a work defending the principles of the French Revolution. He also wrote *The Age of Reason* (1793–1795), criticizing both atheism and orthodox Christianity and calling for a religion based on reason. Though sympathetic to the French Revolution, Paine opposed the execution of King Louis XVI and was appalled by the Reign of Terror that accompanied the Revolution. In the end he was thrown in prison and sentenced to the guillotine; but he was saved by the intervention of the American minister in France, James Monroe. In 1802 he returned to America; but his attacks on George Washington while in France and his religious radicalism made him an outcast. He died in New York, lonely, poverty-stricken, and largely forgotten, in 1809.

**Questions to Consider.**  Paine is eminently quotable. Do you find any passages in the essay below that seem especially eloquent? Do you think Paine's appeal rests on substance as well as style? How did he attempt to whip up enthusiasm for the American cause despite reverses on the battlefield? Do you think his handling of Tories, that is, Americans who were sympathetic to Britain, was effective? Do you think he was just to the Loyalists, to King George III, and to General William Howe? Were his appeals to God likely to impress religious people in America? What parts of the essay do you think George Washington chose to have read to his troops?

# The Crisis, Number One (1776)

THOMAS PAINE

These are the times that try men's souls. The summer soldier and the sunshine patriot will, in this crisis, shrink from the service of his country; but he that stands it NOW, deserves the love and thanks of man and woman. Tyranny, like hell, is not easily conquered; yet we have this consolation with

From Daniel E. Wheeler, ed., *Life and Writings of Thomas Paine* (10 v., V. Parke and Co., New York, 1915), III: 1–16.

**The destruction of the statue of King George in New York City, July 9, 1776.** The statue stood in Bowling Green at the tip of Manhattan Island. Soldiers and artisans, provoked by the words of anti-British firebrands such as Tom Paine and Patrick Henry, did most of the damage, after a public reading of the Declaration of Independence. In this imaginative engraving, a well-dressed woman, possibly of Tory sympathies, watches this violent mob behavior in apparent alarm. (Chicago Historical Society)

us, that the harder the conflict, the more glorious the triumph. What we obtain too cheap, we esteem too lightly: 'Tis dearness only that gives every thing its value. Heaven knows how to put a proper price upon its goods; and it would be strange indeed, if so celestial an article as FREEDOM should not be highly rated. Britain, with an army to enforce her tyranny, has declared that she has a right (*not only to* TAX) but "*to* BIND *us in* ALL CASES WHATSOEVER," and if being *bound in that manner,* is not slavery, then is there not such a thing as slavery upon earth. Even the expression is impious, for so unlimited a power can belong only to GOD. . . .

I have as little superstition in me as any man living, but my secret opinion has ever been, and still is, that God Almighty will not give up a people to military destruction, or leave them unsupportedly to perish, who had so earnestly and so repeatedly sought to avoid the calamities of war, by every decent method which wisdom could invent. Neither have I so much of the infidel in me, as to suppose that HE has relinquished the government of the world, and given us up to the care of devils; and as I do not, I cannot see on what grounds the king of Britain can look up to Heaven for help against us: A common murderer, a highwayman, or a house-breaker has as good a pretence as he. . . .

I shall not now attempt to give all the particulars of our retreat to the Delaware; suffice it for the present to say, that both officers and men, though greatly harassed and fatigued, frequently without rest, covering, or provision, the inevitable consequences of a long retreat, bore it with a manly and a martial spirit. All their wishes were one, which was, that the country would turn out and help them to drive the enemy back. Voltaire has remarked that King William never appeared to full advantage but in difficulties and in action; the same remark may be made on George Washington, for the character fits him. There is a natural firmness in some minds which cannot be unlocked by trifles, but which, when unlocked, discovers a cabinet of fortitude; and I reckon it among those kind of public blessings, which we do not immediately see, that GOD hath blest him with uninterrupted health, and given him a mind that can even flourish upon care.

I shall conclude this paper with some miscellaneous remarks on the state of our affairs; and shall begin with asking the following question, Why is it that the enemy have left the New-England provinces, and made these middle ones the seat of war? The answer is easy: New-England is not infested with tories, and we are. I have been tender in raising the cry against these men, and used numberless arguments to shew them their danger, but it will not do to sacrifice a world to either their folly or their baseness. The period is now arrived, in which either they or we must change our sentiments, or one or both must fall. And what is a tory? Good GOD! what is he? I should not be afraid to go with an hundred whigs against a thousand tories, were they to attempt to get into arms. Every tory is a coward, for a servile, slavish, self-interested fear is the foundation of toryism; and a man under such influence, though he may be cruel, never can be brave.

But, before the line of irrecoverable separation be drawn between us, let us reason the matter together: Your conduct is an invitation to the enemy, yet not one in a thousand of you has heart enough to join him. [General William] Howe is as much deceived by you as the American cause is injured by you. He expects you will all take up arms, and flock to his standard with muskets on your shoulders. Your opinions are of no use to him, unless you support him personally, for 'tis soldiers, and not tories, that he wants.

I once felt all that kind of anger, which a man ought to feel, against the mean principles that are held by the tories: A noted one, who kept a tavern at Amboy, was standing at his door, with as pretty a child in his hand, about eight or nine years old, as most I ever saw, and after speaking his mind as freely as he thought was prudent, finished with this unfatherly expression, *"Well! give me peace in my day."* Not a man lives on the continent but fully believes that a separation must some time or other finally take place, and a generous parent should have said, *"If there must be trouble, let it be in my day that my child may have peace"* and this single reflection, well applied, is sufficient to awaken every man to duty. Not a place upon earth might be so happy as America. Her situation is remote from all the wrangling world, and she has nothing to do but to trade with them. A man may easily distinguish in himself between temper and principle, and I am as confident, as I am that GOD governs the world, that America will never be happy till she gets clear of foreign dominion. Wars, without ceasing, will break out till that period arrives, and the continent must in the end be conqueror; for though the flame of liberty may sometimes cease to shine, the coal never can expire. . . .

Not all the treasures of the world, so far as I believe, could have induced me to support an offensive war, for I think it murder; but if a thief break into my house, burn and destroy my property, and kill or threaten to kill me, or those that are in it, and to *"bind me in all cases whatsoever,"* to his absolute will, am I to suffer it? What signifies it to me, whether he who does it, is a king or a common man; my countryman or not my countryman? whether it is done by an individual villain, or an army of them? If we reason to the root of things we shall find no difference; neither can any just cause be assigned why we should punish in the one case and pardon in the other. Let them call me rebel, and welcome. I feel no concern from it; but I should suffer the misery of devils, were I to make a whore of my soul by swearing allegiance to one whose character is that of a sottish, stupid, stubborn, worthless, brutish man. I conceive likewise a horrid idea in receiving mercy from a being, who at the last day shall be shrieking to the rocks and mountains to cover him, and fleeing with terror from the orphan, the widow, and the slain of America.

There are cases which cannot be overdone by language, and this is one. There are persons too who see not the full extent of the evil which threatens them, they solace themselves with hopes that the enemy, if they succeed, will be merciful. It is the madness of folly to expect mercy from those who have refused to do justice; and even mercy, where conquest is the object, is only a trick of war: The cunning of the fox is as murderous as the violence of the wolf; and we ought to guard equally against both. Howe's first object is partly by threats and partly by promise, to terrify or seduce the people to deliver up their arms, and receive mercy. The ministry recommended the same plan to [General Thomas] Gage, and this is what the tories call making their peace: *"a peace which passeth all understanding"* indeed! A peace which would be the immediate forerunner of a worse ruin than any we have yet thought of. Ye men of Pennsylvania, do reason upon these things! Were the back counties to give up their arms, they would fall an easy prey to the Indians, who are all alarmed. This perhaps is what some tories would not be sorry for. Were the home counties to deliver up their arms, they would be exposed to the resentment of the back counties, who would then have it in their power to chastise their defection at pleasure. And were any one state to give up its arms, THAT state must be garrisoned by all Howe's army of Britons and Hessians to preserve it from the anger of the rest. Mutual fear is a principal link in the chain of mutual love, and woe be to that state that breaks the compact. Howe is mercifully inviting you to barbarous destruction, and men must be either rogues or fools that will not see it. I dwell not upon the powers of imagination; I bring reason to your ears; and in language as plain as A, B, C, hold up truth to your eyes.

I thank GOD that I fear not. I see no real cause for fear. I know our situation well, and can see the way out of it. While our army was collected, Howe dared not risk a battle, and it is no credit to him that he decamped from the White Plains, and waited a mean opportunity to ravage the defenceless Jerseys; but it is great credit to us, that, with a handful of men, we sustained an orderly retreat for near an hundred miles, brought off our ammunition, all our field-pieces, the greatest part of our stores, and had four rivers to pass. None can say that our retreat was precipitate, for we were near three weeks in performing it, that the country might have time to come in. Twice we marched back to meet the enemy and remained out till dark. The sign of fear was not seen in our camp, and had not some of the cowardly and disaffected inhabitants spread false alarms through the country, the Jerseys had never been ravaged. Once more we are again collected and collecting; our new army at both ends of the continent is recruiting fast, and we shall be able to open the next campaign with sixty thousand men, well armed and cloathed. This is our situation, and who will may know it. By perseverance and fortitude we have the prospect of a glorious issue; by cowardice and submission, the sad choice of a variety of evils—a ravaged country—a depopulated city—habitations without safety, and slavery without hope—our homes turned into barracks and bawdy-houses for Hessians, and a future race to provide for whose fathers we shall doubt of. Look on this picture and weep over it! and if there yet remains one thoughtless wretch who believes it not, let him suffer it unlamented.

# 15

## MEN WITH GUNS

Ratification of the new Constitution was no easy matter. By May 1788 conventions in eight states had ratified, including large states in New England (Massachusetts), the Middle Atlantic (Pennsylvania), and the South (South Carolina). But several of these ratified by very narrow margins. Moreover, New York and Virginia had not ratified, and because of their size and strategic location the new nation would be crippled from the outset without them.

A key issue in Virginia, New York, and elsewhere was the absence of a Bill of Rights. James Madison, a key figure at the Philadelphia convention that produced the Constitution, opposed adding a list of guaranteed rights to the framing document, as did most backers of the Constitution, including Alexander Hamilton. But so great was the clamor for guaranteed rights that the Constitutionalists agreed to adopt a Bill of Rights at the first Congress and did so with the first ten amendments.

Most of the amendments reflected recommendations from state conventions such as Virginia's and seemed straightforward. Attention centered on the First Amendment, which guaranteed a range of individual liberties considered vital to political liberty. A set of five amendments (numbers Four through Eight) tried to protect citizens in various ways from the police powers of the government. The Third Amendment prohibited the quartering of troops in private houses, which had been a British practice. Amendments Nine and Ten reserved unspecified rights to "the States respectively" or "the people."

The Second Amendment, the subject of enormous contention in the late twentieth century because of the ambiguous relation between its first part and its second, embodied several features of American experience. First, early Americans were heavily armed. Seventeenth-century Puritan families usually owned a musket for hunting and, eventually, for colonial defense against Catholics and Indians. By the middle of the eighteenth century so did free male colonists elsewhere. Militia units comprising such armed individuals did much of the fighting during the Revolution.

George Washington, his aide-de-camp, Alexander Hamilton, and other commanders deplored this situation because they considered such citizen-soldiers incompetent in serious combat. But many politicians applauded it as a way to avoid having a permanent standing army, which would be both expensive and potentially dangerous to liberty. Following are extracts concerning militias and citizens' right to bear arms from four documents: the Articles of Confederation, the Constitution, the Virginia Constitutional Convention of 1788, and the Second Amendment.

**Questions to Consider.** Do the statements from the Articles, the Constitution, and the Virginia convention clarify the relation between the "militia" and the "right to bear arms" clauses of the Second Amendment? What "security" was the right to bear arms supposed to insure? In light of the assumption embodied in the Articles, does the "right to keep and bear Arms" seem to have been an issue of states' rights or individual rights? What actual latitude did the Articles and the Constitution give states in this matter? In light of the provisions of the Constitution, who is ultimately responsible for insuring a "well regulated" militia? Would the Second Amendment guarantee the right to bear nonmilitary weapons? Would it guarantee the right to bear military weapons of every type? Would the existence of a permanent standing army make the Second Amendment irrelevant?

# The Right to Bear Arms (1777–1789)

## *The Articles of Confederation (1777)*

### Art VI.

. . . No vessels of war shall be kept up in time of peace by any state, except such number only, as shall be deemed necessary by the united states in congress assembled, for the defence of such state, or its trade; nor shall any body of forces be kept up by any state, in time of peace, except such number only, as in the judgment of the united states, in congress assembled, shall be deemed requisite to garrison the forts necessary for the defence of such state; but every state shall always keep up a well regulated and disciplined militia, sufficiently armed and accoutred, and shall provide and constantly have ready for use, in public stores, a due number of field pieces and tents, and a proper quantity of arms, ammunition and camp equipage.

## The Constitution (1787)

We the People of the United States, in Order to form a more perfect Union, establish Justice, insure domestic Tranquility, provide for the common defence, promote the general Welfare, and secure the Blessings of Liberty to ourselves and our Posterity, do ordain and establish this Constitution for the United States of America. . . . *everyone already knows that! Gosh, freakin' idiot!*

### Article. I.

. . . Section. 8. The Congress shall have power To lay and collect Taxes, Duties, Imposts and Excises, to pay the Debts and provide for the common Defence and general Welfare of the United States; . . .

To raise and support Armies, but no Appropriation of Money to that Use shall be for a longer Term than two Years;

To provide and maintain a Navy;

To make Rules for the Government and Regulation of the land and naval Forces;

To provide for calling forth the Militia to execute the Laws of the Union, suppress Insurrections and repel Invasions;

To provide for organizing, arming, and disciplining the Militia, and for governing such Part of them as may be employed in the Service of the United States, reserving to the States respectively, the Appointment of the Officers, and the Authority of training the Militia according to the discipline prescribed by Congress; . . .

*Go eat a tomatoe apple!*

### Article. II.

. . . Section. 2. The President shall be Commander in Chief of the Army and Navy of the United States, and of the Militia of the several States, when called into the actual Service of the United States; . . .

## Virginia's Recommendations for a Bill of Rights (1788)

We the said Delegates in the name and in behalf of the People of Virginia do by these presents assent to and ratify the Constitution recommended on the seventeenth day of September one thousand seven hundred and eighty seven by the Federal Convention for the Government of the United States. . . .

Subsequent Amendments agreed to in Convention as necessary to the proposed Constitution of Government for the United States, recommended

Virginia's Recommendations for a Bill of Rights from *Documentary History of the Constitution* (Department of State, Washington, D.C., 1894–1905).

to the consideration of the Congress which shall first assemble under the said Constitution to be acted upon according to the mode prescribed in the fifth article thereof:

Videlicet [that is to say];

That there be a Declaration or Bill of Rights asserting and securing from encroachment the essential and unalienable Rights of the People in some such manner as the following; . . .

Seventeenth, That the people have a right to keep and bear arms; that a well regulated Militia composed of the body of the people trained to arms is the proper, natural and safe defence of a free State. That standing armies in time of peace are dangerous to liberty, and therefore ought to be avoided, as far as the circumstances and protection of the Community will admit; and that in all cases the military should be under strict subordination to and governed by the Civil power.

## The Bill of Rights (1789)

### Amendment II

A well regulated Militia, being necessary to the security of a free State, the right of the people to keep and bear Arms shall not be infringed.

# 16

## SECURING LIBERTY

*discussed weakening of the Confederation.*

*gained impr. over years.*

In May 1787 delegates from every state except Rhode Island met in Philadelphia to revise the Articles of Confederation. But they disregarded their instructions; by mid-September they had drawn up an entirely new frame of government for the nation that had achieved its independence in 1783. The Constitutional Convention was a distinguished gathering; the states sent their ablest men to Philadelphia. George Washington was there; so were Benjamin Franklin, Alexander Hamilton, and James Madison. For many weeks the delegates labored mightily to construct a constitution that would "form a more perfect union" without jeopardizing liberty. In September they completed their work and submitted the Constitution to the states for ratification. At once a great debate commenced. In countless essays, editorials, pamphlets, and handbills the American people discussed the merits and defects of the new instrument of government offered for their consideration. The most famous of all the commentaries on the Constitution appeared in *The Federalist.*

*The Federalist Papers* consist of eighty-five essays appearing in various New York newspapers between October 1787 and August 1788. Hamilton, who had taken part in the Constitutional Convention, wrote the major portion of them; but James Madison, whose diligence in Philadelphia won him the nickname "Father of the Constitution," wrote a sizable number as well. John Jay, author of the New York State Constitution of 1777, also wrote a few. The essays, which were soon published in book form, discussed the weakness of the Confederation, the powers assigned to the federal government in the new Constitution and the organization of these powers into legislative, executive, and judicial branches of government, and the safeguards that were built into the Constitution to prevent oppression. Thomas Jefferson, who was in Paris at the time as minister to France, wrote to say he read the *Papers* with "care, pleasure, and improvement" and called them the "best commentary on the principles of government which was ever written."

The immediate impact of *The Federalist Papers* was probably not great. Some of the states had completed ratification before many of the essays were published. But the essays may have helped persuade New York and Virginia to ratify the Constitution, and their long-range influence has been profound. Since their first appearance the *Papers* have become a classic of political science. Scholars, legislators, judges, and Supreme Court justices have looked to them time and again for clues to understanding the Constitution that was accepted by the states in 1788. After the Declaration of Independence and the Constitution they are the nation's most important political statement. *The Federalist,* Number Ten, written by Madison, is perhaps the most famous. In it, Madison points out the inevitability of conflicts of interest (particularly economic interest) in free societies and insists that representative government can keep these conflicts from getting out of hand and endangering both private rights and the public good.

James Madison, son of a Virginia planter, was born in Port Conway, Virginia, in 1751, and attended the College of New Jersey (now Princeton). In 1776 he helped frame Virginia's constitution and declaration of rights. Between 1780 and 1783 he was a member of the Continental Congress; after the Revolution he served in Virginia's House of Delegates, where he sponsored legislation to disestablish the Anglican church and provide for religious freedom. As a member of Virginia's delegation to the Philadelphia convention in 1787 he played a major role in shaping the Constitution; his notes on the debates are our main source for information about what was discussed. As a member of the First Congress under Washington he sponsored legislation establishing the State, Treasury, and War Departments and also introduced the first ten amendments to the Constitution (the Bill of Rights) into the House of Representatives. For eight years he served as Thomas Jefferson's secretary of state and succeeded him as president in 1809. His own presidency was a stormy one. Though a man of peace, he presided over the controversial War of 1812 with Britain ("Mr. Madison's War"), which ended with a treaty settling none of the outstanding disputes between the two countries. While he was president, the Republican party gradually accepted the economic program once sponsored by Hamilton and opposed by Jefferson: a second Bank of the United States, a protective tariff, and a large funded debt. In 1817, Madison retired to his estate at Montpelier to manage his farm, pursue his studies, advise James Monroe, his successor in the White House, and warn against disunion. He died in 1836 at the age of eighty-five.

**Questions to Consider.** In the extract from *The Federalist,* Number Ten, presented below, Madison began by singling out factions as the chief problem confronting free nations like the United States. How did he define *faction?* He said there are two ways to prevent factions from forming. What are they? Why did he reject both of them? What did he mean by saying that the "latent causes of faction" are found in human nature? Do you think he was right in his statement that "the most common and durable source of factions has been the various and unequal distribution of property"? What examples did he give of various propertied interests? Did Madison think a "pure democracy" could handle the "mischief of faction"? How did he distinguish a republic from a democracy? Why did he think a republican form of government, such as outlined in the U.S. Constitution, could deal effectively with the problem of factions?

───── ★★✪✪✪★★ ─────

# *The Federalist,* **Number Ten (1787)**

### JAMES MADISON

Among the numerous advantages promised by a well-constructed Union, none deserves to be more accurately developed than its tendency to break and control the violence of faction. The friend of popular governments never finds himself so much alarmed for their character and fate as when he contemplates their propensity to this dangerous vice. He will not fail, therefore, to set a due value on any plan which, without violating the principles to which he is attached, provides a proper cure for it. . . .

By a faction I understand a number of citizens, whether amounting to a majority or minority of the whole, who are united and actuated by some common impulse of passion, or of interest, adverse to the rights of other citizens, or to the permanent and aggregate interests of the community.

There are two methods of curing the mischiefs of faction: the one, by removing its causes; the other, by controlling its effects.

There are again two methods of removing the causes of faction: the one, by destroying the liberty which is essential to its existence; the other, by giving to every citizen the same opinions, the same passions, and the same interests.

It could never be more truly said than of the first remedy that it was worse than the disease. Liberty is to faction what air is to fire, an aliment without which it instantly expires. But it could not be a less folly to abolish liberty, which is essential to political life, because it nourishes faction than it would be to wish the annihilation of air, which is essential to animal life, because it imparts to fire its destructive agency.

The second expedient is as impracticable as the first would be unwise. As long as the reason of man continues fallible, and he is at liberty to exercise

From *The Federalist* (Colonial Press, New York, 1901), 44–52.

**A miniature of James Madison in 1783 at the age of thirty-two.** A small, shy, often sickly Virginia planter and lawyer, Madison commissioned this portrait from Charles Willson Peale—one of the earliest outstanding American artists—as a gift to his fiancée, Kitty Floyd of New York, whom he had met through his friend Thomas Jefferson. Kitty, alas, jilted Madison in favor of one William Clarkson, who "hung round Kitty at the harpsichord." Madison recovered sufficiently to become a chief draftsman of the Constitution and eventually president of the United States and to marry a young Philadelphia widow, Dolley Todd, who would become perhaps the most famous of First Ladies. (Library of Congress)

it, different opinions will be formed. As long as the connection subsists between his reason and his self-love, his opinions and his passions will have a reciprocal influence on each other; and the former will be objects to which the latter will attach themselves. The diversity in the faculties of men, from which the rights of property originate, is not less an insuperable obstacle to a uniformity of interests. The protection of these faculties is the first object of government. From the protection of different and unequal faculties of acquiring property, the possession of different degrees and kinds of property immediately results; and from the influence of these on the sentiments and views of the respective proprietors ensues a division of the society into different interests and parties.

The latent causes of faction are thus sown in the nature of man; and we see them everywhere brought into different degrees of activity, according to the different circumstances of civil society. A zeal for different opinions concerning religion, concerning government, and many other points, as well of speculation as of practice; an attachment to different leaders ambitiously contending for pre-eminence and power; or to persons of other descriptions whose fortunes have been interesting to the human passions, have, in turn, divided mankind into parties, inflamed them with mutual animosity, and rendered them much more disposed to vex and oppress each other than to co-operate for their common good. So strong is this propensity of mankind to fall into mutual animosities that where no substantial occasion presents itself the most frivolous and fanciful distinctions have been sufficient to kindle their unfriendly passions and excite their most violent conflicts. But the most common and durable source of factions has been the various and unequal distribution of property. Those who hold and those who are without property have ever formed distinct interests in society. Those who are creditors, and those who are debtors, fall under a like discrimination. A landed interest, a manufacturing interest, a mercantile interest, a moneyed interest, with many lesser interests, grow up of necessity in civilized nations, and divide them into different classes, actuated by different sentiments and views. . . .

Shall domestic manufacturers be encouraged, and in what degree, by restrictions on foreign manufacturers? are questions which would be differently decided by the landed and the manufacturing classes, and probably by neither with a sole regard to justice and the public good. The apportionment of taxes on the various descriptions of property is an act which seems to require the most exact impartiality; yet there is, perhaps, no legislative act in which greater opportunity and temptation are given to a predominant party to trample on the rules of justice. Every shilling with which they overburden the inferior number is a shilling saved to their own pockets.

It is in vain to say that enlightened statesmen will be able to adjust these clashing interests and render them all subservient to the public good. Enlightened statesmen will not always be at the helm. Nor, in many cases, can such an adjustment be made at all without taking into view indirect and remote considerations, which will rarely prevail over the immediate interest which one party may find in disregarding the rights of another or the good of the whole.

The inference to which we are brought is that the *causes* of faction cannot be removed and that relief is only to be sought in the means of controlling its *effects*.

If a faction consists of less than a majority, relief is supplied by the republican principle, which enables the majority to defeat its sinister views by regular vote. It may clog the administration, it may convulse the society; but it will be unable to execute and mask its violence under the forms of the Constitution. When a majority is included in a faction, the form of popular government, on the other hand, enables it to sacrifice to its ruling passion or interest both the public good and the rights of other citizens. To secure the public good and private rights against the danger of such a faction, and at the same time to preserve the spirit and the form of popular government, is then the great object to which our inquiries are directed. . . .

By what means is this object attainable? Evidently by one of two only. Either the existence of the same passion or interest in a majority at the same time must be prevented, or the majority, having such coexistent passion or interest, must be rendered, by their number and local situation, unable to concert and carry into effect schemes of oppression. . . .

[A] pure democracy, by which I mean a society consisting of a small number of citizens, who assemble and administer the government in person, can admit of no cure for the mischiefs of faction. A common passion or interest will, in almost every case, be felt by a majority of the whole; a communication and concert results from the form of government itself; and there is nothing to check the inducements to sacrifice the weaker party or an obnoxious individual. Hence it is that such democracies have ever been spectacles of turbulence and contention; have ever been found incompatible with personal security or the rights of property; and have in general been as short in their lives as they have been violent in their deaths. . . .

A republic, by which I mean a government in which the scheme of representation takes place, opens a different prospect and promises the cure for which we are seeking. Let us examine the points in which it varies from pure democracy, and we shall comprehend both the nature of the cure and the efficacy which it must derive from the Union.

The two great points of difference between a democracy and a republic are: first, the delegation of the government, in the latter, to a small number of citizens elected by the rest; secondly, the greater number of citizens and greater sphere of country over which the latter may be extended.

The effect of the first difference is, on the one hand, to refine and enlarge the public views by passing them through the medium of a chosen body of citizens, whose wisdom may best discern the true interest of their country and whose patriotism and love of justice will be least likely to sacrifice it to temporary or partial considerations. Under such a regulation it may well happen that the public voice, pronounced by the representatives of the people, will be more consonant to the public good than if pronounced by the people themselves, convened for the purpose. On the other hand, the effect may be inverted. Men of factious tempers, of local prejudices, or of sinister designs, may, by intrigue, by corruption, or by other means, first obtain the suffrages, and then betray the interests of the people. . . .

In the first place it is to be remarked that however small the republic may be the representatives must be raised to a certain number in order to guard against the cabals of a few; and that however large it may be they must be limited to a certain number in order to guard against the confusion of a multitude. . . .

In the next place, as each representative will be chosen by a greater number of citizens in the large than in the small republic, it will be more difficult for unworthy candidates to practise with success the vicious arts by which elections are too often carried; and the suffrages of the people being more free, will be more likely to center on men who possess the most attractive merit and the most diffusive and established characters. . . .

The other point of difference is the greater number of citizens and extent of territory which may be brought within the compass of republican than of democratic government; and it is this circumstance principally which renders factious combinations less to be dreaded in the former than in the latter. The smaller the society, the fewer probably will be the distinct parties and interests composing it; the fewer the distinct parties and interests, the more frequently will a majority be found of the same party; and the smaller the number of individuals composing a majority, and the smaller the compass within which they are placed, the more easily will they concert and execute their plans of oppression. Extend the sphere and you take in a greater variety of parties and interests. . . .

The influence of factious leaders may kindle a flame within their particular States but will be unable to spread a general conflagration through the other States. A religious sect may degenerate into a political faction in a part of the Confederacy; but the variety of sects dispersed over the entire face of it must secure the national councils against any danger from that source. A rage for paper money, for an abolition of debts, for an equal division of property, or for any other improper or wicked project, will be less apt to pervade the whole body of the Union than a particular member of it, in the same proportion as such a malady is more likely to taint a particular county or district than an entire State.

In the extent and proper structure of the Union, therefore, we behold a republican remedy for the diseases most incident to republican government.

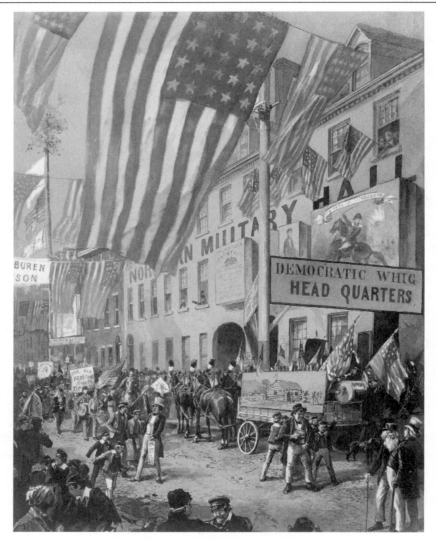

**A political campaign of the Jacksonian era.** (Franklin D. Roosevelt Library)

# CHAPTER THREE

# Nationalists and Partisans

# 17

## THE INDUSTRIAL VISION

Under the new Constitution, Congress had the power to tax, borrow, and regulate trade and money. But the president was also important; he could recommend to Congress "such measures" as he thought "necessary and expedient." While George Washington was president, he established many precedents of economic policy and behavior. Probably the most important recommendations made during his presidency came from Secretary of the Treasury Alexander Hamilton. Hamilton's four reports to Congress on economic and financial policies were crucial in shaping the development of the new nation. In them Hamilton sought to make the Constitution's promise of a "more perfect Union" a reality by recommending governmental policies that fostered private enterprise and economic growth.

Hamilton's first three reports had to do with funding the national debt and creating a national bank. Hamilton wanted the federal government to take over the old Revolutionary debt as well as the debts incurred by the states during the Revolution, convert them into bonds, and pay for the interest on the bonds by levying excise taxes on distilled spirits and by imposing customs duties on such imports as tea, coffee, and wine. Congress adopted his funding proposals; it also accepted his plan for a large national bank that could make loans to businesses and issue currency backed by federal bonds. Hamilton's fourth report, "On Manufactures," urged a system of import taxes ("protective tariffs"), better roads and harbors ("internal improvements"), and subsidies ("bounties") in order to spur manufacturing.

Hamilton's four reports, with their emphasis on national rather than state power, on industry rather than agriculture, and on public spending to promote private enterprise, had a tremendous political impact. First, they triggered the birth of the earliest formal party system: Hamiltonian Federalists urging passage of the program and Democratic Republicans, followers of Secretary of State Thomas Jefferson, trying to modify or block it. Second, the reports helped establish the questions of governmental power and the nature of the economy as basic issues of political debate over the next half-century. Finally,

Hamilton's reports became a veritable fountainhead for Americans concerned with the enhancement of capitalism and national power. Hamiltonian conservatives did not want an uninvolved government; they wanted to forge a partnership between government and business in which federal policies would actively promote business enterprise.

Congress did not immediately adopt Hamilton's recommendations for manufacturing. Protective tariffs, internal improvements, and bounties came much later and were adopted in a piecemeal fashion. Still, "On Manufactures" is important in its preview of the future. Hamilton was perceptive in foreseeing that America's destiny was an industrial one. Long after he had passed from the scene, industrialism did overtake and surpass agriculture (with the encouragement of the states as well as of the federal government) as the driving force of the American economy.

Hamilton himself was concerned more with the political implications of his reports than with their economic effects. His major aim was to strengthen the Union. This strong nationalism probably came from Hamilton's lack of state loyalties. He was born in 1755 in the West Indies (Hamilton claimed 1757). Orphaned at the age of thirteen, he was sent by relatives to the colony of New York in 1772. After preliminary study in New Jersey, he entered King's College (now Columbia University). When war with Britain broke out, he joined the army; in 1777 George Washington made him his aide-de-camp and personal secretary. After the Revolution he studied law, married well, rose rapidly in New York society, and became a dominant force in the Washington administration and the Federalist party. Overbearing and ambitious as well as bright and energetic, he proceeded to alienate important party leaders such as John Adams, and his career declined steadily after Washington left office. In 1804, Vice President Aaron Burr, a long-time political adversary who had just been defeated in the election for governor of New York, demanded a duel of honor with Hamilton because of some alleged derogatory remarks. On July 11, Burr shot Hamilton at their meeting in a field near Weehawken, New Jersey. He died the following day.

**Questions to Consider.** Hamilton argued for manufacturing on the grounds that it would attract immigrants and employ women and children. What does this prediction tell us about the availability and condition of labor in early America and about the attitudes of American leaders toward the work force? Hamilton argued not just for the specialization of labor but even more for the easier application of machinery that would result from labor specialization. What two models did he suggest for combining machinery and labor, and what does his simultaneous use of these two very different models indicate about the state of American industry at the time he was writing? Hamilton thought the spirit of capitalist enterprise must be fostered by govern-ment. Why, if this spirit was so prevalent, did Hamilton feel the need for special measures to promote it? How compatible was Hamilton's economic nationalism with Madison's political federalism?

————————★★🐌🐌🐌★★————————

*Industry to enhance the over economy and agriculture national power*

## On Manufactures (1791)

### ALEXANDER HAMILTON

It is now proper to proceed a step further, and to enumerate the principal circumstances, from which it may be inferred that manufacturing establish-ments not only occasion an augmentation of the produce and revenue of the society, but that they contribute essentially to rendering them greater than they could possibly be without such establishments.

Each of these circumstances has a considerable influence upon the total mass of industrious effort in a community; together, they add to it a degree of energy and effect which is not easily conceived. . . .

### 1. As to the Division of Labor

It has justly been observed, that there is scarcely any thing of greater mo-ment in the economy of a nation than the proper division of labor. The sep-aration of occupations causes each to be carried to a much greater perfection than it could possibly acquire if they were blended. This arises principally from three circumstances:

1st. The greater skill and dexterity naturally resulting from a constant and undivided application to a single object. It is evident that these proper-ties must increase in proportion to the separation and simplification of ob-jects, and the steadiness of the attention devoted to each; and must be less in proportion to the complication of objects, and the number among which the attention is distracted.

2nd. The economy of time, by avoiding the loss of it, incident to a fre-quent transition from operation to another of a different nature. This de-pends on various circumstances: the transition itself, the orderly disposition of the implements, machines, and materials employed in the operation to be relinquished, the preparatory steps to the commencement of a new one, the interruption of the impulse which the mind of the workman acquires from being engaged in a particular operation, the distractions, hesitations,

From Henry Cabot Lodge, ed., *The Works of Alexander Hamilton* (12 v., G. P. Putnam's Sons, New York, 1904), IV: 70–198.

*what is Hamilton's point? why is it Federalist?*
*― ― Jefferson's ? ― ― ― Republican?*

*How/why are they different? ― implications?*

and reluctances which attend the passage from one kind of business to another.

3rd. An extension of the use of machinery. A man occupied on a single object will have it more in his power, and will be more naturally led to exert his imagination, in devising methods to facilitate and abridge labor, than if he were perplexed by a variety of independent and dissimilar operations. Besides this, the fabrication of machines, in numerous instances, becoming itself a distinct trade, the artist who follows it has all the advantages which have been enumerated, for improvement in his particular art; and, in both ways, the invention and application of machinery are extended.

And from these causes united, the mere separation of the occupation of the cultivator from that of the artificer has the effect of augmenting the productive powers of labor, and with them, the total mass of the produce or revenue of a country. In this single view of the subject, therefore, the utility of artificers or manufacturers, towards promoting an increase of productive industry, is apparent.

## 2. As to an Extension of the Use of Machinery, A Point Which, Though Partly Anticipated, Requires to Be Placed in One or Two Additional Lights

The employment of machinery forms an item of great importance in the general mass of national industry. It is an artificial force brought in aid of the natural force of man; and, to all the purposes of labor, is an increase of hands, an accession of strength, unencumbered too by the expense of maintaining the laborer. . . .

The cotton mill, invented in England, within the last twenty years, is a signal illustration of the general proposition which has been just advanced. In consequence of it, all the different processes for spinning cotton are performed by means of machines, which are put in motion by water, and attended chiefly by women and children—and by a smaller number of persons, in the whole, than are requisite in the ordinary mode of spinning. And it is an advantage of great moment, that the operations of this mill continue with convenience during the night as well as through the day. The prodigious effect of such a machine is easily conceived. To this invention is to be attributed, essentially, the immense progress, which has been so suddenly made in Great Britain, in the various fabrics of cotton.

## 3. As to the Additional Employment of Classes of the Community Not Originally Engaged in the Particular Business

This is not among the least valuable of the means by which manufacturing institutions contribute to augment the general stock of industry and pro-

duction. In places where those institutions prevail, besides the persons regularly engaged in them, they afford occasional and extra employment to industrious individuals and families, who are willing to devote the leisure
resulting from the intermissions of their ordinary pursuits to collateral
labours, as a resource for multiplying their acquisitions or their enjoyments.
The husbandman himself experiences a new source of profit and support
from the increased industry of his wife and daughters, invited and stimu-
lated by the demands of the neighboring manufactories.

Besides this advantage of occasional employment to classes having different occupations, there is another, of a nature allied to it, and of a similar
tendency. This is the employment of persons who would otherwise be idle,
and in many cases a burthen on the community, either from the bias of temper, habit, infirmity of body, or some other cause, indisposing or disqualify-
ing them for the toils of the country. It is worthy of particular remark that,
in general, women and children are rendered more useful, and the latter
more early useful by manufacturing establishments, than they would otherwise be. Of the number of persons employed in the cotton manufactories of
Great Britain, it is computed that four sevenths nearly are women and children, of whom the greatest proportion are children, and many of them of a
very tender age. . . .

### 4. As to the Promoting of Emigration from Foreign Countries

Men reluctantly quit one course of occupation and livelihood for another,
unless invited to it by very apparent and proximate advantages. Many who
would go from one country to another, if they had a prospect of continuing
with more benefit the callings to which they have been educated, will often
not be tempted to change their situation by the hope of doing better in some
other way. Manufacturers who, listening to the powerful invitations of a better price for their fabrics, or their labor, of greater cheapness of provisions
and raw materials, of an exemption from the chief part of the taxes, burthens
and restraints, which they endure in the Old World, of greater personal independence and consequence, under the operation of a more equal government, and of what is far more precious than mere religious toleration, a
perfect equality of religious privileges, would probably flock from Europe
to the United States to pursue their own trades or professions, if they were
once made sensible of the advantages they would enjoy, and were inspired
with an assurance of encouragement and employment, will with difficulty,
be induced to transplant themselves, with a view to becoming cultivators of
Land.

If it be true, then, that it is in the interest of the United States to open
every possible avenue to immigration from abroad, it affords a weighty argument for the encouragement of manufactures; which, for the reasons just
assigned, will have the strongest tendency to multiply the inducements to
it. . . .

## 5. As to the Furnishing Greater Scope for the Diversity of Talents and Dispositions, Which Discriminate Men from Each Other

This is a much more powerful means of augmenting the fund of national industry, than may at first sight appear. It is a just observation, that minds of the strongest and most active powers for their proper objects, fall below mediocrity, and labor without effect, if confined to uncongenial pursuits. And it is thence to be inferred, that the results of human exertion may be immensely increased by diversifying its objects. When all the different kinds of industry obtain in a community, each individual can find his proper element, and can call into activity the whole vigor of his nature. And the community is benefited by the services of its respective members, in the manner in which each can serve it with most effect.

If there be any thing in a remark often to be met with, namely, that there is, in the genius of the people of this country, a peculiar aptitude for mechanic improvements, it would operate as a forcible reason for giving opportunities to the exercise of that species of talent, by the propagation of manufactures.

## 6. As to the Affording a More Ample and Various Field for Enterprise

. . . To cherish and stimulate the activity of the human mind, by multiplying the objects of enterprise, is not among the least considerable of the expedients by which the wealth of a nation may be promoted. Even things in themselves not positively advantageous sometimes become so, by their tendency to provoke exertion. Every new scene which is opened to the busy nature of man to rouse and exert itself, is the addition of a new energy to the general stock of effort.

The spirit of enterprise, useful and prolific as it is, must necessarily be contracted or expanded, in proportion to the simplicity or variety of the occupations and productions which are to be found in a society. It must be less in a nation of mere cultivators, than in a nation of cultivators and merchants; less in a nation of cultivators and merchants, than in a nation of cultivators, artificers and merchants.

## 7. As to the Creating, in Some Instances, a New, and Securing in All, a More Certain and Steady Demand for the Surplus Produce of the Soil

This is among the most important of the circumstances which have been indicated. It is a principal means by which the establishment of manufactures contributes to an augmentation of the produce or revenue of a country, and has an immediate and direct relation to the prosperity of agriculture.

It is evident that the exertions of the husbandman will be steady or fluc-
tuating, vigorous or feeble, in proportion to the steadiness or fluctuation,
adequateness or inadequateness, of the markets on which he must depend
for the vent [selling] of the surplus which may be produced by his labor; and
that such surplus, in the ordinary course of things, will be greater or less in
the same proportion.

⊘For the purpose of this vent, a domestic market is greatly to be preferred
to a foreign one; because it is, in the nature of things, far more to be relied
upon⊘

# ★ 18 ★

## A CALL FOR UNITY

The election of 1800 was a stormy one. During the campaign Democratic-Republican Thomas Jefferson was called a dangerous radical and Federalist John Adams a high-toned royalist. The House of Representatives, voting by states in February 1801, finally picked Jefferson as president on the thirty-sixth ballot. Jefferson called his election "the revolution of 1800." Reacting against what he regarded as monarchical tendencies in the Federalists, he insisted on "republican simplicity" in his administration. He stopped using the fancy carriage of state and rode horseback through the streets of Washington like any other citizen. He refused to wear "court dress" when receiving foreign diplomats, and his casual demeanor shocked some of the diplomatic corps. The British minister was so outraged by the informality of dinners at the Executive Mansion that he began refusing invitations to dine with the president.

Jefferson's first inaugural address, given on March 4, 1801, was a beautifully phrased exposition of his republican philosophy. The American republic, he declared, was founded on the sacred principle of majority rule; but the majority, he added, must respect the rights of the minority. He went on to make an appeal for the restoration of good feeling between the Federalists and the Republicans after the bitter campaign of 1800. The two parties differed on many points, he acknowledged, but they agreed on their devotion to the basic principles of the American system of government: equal justice for all; peace and friendship with all nations; support of the state governments in their rights; the right of election by the people; the supremacy of the civil over military authority; freedom of religion, freedom of the press, and freedom of person, under the protection of habeas corpus; and trial by juries impartially selected. "Sometimes," said Jefferson, "it is said that man can not be trusted with government of himself. Can he, then, be trusted with the government of others? Or have we found angels in the form of kings to govern him? Let history answer this question." History, Jefferson thought, showed the failure of undemocratic governments. He placed his faith in the future in governments resting on the consent of the people.

**Questions to Consider.** In reading Jefferson's address several questions come at once to mind. In what ways did Jefferson perceive the United States as different from the countries of Europe? What did he mean by saying that "every difference of opinion is not a difference of principle"? After the bitter political strife of the 1790s, how could Jefferson argue that "we are all Republicans, we are all Federalists"? What role did the accidents of geography—physical separation from Europe and what Jefferson called "a chosen country, with room enough for our descendants"—play in his optimistic expectations? Did any of the themes appearing in Jefferson's inaugural address clash with those put forth by Federalists like Hamilton in 1791 and John Marshall in 1803? Is it possible to summarize Jefferson's "essential principles of our Government" even more than he was able or willing to do? In view of these principles, how could a Massachusetts Federalist like John Adams believe that Jefferson's election as president would produce "the loathsome steam of human victims offered in sacrifice"?

# First Inaugural Address (1801)

THOMAS JEFFERSON

Called upon to undertake the duties of the first executive office of our country, I avail myself of the presence of that portion of my fellow-citizens which is here assembled to express my grateful thanks for the favor with which they have been pleased to look toward me, to declare a sincere consciousness that the task is above my talents, and that I approach it with those anxious and awful presentiments which the greatness of the charge and the weakness of my powers so justly inspire. A rising nation, spread over a wide and fruitful land, traversing all the seas with the rich productions of their industry, engaged in commerce with nations who feel power and forget right, advancing rapidly to destinies beyond the reach of mortal eyes—when I contemplate these transcendent objects, and see the honor, the happiness, and the hopes of this beloved country committed to the issue and the auspices of this day, I shrink from the contemplation, and humble myself before the magnitude of the undertaking. Utterly, indeed, should I despair did not the presence of many whom I here see remind me that in the other high authorities provided by our Constitution I shall find resources of wisdom, of

From James D. Richardson, ed., *A Compilation of the Messages and Papers of the Presidents* (Government Printing Office, Washington, D.C., 1897–1907), I: 309–312.

**Thomas Jefferson on a milk pitcher.** The inscription at the top of the pitcher is from Jefferson's recently delivered inaugural address, which extended the hand of peace to his political opponents. Jefferson's likeness, here ringed with a foliage motif bearing the names of the states, appeared on all types of everyday objects, from pitchers and mugs to bed coverings and wall samplers, which in this way did service as the mass media of the period. (Collection of Janice L. and David J. Frent)

virtue, and of zeal on which to rely under all difficulties. To you, then, gentlemen, who are charged with the sovereign functions of legislation, and to those associated with you, I look with encouragement for that guidance and support which may enable us to steer with safety the vessel in which we are all embarked amidst the conflicting elements of a troubled world.

During the contest of opinion through which we have passed the animation of discussions and of exertions has sometimes worn an aspect which might impose on strangers unused to think freely and to speak and to write what they think; but this being now decided by the voice of the nation, announced according to the rules of the Constitution, all will, of course, arrange themselves under the will of the law, and unite in common efforts for the common good. All, too, will bear in mind this sacred principle, that though the will of the majority is in all cases to prevail, that will to be rightful must be reasonable; that the minority possess their equal rights, which equal law must protect, and to violate would be oppression. Let us, then, fellow-citizens, unite with one heart and one mind. Let us restore to social intercourse that harmony and affection without which liberty and even life itself are but dreary things. And let us reflect that, having banished from our land that religious intolerance under which mankind so long bled and suffered, we have yet gained little if we countenance a political intolerance as despotic, as wicked, and capable of as bitter and bloody persecutions. During the throes and convulsions of the ancient world, during the agonizing spasms of infuriated man, seeking through blood and slaughter his long-lost liberty, it was not wonderful that the agitation of the billows should reach even this distant and peaceful shore; that this should be more felt and feared by some and less by others, and should divide opinions as to measures of safety. But every difference of opinion is not a difference of principle. We have called by different names brethren of the same principle. We are all Republicans, we are all Federalists. If there be any among us who would wish to dissolve this Union or to change its republican form, let them stand undisturbed as monuments of the safety with which error of opinion may be tolerated where reason is left free to combat it. I know, indeed, that some honest men fear that a republican government can not be strong, that this Government is not strong enough; but would the honest patriot, in the full tide of successful experiment, abandon a government which has so far kept us free and firm on the theoretic and visionary fear that this Government, the world's best hope, may by possibility want energy to preserve itself? I trust not. I believe this, on the contrary, the strongest Government on earth. I believe it the only one where every man, at the call of the law, would fly to the standard of the law, and would meet invasions of the public order as his own personal concern. Sometimes it is said that man can not be trusted with government of himself. Can he, then, be trusted with the government of others? Or have we found angels in the forms of kings to govern him? Let history answer this question.

Let us, then, with courage and confidence pursue our own Federal and Republican principles, our attachment to union and representative government. Kindly separated by nature and a wide ocean from the exterminating havoc of one quarter of the globe; too high-minded to endure the degradations of the others; possessing a chosen country, with room enough for our descendants to the thousandth and thousandth generation; entertaining a due sense of our own faculties, to the acquisitions of our own industry, to honor and confidence from our fellow-citizens, resulting not from birth, but from our actions and their sense of them; enlightened by a benign religion, professed, indeed, and practiced in various forms, yet all of them inculcating honesty, truth, temperance, gratitude, and the love of man; acknowledging and adoring an overruling Providence, which by all its dispensations proves that it delights in the happiness of man here and his greater happiness hereafter—with all these blessings, what more is necessary to make us a happy and prosperous people? Still one thing more, fellow-citizens—a wise and frugal Government, which shall restrain men from injuring one another, shall leave them otherwise free to regulate their own pursuits of industry and improvement, and shall not take from the mouth of labor the bread it has earned. This is the sum of good government, and this is necessary to close the circle of our felicities.

About to enter, fellow-citizens, on the exercise of duties which comprehend everything dear and valuable to you, it is proper you should understand what I deem the essential principles of our Government, and consequently those which ought to shape its Administration. I will compress them within the narrowest compass they will bear, stating the general principle, but not all its limitations. Equal and exact justice to all men, of whatever state or persuasion, religious or political; peace, commerce, and honest friendship with all nations, entangling alliances with none; the support of the State governments in all their rights, as the most competent administrations for our domestic concerns and the surest bulwarks against antirepublican tendencies; the preservation of the General Government in its whole constitutional vigor, as the sheet anchor of our peace at home and safety abroad; a jealous care of the right of election by the people—a mild and safe corrective of abuses which are lopped by the sword of revolution where peaceable remedies are unprovided; absolute acquiescence in the decisions of the majority, the vital principle of republics, from which is no appeal but to force, the vital principle and immediate parent of despotism; a well-disciplined militia, our best reliance in peace and for the first moments of war, till regulars may relieve them; the supremacy of the civil over the military authority; economy in the public expense, that labor may be lightly burthened; the honest payment of our debts and sacred preservation of the public faith; encouragement of agriculture, and of commerce as its handmaid; the diffusion of information and arraignment of all abuses at the bar of the public reason; freedom of religion; freedom of the press, and freedom of person under the protection of the habeas corpus, and trial by juries impartially selected. These principles form the bright constellation which has gone before us and guided our steps through an age of revolution and reformation. The wisdom of our sages and blood of our heroes have been devoted to their attainment. They should be the creed of our political faith, the text of civic instruction, the touchstone by which to try the services of those we trust; and should we wander from them in moments of error or of alarm, let us hasten to retrace our steps and to regain the road which alone leads to peace, liberty, and safety. . . .

Relying, then, on the patronage of your good will, I advance with obedience to the work, ready to retire from it whenever you become sensible how much better choice it is in your power to make. And may that infinite Power which rules the destinies of the universe lead our councils to what is best, and give them a favorable issue for your peace and prosperity.

# THE CONSTITUTION PROTECTED

*Fundamental Idea: Why/How is Constitution the
most important?
What implications on gov't /esp. judiciary system?*

*Marbury* v. *Madison* was the first case in which the Supreme Court exercised the right of "judicial review" over laws passed by Congress. In February 1803, Chief Justice John Marshall, a staunch Federalist, speaking for the majority of justices on the Supreme Court, announced his opinion in the case. William Marbury had been appointed justice of the peace for the District of Columbia by John Adams in the last hours of his administration. But because Marbury was a Federalist, James Madison, Jefferson's secretary of state, withheld the commission from him. Marbury appealed to the Supreme Court for a writ of mandamus, that is, a court order compelling Madison to deliver the commission.

Marshall did not believe that Madison was justified in denying Marbury his commission as justice of the peace. But in his opinion he declared that the Supreme Court could not force Madison to deliver the commission. The Constitution, he said, in defining the original jurisdiction of the Supreme Court, did not include the issue of writs to executive officers. Nonetheless, section 13 of the Judiciary Act of 1789 did give the Supreme Court the power to issue such writs, and it was under this law that Marbury had applied to the Court. Marshall, however, declared that section 13 of the Judiciary Act was unconstitutional and that therefore the Court could not render judgment. He then went on to assert the right of the Supreme Court to pass on the constitutionality of laws passed by Congress. "It is a proposition too plain to be contested," he declared, "that the constitution controls any legislative act repugnant to it" and that "a legislative act contrary to the constitution is not law." He added, "It is emphatically the province and duty of the judicial department to say what the law is." And he concluded that "a law repugnant to the constitution is void, and that courts, as well as other departments, are bound by that instrument." By claiming for the Court the duty of deciding whether acts of Congress were constitutional, Marshall upheld the prestige of the judiciary, even though he was unable to do anything for Marbury. But it was not until the *Dred Scott* case, more than half a century later, that the Supreme Court invalidated a congressional act for the second time.

Born in 1755 to well-to-do Virginians, John Marshall received little formal schooling. He studied law, however, and eventually became active in state politics. His service in the army during the American Revolution helped develop his nationalistic outlook. A distant cousin of Thomas Jefferson but a devoted Federalist nonetheless, Marshall served on a commission to France in 1797 and was elected to Congress in 1799. In 1801 President John Adams named him to the U.S. Supreme Court, where he served as chief justice for the next thirty-four years. Among his notable decisions besides *Marbury* v. *Madison* were *McCulloch* v. *Maryland* (1819), which protected federal agencies such as the Bank of the United States from state taxes; *Dartmouth College* v. *Woodward* (1819), which upheld the sanctity of contracts; and *Gibbons* v. *Ogden* (1824), which established federal authority over interstate and foreign commerce. In these and other cases Marshall sought to protect the rights of property, increase the power of the federal government, and raise the prestige of the federal judiciary. Personally convivial, gossipy, courtly with women, and generally reveling in the social life of the slaveholding gentry, Marshall in public remained a figure of controversy throughout his career. He died in Philadelphia in 1835.

**Questions to Consider.** Why, according to Chief Justice Marshall, should the Constitution and its principles be considered permanent? How important was it to Marshall's argument that the U.S. Constitution was written? What alternative did he have in mind, and why did he feel compelled to assert the special character of a written document? Why did he single out the legislative branch as opposed to the executive (or judiciary) as the chief danger to the permanence of the Constitution and its principles? On what grounds, according to Marshall, did the judiciary become the final arbiter of constitutional quarrels with the right to annul legislation? Why was Marshall's decision seen as a political victory for the Federalist party?

# *Marbury* v. *Madison* (1803)

### JOHN MARSHALL

The question whether an act repugnant to the constitution can become the law of the land is a question deeply interesting to the United States; but,

From 1 *Craven* 137 (1803).

happily not of an intricacy proportioned to its interest. It seems only necessary to recognize certain principles supposed to have been long and well established, to decide it.

That the people have an original right to establish for their future government such principles as, in their opinion, shall most conduce to their own happiness, is the basis on which the whole American fabric has been erected. The exercise of this original right is a very great exertion, nor can it nor ought it to be frequently repeated. The principles therefore so established are deemed fundamental. And as the authority from which they proceed is supreme and can seldom act, they are designed to be permanent.

This original and supreme will organizes the government, and assigns to different departments their respective powers. It may either stop here or establish certain limits not to be transcended by those departments.

The government of the United States is of the latter description. The powers of the legislature are defined and limited; and that those limits may not be mistaken or forgotten, the constitution is written. To what purpose are powers limited, and to what purpose is that limitation committed to writing, if these limits may, at any time, be passed by those intended to be restrained? The distinction between a government with limited and unlimited powers is abolished if those limits do not confine the persons on whom they are imposed and if acts prohibited and acts allowed are of equal obligation. It is a proposition too plain to be contested, that the constitution controls any legislative act repugnant to it; or the legislature may alter the constitution by an ordinary act.

Between these alternatives there is no middle ground. The constitution is either a superior paramount law, unchangeable by ordinary means, or it is on a level with ordinary legislative acts, and, like other acts, is alterable when the legislature shall please to alter it.

If the former part of the alternative be true, then a legislative act contrary to the constitution is not law; if the latter part be true, then written constitutions are absurd attempts, on the part of the people, to limit a power in its own nature illimitable.

Certainly all those who have framed written constitutions contemplate them as forming the fundamental and paramount law of the nation, and consequently the theory of every such government must be that an act of the legislature repugnant to the constitution is void.

This theory is essentially attached to a written constitution, and is consequently to be considered, by this court, as one of the fundamental principles of our society. It is not, therefore, to be lost sight of in the further consideration of this subject.

If an act of the legislature repugnant to the constitution is void, does it, notwithstanding its invalidity, bind the courts and oblige them to give it effect? Or, in other words, though it be not law, does it constitute a rule as operative as if it was a law? This would be to overthrow in fact what was established in theory, and would seem, at first view, an absurdity too gross to be insisted on. It shall, however, receive a more attentive consideration.

It is emphatically the province and duty of the judicial department to say what the law is. Those who apply the rule to particular cases must of necessity expound and interpret that rule. If two laws conflict with each other, the courts must decide on the operation of each.

So if a law be in opposition to the constitution; if both the law and the constitution apply to a particular case, so that the court must either decide that case conformably to the law, disregarding the constitution, or conformably to the constitution, disregarding the law, the court must determine which of these conflicting rules governs the case. This is of the very essence of judicial duty.

If, then, the courts are to regard the constitution, and the constitution is superior to any ordinary act of the legislature, the constitution, and not such ordinary act, must govern the case to which they both apply.

Those, then, who controvert the principle that the constitution is to be considered in court as a paramount law, are reduced to the necessity of maintaining that courts must close their eyes on the constitution and see only the law.

This doctrine would subvert the very foundation of all written constitutions. It would declare that an act which, according to the principles and theory of our government, is entirely void, is yet, in practice, completely obligatory. It would declare that if the legislature shall do what is expressly forbidden, such act, notwithstanding the express prohibition, is in reality effectual. It would be giving to the legislature a practical and real omnipotence with the same breath which professes to restrict their powers within narrow limits. It is prescribing limits and declaring that those limits may be passed at pleasure.

That it thus reduces to nothing what we have deemed the greatest improvement on political institutions, a written constitution, would of itself be sufficient, in America, where written constitutions have been viewed with so much reverence, for rejecting the construction. But the peculiar expressions of the constitution of the United States furnish additional arguments in favor of its rejection.

The judicial power of the United States is extended to all cases arising under the constitution.

Could it be the intention of those who gave this power to say that in using it the constitution should not be looked into? That a case arising under the constitution should be decided without examining the instrument under which it arises?

This is too extravagant to be maintained.

In some cases, then, the constitution must be looked into by the judges. And if they can open it at all, what part of it are they forbidden to read or to obey?

There are many other parts of the constitution which serve to illustrate this subject.

It is declared that "no tax or duty shall be laid on articles exported from any state." Suppose a duty on the export of cotton, of tobacco, or of flour, and a suit instituted to recover it, ought judgment to be rendered in such a case? Ought the judges to close their eyes on the constitution, and only see the law?

The constitution declares "that no bill of attainder or *ex post facto* law shall be passed." If, however, such a bill should be passed, and a person should be prosecuted under it, must the court condemn to death those victims whom the constitution endeavors to preserve?

"No person," says the constitution, "shall be convicted of treason unless on the testimony of two witnesses to the same overt act, or on confession in open court."

Here the language of the constitution is addressed especially to the courts. It prescribes, directly for them, a rule of evidence not to be departed from. If the legislature should change that rule, and declare one witness, or a confession out of court, sufficient for conviction, must the constitutional principle yield to the legislative act?

From these, and many other selections which might be made, it is apparent that the framers of the constitution contemplated that instrument as a rule for the government of *courts,* as well as of the legislature. Why otherwise does it direct the judges to take an oath to support it? This oath certainly applies in an especial manner to their conduct in their official character. How immoral to impose it on them if they were to be used as the instruments, and the knowing instruments, for violating what they swear to support!

The oath of office, too, imposed by the legislature, is completely demonstrative of the legislative opinion on this subject. It is in these words: "I do solemnly swear that I will administer justice without respect to persons, and do equal right to the poor and to the rich; and that I will faithfully and impartially discharge all the duties incumbent on me as ———, according to the best of my abilities and understanding, agreeably to *the constitution* and laws of the United States." Why does a judge swear to discharge his duties agreeably to the constitution of the United States, if that constitution forms no rule for his government—if it is closed upon him, and cannot be inspected by him?

If such be the real state of things, this is worse than solemn mockery. To prescribe, or to take this oath, becomes equally a crime.

It is also not entirely unworthy of observation, that in declaring what shall be the *supreme* law of the land, the constitution itself is first mentioned, and not the laws of the United States generally, but those only which shall be made in *pursuance* of the constitution, have that rank.

Thus, the particular phraseology of the constitution of the United States confirms and strengthens the principle, supposed to be essential to all written constitutions, that a law repugnant to the constitution is void, and that courts, as well as other departments, are bound by that instrument.

# 20

## THE WIDE MISSOURI

Thomas Jefferson's presidency did not usher in the wide-eyed revolutionary radicalism that some Federalist party orators had warned against, but "Long Tom" did prove reluctant to have the central government promote trade and manufacturing. More solicitous of states' rights than the Federalists, Jefferson hesitated to assert the government's authority in economic matters. More solicitous of farming than of industry as a way of life, he also hesitated to encourage commerce at the expense of agriculture. Ironically enough, it was precisely this agrarian vision, this belief that America should remain predominantly rural, that led Jefferson to purchase the Louisiana Territory from France in 1803, thus doubling the nation's size by means of a maneuver that some observers felt was unconstitutional and underhanded.

This vision of America as a land of farmers also prompted the president to sponsor the exploration of the upper Louisiana Territory and the great Columbia River region beyond. Jefferson's interest in the West was long-standing—he asked Congress to authorize an expedition into the Pacific Northwest months before the United States actually bought the Louisiana Territory—and besides, he never lost an opportunity to slake his immense thirst for scientific knowledge. What better opportunity could arise? Ever the politician, however, he was also careful to stress (for the benefit of stray Federalist voters) that the venture might open vast new trading horizons as well as vast new agricultural regions.

The leaders of this first expedition were U.S. Army captains Meriwether Lewis, a noted woodsman who had once been Jefferson's private secretary, and William Clark, an Indian fighter from Kentucky. In the spring of 1804, Lewis and Clark started from St. Louis up the Missouri River with a large party in three well-stocked boats "under a gentle breeze"; Lewis, in nominal command, fully shared responsibility with Clark. After wintering in present-day North Dakota in 40°-below temperatures, nine hand-picked men plus a Shoshone and a French-Canadian guide traversed the Rocky Mountains; they survived on horse meat and tallow, and in November reached "this great Pacific Ocean. O the joy!" Back in St. Louis by the following September, Lewis sent the eagerly awaited letter excerpted below, the party's first communication with government and country in a year. Enthusiastically received, this report whetted American interest in the new territory to a keen edge, leading not only to more exploration and extensive fur trading but to formal U.S. interest in the Oregon Territory and its ultimate wresting in 1845 from the grip of long-time foe Great Britain.

Meriwether Lewis, the youthful head of the great expedition, was born in 1774 in Albemarle County, Virginia, not far from Jefferson's home. Although his family eventually settled in the state of Georgia, Lewis returned alone at age thirteen to Virginia where, after sporadic private study, he enlisted in the local militia in time to be sent to help suppress the Pennsylvania Whisky Rebellion in 1794. The next year, lacking better prospects and having acquired a taste for bivouacking, Lewis joined the regular army. But when President Jefferson offered to make him presidential secretary, he eagerly, and wisely, accepted. So close did the two men become that for two years Lewis lived in the executive mansion, helping plan the expedition. He prepared himself to lead it by studying mapmaking, firearms design, and other skills. In late 1806, on the heels of his remarkable expeditionary triumph, Jefferson appointed Lewis governor of the Louisiana Territory. In 1809 while journeying to Washington on administrative business, Lewis died under mysterious circumstances near Nashville, Tennessee.

**Questions to Consider.** Because Meriwether Lewis was eager to send word to the East, he could not in this first letter afford to compile a full report. He had to make decisions, in other words, about what information to include and what not to include. Are you in any way surprised at the letter's contents? What might he have emphasized that he did not? What impression of the journey and the territory was he trying to leave with his reader? Although addressed to Jefferson personally, the letter was quickly publicized and widely read throughout the United States. Does Lewis seem to have been writing for other eyes as well as Jefferson's? Do you think Lewis understood the implications of his message for future American development and foreign policy?

# Report on the Missouri and Columbia Rivers (1806)

MERIWETHER LEWIS

It is with pleasure that I announce to you the safe arrival of myself and party at 12 o'clock today at this place with our papers and baggage. In obedience to your orders we have penetrated the continent of North America to the

Pacific Ocean, and sufficiently explored the interior of the country to affirm with confidence that we have discovered the most practicable route which does exist across the continent by means of the navigable branches of the Missouri and Columbia Rivers. . . .

We view this passage across the continent as affording immense advantages to the fur trade, but fear that the advantages which it offers as a communication for the productions of the East Indies to the United States and thence to Europe will never be found equal on an extensive scale to that by way of the Cape of Good Hope; still we believe that many articles not bulky, brittle nor of a very perishable nature may be conveyed to the United States by this route with more facility and at less expense than by that at present practiced.

The Missouri and all its branches from the Cheyenne upwards abound more in beaver and common otter, than any other streams on earth, particularly that proportion of them lying within the Rocky Mountains. The furs of all this immense tract of country including such as may be collected on the upper portion of the River St. Peters, Red River, and the Assinniboin with the immense country watered by the Columbia, may be conveyed to the mouth of the Columbia by the 1st of August in each year and from thence be shipped to, and arrive in Canton [China] earlier than the furs at present shipped from Montreal annually arrive in London. The British N. West Company of Canada were they permitted by the United States might also convey their furs collected in the Athabaske, on the Saskashawan, and south and west of Lake Winnipic by that route within the period before mentioned. The productions of nine-tenths of the most valuable fur country of America could be conveyed by the route proposed to the East Indies.

In the infancy of the trade across the continent, or during the period that the trading establishments shall be confined to the Missouri and its branches, the men employed in this trade will be compelled to convey the furs collected in that quarter as low on the Columbia as tide water [near the ocean], in which case they could not return to the falls of the Missouri until about the 1st of October, which would be so late in the season that there would be considerable danger of the river being obstructed by ice before they could reach this place and consequently that the commodities brought from the East Indies would be detained until the following spring; but this difficulty will at once vanish when establishments are also made on the Columbia, and a sufficient number of men employed at them to convey annually the productions of the East Indies to the upper establishment on the Kooskooske, and there exchange them with the men of the Missouri for their furs in the beginning of July. By this means the furs not only of the Missouri but those also of the Columbia may be shipped to the East Indies by the sea-

From Reuben Gold Thwaites, ed., *Original Journals of the Lewis and Clark Expedition* (New York, 1904–1905), VII: 334–337.

**Lewis (standing) and Clark with York, Clark's slave, and Sacajawea, an Indian woman.** York was an accomplished linguist and an effective interpreter and ambassador of good will to the Indian tribes, who were amazed at his color. Sacajawea served the expedition as a guide. (Montana State Capitol)

son before mentioned, and the commodities of the East Indies arrive at St. Louis or the mouth of the Ohio by the last of September in each year.

Although the Columbia does not as much as the Missouri abound in beaver and otter, yet it is by no means despicable in this respect, and would furnish a valuable fur trade distinct from any other consideration in addition to the otter and beaver which it could furnish. There might be collected considerable quantities of the skins of three species of bear affording a great variety of colours and of superior delicacy, those also of the tiger cat, several species of fox, martin and several others of an inferior class of furs, besides the valuable sea otter of the coast.

If the government will only aid, even in a very limited manner, the enterprise of her citizens I am fully convinced that we shall shortly derive the benefits of a most lucrative trade from this source, and that in the course of ten or twelve years a tour across the continent by the route mentioned will be undertaken by individuals with as little concern as a voyage across the Atlantic is at present.

The British N. West Company of Canada has for several years carried on a partial trade with the Minnetares, Ahwayhaways and Mandans on the Missouri from their establishments on the Assinniboin at the entrance of Mouse River; at present I have good reason for believing that they intend shortly to form an establishment near those nations with a view to engross the fur trade of the Missouri. The known enterprise and resources of this company, latterly strengthened by an union with their powerful rival the X. Y. Company, renders them formidable in that distant part of the continent to all other traders; and in my opinion if we are to regard the trade of the Missouri as an object of importance to the United States, the strides of this company towards the Missouri cannot be too vigilantly watched nor too firmly and speedily opposed by our government. The embarrassments under which the navigation of the Missouri at present labours from the unfriendly dispositions of the Kancez, the several bands of Tetons, Assinniboins, and those tribes that resort to the British establishments on the Saskashawan is also a subject which requires the earliest attention of our government. As I shall shortly be with you I have deemed it unnecessary here to detail the several ideas which have presented themselves to my mind on those subjects, more especially when I consider that a thorough knowledge of the geography of the country is absolutely necessary to their being understood, and leisure has not yet permitted us to make but one general map of the country which I am unwilling to risk by the mail. . . .

I have brought with me several skins of the sea otter, two skins of the native sheep of America, five skins and skeletons complete of the Bighorn or mountain ram, and a skin of the mule deer besides the skins of several other quadrapeds and birds native of the countries through which we have passed. I have also preserved a pretty extensive collection of plants, and collected nine other vocabularies [of Indian tribes].

I have prevailed on the great chief of the Mandan nation to accompany me to Washington; he is now with my friend and colleague Capt. Clark at this place, in good health and spirits, and very anxious to proceed. . . .

The route by which I purpose traveling from hence to Washington is by way of Cahokia, Vincennes, Louisville, Ky., the Crab Orchard, Abington, Fincastle, Stanton and Charlottesville. Any letters directed to me at Louisville ten days after the receipt of this will most probably meet me at that place. I am very anxious to learn the state of my friends in Albemarle, particularly whether my mother is yet living. I am with every sentiment of esteem your Obt. and very Humble servant.

# 21

## THE SECTIONAL SPECTER

The first great sectional struggle in the United States (after the Missouri crisis over slavery) was over the tariff. Northern industrialists favored high tariffs to protect their products from foreign competition. But the South was an agricultural region, and Southerners complained that protective tariffs raised the price of manufactured goods and prevented them from importing low-priced goods from abroad. On May 20, 1828, Congress passed a tariff bill with rates so high that South Carolina's John C. Calhoun (vice-president at the time) called it a "Tariff of Abominations." He presented a lengthy statement of the Southern position on tariffs in which he developed his theory of nullification.

Calhoun believed in the "compact" theory of the Union. He maintained that the Constitution was a contract into which the states had entered of their own free will. The states retained their sovereignty, and the federal government was merely their agent for general purposes. If the federal government exceeded its authority and encroached on the powers of the states, the states had a right to resist. Calhoun thought the constitutionality of acts of Congress should be decided by state conventions called for that purpose. If such a convention declared an act of Congress in violation of the Constitution, that act became null and void within the borders of that state. Calhoun insisted that the Constitution did not give Congress the right to levy protective tariffs and that the states had a right to nullify tariff legislation.

On December 19, 1828, the South Carolina legislature published Calhoun's statement (without mentioning his name) as "South Carolina Exposition and Protest," together with resolutions, reproduced below, condemning the tariff. For the time being, South Carolina contented itself with making this protest, hoping that the tariff would be revised after Andrew Jackson became president. But in July 1832, when a new tariff bill was passed by Congress and signed by Jackson, South Carolinians decided to put Calhoun's theory into practice. On November 4, 1832, a special state convention met in Columbia, adopted an ordinance declaring the tariffs of 1828 and 1832 unconstitutional, and announced that no tariff duties would be collected in the state after February 1, 1833. Jackson at once denounced South Carolina's action and asked Congress to give him authority to use the army and navy, if necessary, to compel South Carolina to obey the law. South Carolina continued defiant. When Congress passed a compromise bill lowering the tariff rate, the "nullies" (as they were called) repealed the nullification ordinance. But they did not disavow the nullification theory.

Calhoun was born in South Carolina in 1782 to an upcountry farmer. After graduating from Yale College, he practiced law briefly. He then married a wealthy Charleston woman and began a political climb that led to Congress, a post in James Monroe's cabinet, and the vice presidency under both John Quincy Adams and Andrew Jackson. He began as a vigorous nationalist, favoring the protective tariff, but moved to states' rights and an antitariff position when it became clear that South Carolina had more to gain from free trade. During the nullification crisis he resigned from the vice presidency in December 1832 for a seat in the Senate. There he became one of the "great triumvirate" (along with Henry Clay and Daniel Webster); an implacable foe of Jackson; and a staunch supporter of South Carolina, the South, and slavery. He died in Washington, D.C., in early 1850.

**Questions to Consider.** Why was a protective tariff considered so threatening to the Carolinians? Were they fearful of higher prices for imported goods or of reduced markets for their own product, cotton? Why did the "encouragement of domestic industry," originally urged by Alexander Hamilton in 1791, cause such a fierce blowup in 1828 but not before? Was Calhoun trying to speak for all of American agriculture or only for a certain kind? Was it the threat to agriculture or to something else that most disturbed Calhoun? Which of the eight articles of the "Protest" furnishes the best clue to the situation in South Carolina? As to the political issue, why did Calhoun fear what he called "simple consolidated government" as a threat to freedom?

# South Carolina Exposition and Protest (1828)

### JOHN C. CALHOUN

The Senate and House of Representatives of South Carolina, now met, and sitting in General Assembly, through the Hon. William Smith and the Hon. Robert Y. Hayne, the representatives in the Senate of the United States, do,

Jonathan Elliot, ed., *The Debates in the Several State Conventions on the Adoption of the Federal Constitution,* &c (5 v., J. B. Lippincott, Philadelphia, 1836), IV: 580–582.

**John C. Calhoun.** Calhoun, who served as congressman, vice-president under Andrew Jackson, and then senator from South Carolina, started out as a strong nationalist and then became one of the most vigorous states' righters in the nation. He insisted that sovereignty (supreme power) resided in "the people of the several states" rather than in the people making up the nation as a whole, and that the people of the states had the right to nullify any federal laws they thought threatened their state's welfare. Calhoun developed his doctrine of nullification as a reaction against protective-tariff measures designed to encourage Northern industries but which he thought hurt South Carolina and other Southern states with little or no manufacturing. He was also a states' righter because he wanted to safeguard the institution of slavery from interference by antislavery crusaders in the North. (National Portrait Gallery/Smithsonian Institution, Washington, D.C.)

in the name and on behalf of the good people of the said commonwealth, solemnly PROTEST against the system of protecting duties, lately adopted by the federal government, for the following reasons:—

1st. *Because* the good people of this commonwealth believe that the powers of Congress were delegated to it in trust for the accomplishment of certain specified objects which limit and control them, and that every exercise of them for any other purpose, is a violation of the Constitution as unwarrantable as the undisguised assumption of substantive, independent powers not granted or expressly withheld.

2d. *Because* the power to lay duties on imports is, and in its very nature can be, only a means of effecting objects specified by the Constitution; since no free government, and least of all a government of enumerated powers, can of right impose any tax, any more than a penalty, which is not at once justified by public necessity, and clearly within the scope and purview of the social compact; and since the right of confining appropriations of the public money to such legitimate and constitutional objects is as essential to the liberty of the people as their unquestionable privilege to be taxed only by their own consent.

3d. *Because* they believe that the tariff law passed by Congress at its last session, and all other acts of which the principal object is the protection of manufactures, or any other branch of domestic industry, if they be considered as the exercise of a power in Congress to tax the people at its own good will and pleasure, and to apply the money raised to objects not specified in the Constitution, is a violation of these fundamental principles, a breach of a well-defined trust, and a perversion of the high powers vested in the federal government for federal purposes only.

4th. *Because* such acts, considered in the light of a regulation of commerce, are equally liable to objection; since, although the power to regulate commerce may, like all other powers, be exercised so as to protect domestic manufactures, yet it is clearly distinguishable from a power to do so *eo nomine*,[1] both in the nature of the thing and in the common acception of the terms; and because the confounding of them would lead to the most extravagant results, since the encouragement of domestic industry implies an absolute control over all the interests, resources, and pursuits of a people, and is inconsistent with the idea of any other than a simple, consolidated government.

5th. *Because*, from the contemporaneous exposition of the Constitution in the numbers of the *Federalist*, (which is cited only because the Supreme Court has recognized its authority), it is clear that the power to regulate commerce was considered by the Convention as only incidentally connected with the encouragement of agriculture and manufactures; and because the power of laying imposts and duties on imports was not understood to justify in any case, a prohibition of foreign commodities, except as a means of extending commerce, by coercing foreign nations to a fair reciprocity in their intercourse with us, or for some *bona fide* commercial purpose.

6th. *Because*, whilst the power to protect manufactures is nowhere expressly granted to Congress, nor can be considered as necessary and proper to carry into effect any specified power, it seems to be expressly reserved to the states, by the 10th section of the 1st article of the Constitution.

---

1. **eo nomine:** "by that name" (Latin).—*Eds.*

7th. *Because* even admitting Congress to have a constitutional right to protect manufactures by the imposition of duties, or by regulations of commerce, designed principally for that purpose, yet a tariff of which the operation is grossly unequal and oppressive, is such an abuse of power as is incompatible with the principles of a free government and the great ends of civil society, justice, and equality of rights and protection.

8th. *Finally*, because South Carolina, from her climate, situation, and peculiar institutions, is, and must ever continue to be, wholly dependent upon agriculture and commerce, not only for her prosperity, but for her very existence as a state; because the valuable products of her soil—the blessings by which Divine Providence seems to have designed to compensate for the great disadvantages under which she suffers in other respects—are among the very few that can be cultivated with any profit by slave labor; and if, by the loss of her foreign commerce, these products should be confined to an inadequate market, the fate of this fertile state would be poverty and utter desolation; her citizens, in despair, would emigrate to more fortunate regions, and the whole frame and constitution of her civil policy be impaired and deranged, if not dissolved entirely.

Deeply impressed with these considerations, the representatives of the good people of this commonwealth, anxiously desiring to live in peace with their fellow-citizens, and to do all that in them lies to preserve and perpetuate the union of the states, and liberties of which it is the surest pledge, but feeling it to be their bounden duty to expose and resist all encroachments upon the true spirit of the Constitution, lest an apparent acquiescence in the system of protecting duties should be drawn into precedent—do, in the name of the commonwealth of South Carolina, claim to enter upon the Journal of the Senate their *protest* against it as unconstitutional, oppressive, and unjust.

# 22

## THE TRAIL OF TEARS

American attitudes toward the Native American nations varied widely in the first part of the nineteenth century. Some people urged a policy of assimilation; others proposed the voluntary removal of the Native Americans to lands in the West. But land-hungry Americans in the South and West wanted to push the indigenous peoples off their ancestral lands by force, and a few even favored extermination. When Andrew Jackson, an old "Indian fighter," became president in March 1829, he adopted a policy of forcing the tribes to move to the trans-Mississippi West. The Removal Act of 1830, passed by Congress with his encouragement, proposed that the tribes trade their lands in the United States for new homes in federal territory west of the Mississippi River.

Native Americans everywhere objected to the removal policy, but there was little they could do about it. In Illinois and Florida, they put up forceful resistance, but after several years of bloody warfare they were finally subdued. In Georgia, the Cherokees, a nation in the northwestern part of the state, tried to protect their rights peacefully. Belying the average white's contention that "Indians are savages," the Cherokees had become skilled in agriculture, built fine homes and roads, accepted Christian missionaries, adopted a constitution, and published books in an alphabet invented by Sequoya, a talented hunter who had become a silversmith and a scholar. The Cherokees had treaty commitments from the U.S. government, but neither President Jackson nor the state of Georgia was willing to respect them. In July 1830, when Georgia decided to take over their lands, the Cherokees made a moving appeal to the American people to respect their "national and individual rights" and permit them "to remain on the land of our fathers."

The Cherokees' appeal was in vain. Although some northeastern humanitarians sympathized with the Cherokees, and the Supreme Court in two decisions written by Chief Justice John Marshall ruled in the Cherokees' favor, the state of Georgia asserted its sovereignty over their territory. Jackson sent an army of 7,000 to drive them westward at bayonet point. Over 4,000 of the 15,000 Cherokees who went west along the Trail of Tears in 1838 perished en route. By the time Jackson left office he could boast that his removal policy was rapidly nearing completion.

The "shotgun removal," as it was called, shocked Ralph Waldo Emerson, one of America's greatest writers. "Such a dereliction of all faith and virtue," he cried, "such a denial of justice, and such deafness to screams for mercy were never heard of in time of peace and in the dealing of a nation with its own allies and wards, since the earth was made."

**Questions to Consider.** In the final section of the appeal, which appears below, note the style in which the Cherokees state their case. Is it coolly argued or does it contain deep-seated feelings? How united were the Cherokees? What rights did they cite? What were their major objections to moving to a new location?

*Basis of argument: the law*

*concern of the future*

———————— ★ ★ 🎗🎗🎗🎗 ★ ★ ————————

# Appeal of the Cherokee Nation (1830)

We are aware that some persons suppose it will be for our advantage to remove beyond the Mississippi. We think otherwise. Our people universally think otherwise. Thinking that it would be fatal to their interests, they have almost to a man sent their memorial to Congress, deprecating the necessity of a removal. This question was distinctly before their minds when they signed their memorial. Not an adult person can be found, who has not an opinion on the subject; and if the people were to understand distinctly, that they could be protected against the laws of the neighboring States, there is probably not an adult person in the nation, who would think it best to remove; though possibly a few might emigrate individually. There are doubtless many who would flee to an unknown country, however beset with dangers, privations and sufferings, rather than be sentenced to spend six years in a Georgia prison for advising one of their neighbors not to betray his country. And there are others who could not think of living as outlaws in their native land, exposed to numberless vexations, and excluded from being parties or witnesses in a court of justice. It is incredible that Georgia should ever have enacted the oppressive laws to which reference is here made, unless she had supposed that something extremely terrific in its character was necessary, in order to make the Cherokees willing to remove. We are not willing to remove; and if we could be brought to this extremity, it would be, not by argument; not because our judgment was satisfied; not because our condition will be improved—but only because we cannot endure to be deprived of our national and individual rights, and subjected to a process of intolerable oppression.

We wish to remain on the land of our fathers. We have a perfect and original right to claim this, without interruption or molestation. The treaties with us, and laws of the United States made in pursuance of treaties, guaranty our residence, and our privileges, and secure us against intruders. Our only request is, that these treaties may be fulfilled, and these laws executed.

From E. C. Tracy, *Memoir of the Life of Jeremiah Evarts* (Boston, 1845), 149–158.

**The Trail of Tears.** In Robert Lindneux's dramatic painting, the Cherokee move toward reservation territory west of the Mississippi River in 1838. Some 4,000 of the 15,000 who began the trip died. But 15,000 was actually only a small portion of the 100,000 Indians driven out of the southeastern United States between 1820 and 1845, and 4,000 was only a small portion of the 25,000 to 30,000 killed in the process. ("Trail of Tears" by Robert Lindneux. Woolaroc Museum, Bartlesville, Oklahoma)

But if we are compelled to leave our country, we see nothing but ruin before us. The country west of the Arkansas territory is unknown to us. From what we can learn of it, we have no prepossessions in its favor. All the inviting parts of it, as we believe, are preoccupied by various Indian nations, to which it has been assigned. They would regard us as intruders, and look upon us with an evil eye. The far greater part of that region is, beyond all controversy, badly supplied with wood and water; and no Indian tribe can live as agriculturists without these articles. All our neighbors, in case of our removal, though crowded into our near vicinity, would speak a language totally different from ours, and practice different customs. The original possessors of that region are now wandering savages, lurking for prey in the neighborhood. They have always been at war, and would be easily tempted to turn their arms against peaceful emigrants. Were the country to which we are urged much better than it is represented to be, and were it free from the objections which we have made to it, still it is not the land of our birth, nor of our affections. It contains neither the scenes of our childhood, nor the graves of our fathers.

# 23

## ASSAULTING MONOPOLY

The Second Bank of the United States (BUS), chartered by Congress in 1816 for twenty years, was a powerful institution. It performed several important functions: it served as a depository for government funds, it marketed government securities, it made loans to businesses, and, by maintaining specie payments (gold and silver) on its bank notes, it provided the country with a sound currency. With headquarters in Philadelphia and twenty-nine branches in other cities, the BUS contained private funds as well as government money. It controlled one-fifth of the bank notes and one-third of the bank deposits and specie of the country. Advocates of "cheap money"—state bankers, land speculators, and some small businessowners—were hostile to the bank because it restricted the amount of paper money in circulation. They hoped to benefit from an abundance of paper currency. But those who favored "hard money" also disliked the bank. Eastern working people were suspicious of wages paid in paper money, and Southern planters and Western farmers tended to look on any money but gold and silver as dishonest. Andrew Jackson, who had an unpleasant experience with banks as a young man, was a hard-money man and distrustful of all banks.

In the spring of 1832, friends of the BUS in Congress, particularly Henry Clay, urged Nicholas Biddle, the bank's president, to seek a renewal of the bank's charter. The charter did not actually expire until 1836, but Clay was sure that Congress would approve a new charter at once. He was right; after investigating the bank's operations, Congress passed a recharter bill by large majorities. But on July 10, 1832, President Jackson vetoed the bill. In his veto message, he denounced the bank bill as an unconstitutional violation of states' rights as well as an endorsement of a dangerous monopoly whose profits came from "the earnings of the American people" and went to the benefit of foreign stockholders and "a few hundred of our own citizens, chiefly of the richest class."

When Jackson ran for reelection in 1832 the BUS was the main campaign issue. Henry Clay, the candidate of the National Republicans, was a strong supporter of the bank, and so were most eastern merchants and businessmen. They insisted that the bank performed an essential function in managing the country's finances. But working people in the East and farmers in the West tended to support Jackson. They felt that Nicholas Biddle followed policies that favored the rich and powerful at the expense of the plain people. Biddle himself continually boasted about the great powers at his disposal and made no secret of his contempt for popular government. During the 1832 campaign he worked hard to defeat Jackson by lending large sums of money to Jackson's opponents. Biddle's behavior convinced the Jacksonians that the BUS represented a dangerous "concentration of power in the hands of a few men irresponsible to the people."

After his triumphant reelection, Jackson decided to move against the bank at once without waiting for its charter to expire. He directed Secretary of the Treasury Roger B. Taney to place government funds in state banks rather than in the BUS, where they were usually deposited. By the end of 1833, some twenty-three state banks, called "pet banks" by Jackson's enemies, were handling funds of the federal government. Jackson's withholding of federal funds effectively killed Biddle's bank, although it remained in operation until its charter expired in 1836. In 1836 it was reorganized as a state bank in Pennsylvania. The decline of the BUS was accompanied by increasing disarray in the nation's economy. In 1837 came a financial panic, followed by the country's worst depression up to that time.

Andrew Jackson was born in 1767 on the Carolina frontier; his parents were poor Scotch-Irish immigrants. But Jackson climbed rapidly to wealth and status through land speculation and law practice. In 1795, before he was thirty, he established the Hermitage, a splendid plantation near Nashville, Tennessee, and he headed for Congress the next year. As major-general of his state's militia, Jackson won a victory over the British at the Battle of New Orleans in 1815 that catapulted him to national prominence and led to a Senate seat in 1823 and the presidency in 1828. Known as Old Hickory and famous as a champion of the West and the common man, Jackson quarreled with John C. Calhoun over nullification as well as with Biddle over the BUS. These conflicts added to his popularity and enabled him to build a strong Democratic party based on patronage and personality as well as on appeals to regional and class interests. Having survived the first attempt to assassinate a president when an unemployed housepainter attacked him in 1835, Jackson retired at the end of his second term to the Hermitage, where he died in 1845.

**Questions to Consider.** Jackson, as you will see, opposed the BUS as a monopoly. Why did he attack monopolies so strongly? Did banks in general trouble Jackson, or only this particular bank? How did his castigation of foreign control strengthen Jackson's position with the people? Note, too, the president's concern for the right of states to tax the bank and of state-chartered banks to prosper. Is it surprising that a vigorous chief executive and strong opponent of nullification should here be a champion of states' rights? With whom was Jackson quarreling in his remarks near the end of the message about "necessary" and "proper"? Consider, finally, Jackson's championing of the low and poor against the high and rich. Did this appeal to class differences, as opposed to occupational or sectional ones, signal a new turn in American politics? If so, why do you suppose it occurred in 1832 rather than, say, in 1816 or 1824? Who were Jackson's poor, anyway?

# Bank Veto Message (1832)

ANDREW JACKSON

The bill "to modify and continue" the act entitled "An act to incorporate the subscribers to the Bank of the United States" was presented to me on the 4th July instant. Having . . . come to the conclusion that it ought not to become a law, I herewith return it to the Senate, in which it originated, with my objections.

A bank of the United States is in many respects convenient for the Government and useful to the people. Entertaining this opinion, and deeply impressed with the belief that some of the powers and privileges possessed by the existing bank are unauthorized by the Constitution, subversive of the rights of the States, and dangerous to the liberties of the people, I felt it my duty at an early period of my Administration to call the attention of Congress to the practicability of organizing an institution combining all its advantages and obviating these objections. I sincerely regret that in the act before me I can perceive none of these modifications of the bank charter which are necessary, in my opinion, to make it compatable with justice, with sound policy, or with the Constitution of our country.

The present corporate body . . . enjoys an exclusive privilege of banking under the authority of the General Government, a monopoly of its favor and support, and, as a necessary consequence, almost a monopoly of the foreign and domestic exchange. The powers, privileges, and favors bestowed upon it in the original charter, by increasing the value of the stock far above its par value, operated as a gratuity of many millions to the stockholders. . . .

The act before me proposes another gratuity to the holders of the same stock. . . . On all hands it is conceded that its passage will increase at least

From James D. Richardson, ed., *A Compilation of the Messages and Papers of the Presidents* (Government Printing Office, Washington, D.C., 1897–1907), II: 217–218.

20 or 30 per cent more the market price of the stock, subject to the payment of the annuity of $200,000 per year secured by the act, thus adding in a moment one-fourth to its par value. It is not our own citizens only who are to receive the bounty of our Government. More than eight millions of the stock of this bank are held by foreigners. By this act the American Republic proposes virtually to make them a present of some millions of dollars. For these gratuities to foreigners and to some of our own opulent citizens the act secures no equivalent whatever. . . .

Every monopoly and all exclusive privileges are granted at the expense of the public, which ought to receive a fair equivalent. The many millions which this act proposes to bestow on the stockholders of the existing bank must come directly or indirectly out of the earnings of the American people. It is due to them, therefore, if their Government sell monopolies and exclusive privileges, that they should at least exact for them as much as they are worth in open market. . . .

The modifications of the existing charter proposed by this act are not such, in my view, as make it consistent with the rights of the States or the liberties of the people. The qualification of the right of the bank to hold real estate, the limitation of its power to establish branches, and the power reserved to Congress to forbid the circulation of small notes are restrictions comparatively of little value or importance. All the objectionable principles of the existing corporation, and most of its odious features, are retained without alleviation. . . .

Is there no danger to our liberty and independence in a bank that in its nature has so little to bind it to our country? The president of the bank has told us that most of the State banks exist by its forbearance. Should its influence become concentrated, as it may under the operation of such an act as this, in the hands of a self-elected directory whose interests are identified with those of the foreign stockholders, will there not be cause to tremble for the purity of our elections in peace and for the independence of our country in war? Their power would be great whenever they might choose to exert it; but if this monopoly were regularly renewed every fifteen or twenty years on terms proposed by themselves, they might seldom in peace put forth their strength to influence elections or control the affairs of the nation. But if any private citizen or public functionary should interpose to curtail its powers or prevent a renewal of its privileges, it can not be doubted that he would be made to feel its influence. . . .

If we must have a bank with private stockholders, every consideration of sound policy and every impulse of American feeling admonishes that it should be *purely American*. Its stockholders should be composed exclusively of our own citizens, who at least ought to be friendly to our Government and willing to support it in times of difficulty and danger. . . .

The bank is professedly established as an agent of the executive branch of the Government, and its constitutionality is maintained on that ground. Neither upon the propriety of present action nor upon the provisions of this act was the Executive consulted. It has had no opportunity to say that it neither needs nor wants an agent clothed with such powers and favored by such exemptions. There is nothing in its legitimate functions which makes it necessary or proper. Whatever interest or influence, whether public or private, has given birth to this act, it can not be found either in the wishes or necessities of the executive department, by which present action is deemed premature, and the powers conferred upon its agent not only unnecessary, but dangerous to the Government and country. . . .

It is to be regretted that the rich and powerful too often bend the acts of government to their selfish purposes. Distinctions in society will always exist under every just government. Equality of talents, of education, or of wealth can not be produced by human institutions. In the full enjoyment of the gifts of Heaven and the fruits of superior industry, economy, and virtue, every man is equally entitled to protection by law; but when the laws undertake to add to these natural and just advantages artificial distinctions, to grant titles, gratuities, and exclusive privileges, to make the rich richer and the potent more powerful, and the humble members of society—the farmers, mechanics, and laborers—who have neither the time nor the means of securing like favors to themselves, have a right to complain of the injustice of their Government.

There are no necessary evils in government. Its evils exist only in its abuse. If it would confine itself to equal protection, and, as Heaven does its rains, shower its favors alike on the high and the low, the rich and the poor, it would be an unqualified blessing. In the act before me there seems to be a wide and unnecessary departure from these just principles. . . .

Experience should teach us wisdom. Most of the difficulties our Government now encounters and most of the dangers which impend over our Union have sprung from an abandonment of the legitimate objects of Government by our national legislation, and the adoption of such principles as are embodied in this act. Many of our rich men have not been content with equal protection and equal benefits, but have besought us to make them richer by act of Congress. By attempting to gratify their desires we have in the results of our legislation arrayed section against section, interest against interest, and man against man, in a fearful commotion which threatens to shake the foundations of our Union. It is time to pause in our career to review our principles, and if possible revive that devoted patriotism and spirit of compromise which distinguished the sages of the Revolution and the fathers of our Union.

# 24

# EMPIRE

When James K. Polk ran for president in 1844, the Democrats campaigned for the reannexation of Texas and the reoccupation of Oregon. Texas, they maintained, had been acquired through the Louisiana Purchase of 1803 and had been unwisely given back. The Oregon country, too, they argued, was part of the United States by virtue of American settlements there in the early nineteenth century; British claims were unjustified. Polk heartily agreed with the Democratic platform on both issues.

Polk compromised with Britain on Oregon, signing a treaty in 1846 that fixed the boundary at the 49th parallel. But his administration went to war with Mexico that same year over Texas and ended by acquiring California and the Southwest for the United States. In fact, Polk had vowed to obtain these territories at any price. When the Mexican government refused to sell them, he maneuvered the United States into war by ordering General Zachary Taylor into a hotly disputed area to provoke a Mexican attack. When that attack came, Polk declared that Mexico "has invaded our territory and shed American blood upon the American soil. . . . War exists by the act of Mexico herself."

Polk's territorial conquests, which mark him as one of the great imperialists of the age, comparable to Disraeli in Britain or the Russian czars, produced a lively debate over the meaning of expansion. Some people, especially New Englanders, thought the Mexican War had been inspired by Southern planters (like Polk himself) greedy for new lands into which to extend slavery. Senator Charles Sumner of Massachusetts called it "a War to Strengthen the 'Slave Power'. . . [and] a War Against the Free States." Others saw both Oregon and the Southwest as tokens in a Northern drive for more farmland and for harbors on the West Coast for the China trade.

The largest group of all saw expansion in terms of what John L. O'Sullivan, the most influential spokesman for westward expansion, called "manifest destiny." According to O'Sullivan, a Democratic editor in New York, the single most important state in national politics, manifest destiny was the "design of Providence"—the right of a teeming, vigorous American nation to take possession of an entire continent and extend the sphere of Anglo-Saxon institutions from sea to sea. By "destiny" O'Sullivan meant that this was foreordained, decreed by fate, bound to happen. By "manifest" he meant that this fate was obvious, that anyone should be able to see it and therefore stand aside and let it happen. That parts of the continent were already occupied by "inferior" Native Americans or held by "imbecile" Mexico was, O'Sullivan insisted, irrelevant. Nature itself would see to it that some day the peoples of the Atlantic and Pacific would "flow together into one."

O'Sullivan's fierce nationalism was perfectly in tune with the mid-nineteenth-century expansionist inclinations of most Americans. From the beginning of settlement, Americans had been lured westward. With Jefferson's acquisition of the Louisiana Territory, they began to harbor visions of a vast American "empire." The War of 1812 partly resulted from land hunger. With the Monroe Doctrine of 1823, Americans declared their special claim to the whole Western Hemisphere.

That claim was made most belligerently in the Mexican War—so belligerently, in fact, that as part of the postwar settlement, the American government offered to pay Mexico $15 million in what Henry David Thoreau and others called "conscience money." But just as its opponents had predicted, the Mexican War divided the victors, triggering an agonizing controversy between North and South over where and whether slavery would be permitted to invade the newly acquired territories.

Born in Ireland in 1813, John L. O'Sullivan immigrated at an early age to New York City, where he became a lawyer, journalist, and ardent Jacksonian. In 1841 O'Sullivan established the *United States Magazine and Democratic Review*, New York's chief Democratic propaganda organ and one of the most jingoistic magazines of the era. O'Sullivan first used the phrase "manifest destiny" in the *Democratic Review* in 1845. Like many Jacksonians, O'Sullivan was tolerant of immigrants and Catholics, but rabidly anti-English and racist. Rewarded with patronage appointments, O'Sullivan at one point joined an expedition to seize Cuba as a slave territory for the United States. He was a Confederate sympathizer during the Civil War. He died in 1895.

**Questions to Consider.** What specific factors did O'Sullivan cite in arguing that the United States was destined to "overspread the continent"? Why was he so concerned to defend the United States from charges of "spoliation" and "conquest"? How important was sheer population growth to O'Sullivan's argument? Were his numbers accurate? How important were new means of transportation and communication to his vision? Why, given O'Sullivan's strident hostility to

England, did he refer constantly to the superiority of "Anglo-Saxon" peoples and institutions and applaud the weight of the "Anglo-Saxon foot"?

*why does U.S. have a right*
*what's wrong w/ Mexico*

★ ★ 🌀🌀🌀🌀 ★ ★

*Manifest Destiny*

## Annexation (1845)

JOHN L. O'SULLIVAN

*mwahahahaha!*

Texas is now ours. Already, before these words are written, her Convention has undoubtedly ratified the acceptance, by her Congress, of our proffered invitation into the Union; and made the requisite changes in her already republican form of constitution to adopt it to its future federal relations. Her star and her stripe may already be said to have taken their place in the glorious blazon of our common nationality; and the sweep of our eagle's wing already includes within its circuit the wide extent of her fair and fertile land. She is no longer to us a mere geographical space—a certain combination of coast, plain, mountain, valley, forest and stream. She is no longer to us a mere country on the map. She comes within the dear and sacred designation of Our Country; no longer a *"pays,"* she is a part of *"la patrie"*; and that which is at once a sentiment and a virtue, Patriotism, already begins to thrill for her too within the national heart. . . .

Why, were other reasoning wanting, in favor of now elevating this question of the reception of Texas into the Union, out of the lower region of our past party dissensions, up to its proper level of a high and broad nationality, it surely is to be found, found abundantly, in the manner in which other nations have undertaken to intrude themselves into it, between us and the proper parties to the case, in a spirit of hostile interference against us, for the avowed object of thwarting our policy and hampering our power, limiting our greatness and checking the fulfilment of our manifest destiny to overspread the continent allotted by Providence for the free development of our yearly multiplying millions. . . .

It is wholly untrue, and unjust to ourselves, the pretence that the Annexation has been a measure of spoliation, unrightful and unrighteous—of military conquest under forms of peace and law—of territorial aggrandizement at the expense of justice, and justice due by a double sanctity to the weak. This view of the question is wholly unfounded, and has been before so amply refuted in these pages, as well as in a thousand other modes, that we shall not again dwell upon it. The independence of Texas was complete and absolute. It was an independence, not only in fact but of right. No obligation of duty towards Mexico tended in the least degree to restrain our right to effect the desired recovery of the fair province once our own—whatever motives of policy might have prompted a more deferential consideration of her feelings and her pride, as involved in the question. If Texas became peopled with an American population, it was by no contrivance of our government, but on the express invitation of that of Mexico herself; accompanied with such guaranties of State independence, and the maintenance of a federal system analogous to our own, as constituted a compact fully justifying the strongest measures of redress on the part of those afterwards deceived in this guaranty, and sought to be enslaved under the yoke imposed by its violation. She was released, rightfully and absolutely released, from all Mexican allegiance, or duty of cohesion to the Mexican political body, by the acts and fault of Mexico herself, and Mexico alone. There never was a clearer case. It was not revolution; it was resistance to revolution; and resistance under such circumstances as left independence the necessary resulting state, caused by the abandonment of those with whom her former federal association had existed. What then can be more preposterous than all this clamor by Mexico and the Mexican interest, against Annexation, as a violation of any rights of hers, any duties of ours? . . .

Nor is there any just foundation of the charge that Annexation is a great pro-slavery measure—calculated to increase and perpetuate that institution. Slavery had nothing to do with it. . . . The country which was the subject of Annexation in this case, from its geographical position and relations, happens to be—or rather the portion of it now actually settled, happens to be—a slave country. But a similar process might have taken place in proximity to a different section of our Union; and indeed there is a great deal of Annexation yet to take place, within the life of the present generation, along the whole line of our northern border. Texas has been absorbed into the Union in the inevitable fulfillment of the general law which is rolling our population westward; the connexion of which with that ratio of growth in population which is destined within a hundred years to swell our numbers to the enormous population of *two hundred and fifty millions* (if not more), is too evident to leave us in doubt of the manifest design of Providence in regard to the occupation of this continent. It was disintegrated from Mexico in the natural course of events, by a process perfectly legitimate on its own part, blameless on ours; and in which all the censures due to wrong, perfidy and folly, rest on Mexico alone. And possessed as it was by a population which was in truth but a colonial detachment from our own, and which was still bound by myriad ties of the very heartstrings to its old relations, domestic and political, their incorporation into the Union was not only inevitable, but the most natural, right and proper thing in the world—and it is only astonishing that there should be any among ourselves to say it nay. . . .

California will, probably, next fall away from the loose adhesion which, in such a country as Mexico, holds a remote province in a slight equivocal kind of dependence on the metropolis. Imbecile and distracted, Mexico never can exert any real governmental authority over such a country. The impotence of the one and the distance of the other, must make the relation one of virtual independence; unless, by stunting the province of all natural growth, and forbidding that immigration which can alone develope its capabilities and fulfill the purposes of its creation, tyranny may retain a military dominion which is no government in the legitimate sense of the term. In the case of California this is now impossible. The Anglo-Saxon foot is already on its borders. Already the advance guard of the irresistible army of Anglo-Saxon emigration has begun to pour down upon it, armed with the plough and the rifle, and marking its trail with schools and colleges, courts and representative halls, mills and meeting-houses. A population will soon be in actual occupation of California, over which it will be idle for Mexico to dream of dominion. They will necessarily become independent. All this without agency of our government, without responsibility of our people— in the natural flow of events, the spontaneous working of principles, and the adaptation of the tendencies and wants of the human race to the elemental circumstances in the midst of which they find themselves placed. And they will have a right to independence—to self-government—to the possession of the homes conquered from the wilderness by their own labors and dangers, sufferings and sacrifices—a better and a truer right than the artificial title of sovereignty in Mexico a thousand miles distant, inheriting from Spain a title good only against those who have none better. Their right to independence will be the natural right of self-government belonging to any community strong enough to maintain it—distinct in position, origin and character, and free from any mutual obligations of membership of a common political body, binding it to others by the duty of loyalty and compact of public faith. This will be their title to independence; and by this title, there can be no doubt that the population now fast streaming down upon California will both assert and maintain that independence. Whether they will then attach themselves to our Union or not, is not to be predicted with any certainty. Unless the projected rail-road across the continent to the Pacific be carried into effect, perhaps they may not; though even in that case, the day is not distant when the Empires of the Atlantic and Pacific would again flow together into one, as soon as their inland border should approach each other. But that great work, colossal as appears the plan on its first suggestion, cannot remain long unbuilt. Its necessity for this very purpose of binding and holding together in its iron clasp our fast settling Pacific region with that of the Mississippi valley—the natural facility of the route—the ease with which any amount of labor for the construction can be drawn in from the overcrowded populations of Europe, to be paid in the lands made valuable by the progress of the work itself—and its immense utility to the commerce of the world with the whole eastern coast of Asia, alone almost sufficient for the support of such a road—these considerations give assurance that the day cannot be distant which shall witness the conveyance of the representatives from Oregon and California to Washington within less time than a few years ago was devoted to a similar journey by those from Ohio; while the magnetic telegraph will enable the editors of the "San Francisco Union," the "Astoria Evening Post," or the "Nootka Morning News" to set up in type the first half of the President's Inaugural, before the echoes of the latter half shall have died away beneath the lofty porch of the Capitol, as spoken from his lips.

Away, then, with all idle French talk *of balances of power* on the American Continent. There is no growth in Spanish America! Whatever progress of population there may be in the British Canadas, is only for their own early severance of their present colonial relation to the little island three thousand miles across the Atlantic; soon to be followed by Annexation, and destined to swell the still accumulating momentum of our progress. And whatsoever may hold the balance, though they should cast into the opposite scale all the bayonets and cannon, not only of France and England, but of Europe entire, how would it kick the beam against the simple solid weight of the two hundred and fifty or three hundred millions—and American millions—destined to gather beneath the flutter of the stripes and stars, in the fast hastening year of the Lord 1945?

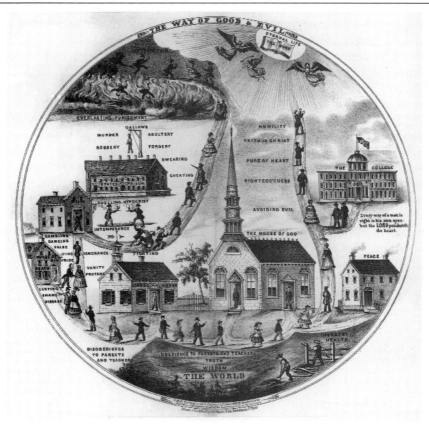

**Reform dreams and nightmares.** In this drawing, education, worship, and work are the foundations of the good life. The path to evil, by contrast, begins with disobedience to parents and teachers, and then it leads through vanity, fighting, gambling, dueling, and other bad behavior to, finally, the saloon, the prison, and the fires of everlasting punishment. (Library of Congress)

CHAPTER FOUR

# The Age of Reform

# 25

## LONGING FOR FREEDOM

During the wave of early-nineteenth-century revivalism known as the "Second Great Awakening," Baptists and Methodists made great progress in their efforts to convert African slaves to Christianity. Exactly how many were converted is unclear. What is clear is that in adopting the religion of their masters, the slaves filled it with ideas that, born of the shattering experience of enslavement, were uniquely their own.

There was much in Christianity for slaves to find appealing. They saw themselves, for example, in the Old Testament stories about the Hebrews, a chosen people enslaved by the Egyptians and led to the promised land by Moses. In the New Testament's promises of justice they found reason to believe that they, too, would eventually be redeemed. After Nat Turner, a Christian preacher, led a band of black slaves who murdered sixty white men, women, and children in Virginia in 1831, "slaves codes" made it illegal for blacks and whites to worship together, a practice that slaveholders had previously permitted within limits. Ironically, this enforced segregation gave black Christians a certain latitude to develop even more distinctive kinds of worship.

There was, for example, the call-and-response sermon, in which the preacher would deliver a vivid sermon packed with biblical stories and characters, and the congregation would shout out its encouragement and support, calling "That's right, Brother!" and "Oh, yes, oh yes!" as the spirit moved them. There were also the "spirituals," examples of which appear below.

It is impossible to credit any particular spiritual hymn to a particular person or group. These were essentially folk songs, full of heartfelt, deeply emotional religious convictions, that emerged from the collective consciousness of a people who believed that a righteous God was going to notice their suffering. They were confident that true freedom would be found, if not in this world—"I ain't got long to stay here"—then surely in the next, in "heab'n." The antebellum slave world produced two forms of singing: work songs, which would become the "blues" after the Civil War, and spirituals, which would become "gospel" music. It is in the spirituals that we can see most clearly the slaves' intense longing for salvation as well as their idiosyncratic and triumphal joy: "Way down yonder in the graveyard walk, I thank God I'm free at last."

**Questions to Consider.** Some spirituals were sorrowful, others full of joy. Which of the following songs seem to have been "sorrow" songs, and which ones songs of joy? To what extent does the imagery of the songs seem to have reflected the plantation world that the slaves knew? What images seem drawn from the Bible? Did the spirituals refer to more stories from the Old Testament or the New? Why might this have been so? Would the hymns of poor Southern whites, who also joined the Baptist and Methodist churches in large numbers at this time, have resembled slave spirituals?

# Spirituals (ca. 1800–1830)

### GO DOWN, MOSES

Go down, Moses,
'Way down in Egypt land,
Tell ole Pharaoh,
To let my people go.

Go down, Moses,
'Way down in Egypt land,
Tell ole Pharaoh,
To let my people go.

When Israel was in Egypt land,
Let my people go,
Oppressed so hard they could not stand,
Let my people go.

Thus spoke the Lord, bold Moses said,
Let my people go,
If not I'll smite your first-born dead,
Let my people go.

Go down, Moses,
'Way down in Egypt land,

From Thomas R. Frazier, ed., *Afro-American History: Primary Sources* (Dorsey Press, Chicago, 1988), 82–85. Coypyright © 1988 by Dorsey Press.

Tell ole Pharaoh,
To let my people go.

## ALL GOD'S CHILLUN GOT WINGS

I got a robe, you got a robe,
All o' God's chillun got a robe.
When I get to heab'n, goin' to put on my robe,
I'm goin' to shout all ovah God's heab'n,
Heab'n, heab'n,
Ev'rybody talkin' 'bout heab'n ain't goin' dere;
Heab'n, heab'n,
I'm goin' to shout all ovah God's heab'n.

I got-a wings, you got-a wings,
All o' God's chillun got-a wings.
When I get to heab'n, goin' to put on my wings,
I'm goin' to fly all ovah God's heab'n,
Heab'n, heab'n,
Ev'rybody talkin' 'bout heab'n ain't goin' dere;
Heab'n, heab'n,
I'm goin' to fly all ovah God's heab'n.

I got a harp, you got a harp,
All o' God's chillun got a harp.
When I get to heab'n, goin' to play on my harp,
I'm goin' to play all ovah God's heab'n,
Heab'n, heab'n,
Ev'rybody talkin' 'bout heab'n ain't goin' dere;
Heab'n, heab'n,
I'm goin' to play all ovah God's heab'n.

I got-a shoes, you got-a shoes,
All o' God's chillun got-a shoes.
When I get to heab'n, goin' to put on my shoes,
I'm goin' to walk all ovah God's heab'n,
Heab'n, heab'n,
Ev'rybody talkin' 'bout heab'n ain't goin' dere;
Heab'n, heab'n,
I'm goin' to walk all ovah God's heab'n.

## STEAL AWAY TO JESUS

Steal away, steal away, steal away to Jesus!
Steal away, steal away home,
I ain't got long to stay here.

**Banjo-like instrument painted by Samuel Jennings, an artist active in Philadelphia at the end of the eighteenth century.** (Library Company of Philadelphia)

My Lord, He calls me, He calls me by the thunder,
The trumpet sounds within-a my soul,
I ain't got long to stay here.

Steal away, steal away, steal away to Jesus!
Steal away, steal away home,d
I ain't got long to stay here.

Green trees a-bending, po' sinner stand a-trembling,
The trumpet sounds within-a my soul,
I ain't got long to stay here.

Steal away, steal away, steal away to Jesus!
Steal away, steal away home,
I ain't got long to stay here.

## DIDN'T MY LORD DELIVER DANIEL

Didn't my Lord deliver Daniel,
    deliver Daniel, deliver Daniel,
Didn't my Lord deliver Daniel,
An' why not every man.

He delivered Daniel from the lion's den,
Jonah from the belly of the whale,
An' the Hebrew chillun from the fiery furnace,
An' why not every man.

Didn't my Lord deliver Daniel,
    deliver Daniel, deliver Daniel,
Didn't my Lord deliver Daniel,
An' why not every man.

The moon run down in a purple stream,
The sun forbear to shine,
An' every star disappear,
King Jesus shall-a be mine.

The win' blows eas' an' the win' blows wes',
It blows like the judg-a-ment day,
An' ev'ry po' soul that never did pray'll
Be glad to pray that day.

Didn't my Lord deliver Daniel,
    deliver Daniel, deliver Daniel,
Didn't my Lord deliver Daniel,
An' why not every man.

## I THANK GOD I'M FREE AT LAST

Free at last, free at last,
I thank God I'm free at last.
Free at last, free at last,
I thank God I'm free at last.

Way down yonder in the graveyard walk,
I thank God I'm free at last,

Me and my Jesus gonna meet an' talk,
I thank God I'm free at last.

On-a my knees when the light pass by,
I thank God I'm free at last,
Thought my soul would rise an' fly,
I thank God I'm free at last.

One o' these mornin's bright an' fair,
I thank God I'm free at last,
Gonna meet my Jesus in the middle o' the air,
I thank God I'm free at last.

Free at last, free at last,
I thank God I'm free at last,
Free at last, free at last,
I thank God I'm free at last.

# 26

## A CALL TO ARMS

With the publication in Boston of the first issue of William Lloyd Garrison's *Liberator* in January 1831, the antislavery movement turned toward militancy. But Garrison's call for immediate emancipation was preceded by David Walker's *Appeal to the Coloured Citizens of the World,* published in September 1829. In one place in his impassioned pamphlet, not appearing in the excerpt below, Walker called African-Americans the "most wretched, degraded, and abject sort of beings that ever lived since the world began." He blasted American whites for their condescension, insensitivity, and cruelty and demanded that they end slavery and begin treating blacks as human beings with all the rights of other citizens. "Treat us like men," he cried, "and we will be friends."

In composing his *Appeal* Walker knew whereof he wrote. A free black man born in North Carolina in 1785, he managed to get an education. He traveled widely in the South observing slavery before he settled in Boston in 1827 and opened a shop that sold old clothes. When *Freedom's Journal,* the first American black newspaper, began publication in New York in 1827, Walker began contributing articles to it; he also lectured against slavery to small groups in Boston. He wrote his *Appeal* at high speed, printed it at his own expense, and saw to it that copies made their way into the South. The reaction to the *Appeal* was not surprising. Prominent Southerners demanded its suppression; even Bostonians called it "wicked and inflammatory." Garrison himself praised its "impassioned and determined spirit," but regretted its publication; later he changed his mind and reprinted most of it in the *Liberator.* Though there were threats on his life, Walker prepared new editions of his *Appeal.* But on June 28, 1830, he was found dead near the doorway of his shop, possibly the victim of poisoning.

**Questions to Consider.** Why do you suppose Walker's *Appeal* shocked even those whites opposed to slavery? To whom was he addressing his plea: to slaves, free blacks, or whites? Do you think he was exaggerating the misery of blacks in the United States? How radical does his *Appeal* sound today? What kind of action did he call upon black Americans to take? What part did religion play in his view of things?

# Appeal to the Coloured Citizens of the World (1829)

### DAVID WALKER

I know that the blacks, take them half enlightened and ignorant, are more humane and merciful than the most enlightened and refined European that can be found in all the earth. Let no one say that I assert this because I am prejudiced on the side of my colour, and against the whites or Europeans. For what I write, I do it candidly, for my God and the good of both parties: Natural observations have taught me these things; there is a solemn awe in the hearts of the blacks, as it respects *murdering* men; whereas the whites (though they are great cowards) where they have the advantage, or think that there are any prospects of getting it, they murder all before them, in order to subject men to wretchedness and degradation under them. This is the natural result of pride and avarice. . . . Should the lives of such creatures be spared? Are God and Mammon in league? What has the Lord to do with a gang of desperate wretches, who go *sneaking about the country like robbers*—light upon his people wherever they can get a chance, binding them with chains and handcuffs, beat and murder them as they would *rattlesnakes?* Are they not the Lord's enemies? Ought they not to be destroyed? Any person who will save such wretches from destruction, is fighting against the Lord, and will receive his just recompense. . . . The whites have had us under them for more than three centuries, murdering, and treating us like brutes; and, as Mr. Jefferson wisely said, they have never *found us out*—they do not know, indeed, that there is an unconquerable disposition in the breasts of the blacks, which, when it is fully awakened and put in motion, will be subdued, only with the destruction of the animal existence. Get the blacks started, and if you do not have a gang of tigers and lions to deal with, I am a deceiver of the blacks and of the whites.

Now, I ask you, had you not rather be killed than to be a slave to a tyrant, who takes the life of your mother, wife, and dear little children? Look upon your mother, wife and children, and answer God Almighty; and believe this, that it is no more harm for you to kill a man, who is trying to kill you, than it is for you to take a drink of water when thirsty; in fact, the man who will stand still and let another murder him, is worse than an infidel, and, if he

From David Walker, *Walker's Appeal, in Four Articles; Together with a Preamble to Coloured Citizens of the World* (D. Walker, Boston, 1830), 11–87.

**A card from "Stephens' Album Varieties: The Slave in 1863," published in the North during the Civil War.** Slave sales boomed in the 1830s and 1840s as soil exhaustion in the older slave states led landowners to increase their income by selling slaves to settlers in the booming Gulf states of Alabama, Mississippi, Louisiana, and Texas. A great fear of slaves in the Upper South was to be sold "down the river" to the hard-bitten masters of the Deep South, or to see members of their families sold. Here a wife and mother, seeing her husband already in chains for transporting, begs the slave trader, "Buy us, too." Slave sales shattered as many as one-third of all slave families in the antebellum era. All of this became ideal grist for the publicity mill of antislavery activists and Republicans. (Library of Congress)

has common sense, ought not to be pitied. . . . Oh! coloured people of these United States, I ask you, in the name of that God who made us, have we, in consequence of oppression, nearly lost the spirit of man, and, in no very trifling degree, adopted that of brutes? Do you answer, no? I ask you, then, what set of men can you point me to, in all the world, who are so abjectedly employed by their oppressors, as we are by our *natural enemies?* How can, Oh! how can those enemies but say that we and our children are not of the HUMAN FAMILY, but were made by our Creator to be an inheritance to them and theirs for ever? How can the slaveholders but say that they can bribe the best coloured person in the country, to sell his brethren for a trifling sum of money, and take that atrocity to confirm them in their avaricious opinion, that we were made to be slaves to them and their children? . . .

I aver, that when I look over these United States of America, and the world, and see the ignorant deceptions and consequent wretchedness of my brethren, I am brought ofttimes solemnly to a stand, and in the midst of my reflections I exclaim to my God, "Lord didst thou make us to be slaves to our brethren, the whites?" But when I reflect that God is just, and that millions of my wretched brethren would meet death with glory—yea, more, would plunge into the very mouths of cannons and be torn into particles as minute as the atoms which compose the elements of the earth, in preference to a mean submission to the lash of tyrants, I am with streaming eyes, compelled to shrink back into nothingness before my Maker, and exclaim again, thy will be done, O Lord God Almighty.

Men of colour, who are also of sense, for you particularly is my APPEAL designed. Our more ignorant brethren are not able to penetrate its value. I call upon you therefore to cast your eyes upon the wretchedness of your brethren, and to do your utmost to enlighten them—*go to work and enlighten your brethren!*—Let the Lord see you doing what you can to rescue them and yourselves from degradation. Do any of you say that you and your family are free and happy, and what have you to do with the wretched slaves and other people? So can I say, for I enjoy as much freedom as any of you, if I am not quite as well off as the best of you. Look into our freedom and happiness, and see of what kind they are composed!! They are of the very lowest kind—they are the very *dregs!*—they are the most servile and abject kind, that ever a people was in possession of! If any of you wish to know how FREE you are, let one of you start and go through the southern and western States of this country, and unless you travel as a slave to a white man (a servant is a *slave* to the man whom he serves) or have your free papers (which if you are not careful they will get from you) if they do not take you up and put you in jail, and if you cannot give good evidence of your freedom, sell you into eternal slavery, I am not a living man: or any man of colour, immaterial who he is, or where he came from, if he is *the fourth from the negro race!!* (as we are called) the white Christian of America will serve him the same they will sink him into wretchedness and degradation for ever while he lives. And yet some of you have the hardihood to say that you are free and happy! May God have mercy on your freedom and happiness!! I met a coloured man in the street a short time since, with a string of boots on his shoulders; we fell into conversation, and in the course of which, I said to him, what a miserable set of people we are! He asked, why?—Said I, we are so subjected under the whites, that we cannot obtain the comforts of life, but by cleaning their boots and shoes, old clothes, waiting on them, shaving them &c. Said he, (with the boots on his shoulders) "I am completely happy!!! I never want to live any better or happier than when I get a plenty of boots and shoes to clean!!!" Oh! how can those who are actuated by avarice only, but think, that our Creator made us to be an inheritance to them for ever, when they see that our greatest glory is centered in such mean and low objects? Understand me, brethren, I do not mean to speak against the occupations by which we acquire enough and sometimes scarcely that, to render ourselves and families comfortable through life. I am subjected to the same inconvenience, as you all.—My objections are, to our *glorying* and being *happy* in such low employments; for if we are men, we ought to be thankful to the Lord for the past, and for the future. Be looking forward with thankful hearts to higher attainments than *wielding the razor* and *cleaning boots and shoes.* The man whose aspirations are not *above,* and even *below* these, is indeed, ignorant and wretched enough. I advanced it therefore to you, not as a *problematical,* but as an unshaken and for ever immovable *fact,* that your full glory and happiness, as well as all other coloured people under Heaven, shall never be fully consummated, but with the *entire emancipation of your enslaved brethren all over the world.* You may therefore, go to work and do what you can to rescue, or join in with tyrants to oppress them and yourselves, until the Lord shall come upon you all like a thief in the night. For I believe it is the will of the Lord that our greatest happiness shall consist in working for the salvation of our whole body. When this is accomplished a burst of glory will shine upon you, which will indeed astonish you and the world. Do any of you say this never will be done? I assure you that God will accomplish it—if nothing else will answer, he will hurl tyrants and devils into *atoms* and make way for his people. But O my brethren! I say unto you again, you must go to work and prepare the way of the Lord.

# 27

## Freedom Now

David Walker's militant call to arms in 1829 failed to influence most white abolitionists, who wanted to end slavery through persuasion, not violence. Yet, after the rapid spread of the Cotton Kingdom had made slavery so profitable, persuading significant numbers of slaveholders to free their slaves seemed hopeless. It became virtually impossible when Southern states passed laws that outlawed public debates on the issue of slavery and made manumission (voluntarily freeing one's slaves) illegal.

Furthermore, persuading Northerners to support nonviolent abolitionism was almost as difficult as persuading Southerners. The cause appeared hopelessly impractical. In addition, most white Northerners considered blacks inferior and did not want them around, free or otherwise. Recognizing this difficulty, the American Colonization Society had tried—unsuccessfully—to encourage gradual manumission by raising money to send freed slaves to Africa. The problem remained when William Lloyd Garrison of Boston founded the militant American Anti-Slavery Society in 1833. His chief goals were to persuade Northerners on two points: that immediate abolition was feasible; and that slaves, once free, would make acceptable citizens and neighbors.

Women played a major role in nineteenth-century reform movements, including the antislavery struggle. They helped sensitize the Protestant churches to the evils of slavery and organized petition drives urging Congress to abolish the slave trade. At a time when the male-dominant mainstream culture of the United States was intolerant of women who commented on political issues, they wrote and sometimes spoke out against slavery. One of their great early successes was Lydia Maria Child's *An Appeal in Favor of That Class of Americans Called Africans,* which appeared in 1833. Child's book (excerpted below) blended anecdote, logic, and historical scholarship and was written in a clear, compelling style. It helped convert thousands of wavering Northerners to the cause of immediate abolitionism and thus significantly strengthened the role of the Garrisonians in the unfolding antislavery crusade.

Born in 1802 into a family of Massachusetts Unitarians, Lydia Maria Child was, at age 31, already the best-known woman writer in America when *An Appeal* appeared. She had several novels and domestic "how-to" works to her credit and had founded the country's first children's magazine, the *Juvenile Miscellany,* in 1826. Though she was influential with reformers, Child's *Appeal* badly damaged her popularity. Sales of her books fell sharply, and the *Juvenile Miscellany* foundered in 1834. From 1840 to 1849 she and her husband edited the *National Anti-Slavery Standard* in New York City. In 1852 they moved to a Massachusetts farm, where Lydia wrote extensively on religion, women's rights, capital punishment, slavery, and, following the Civil War, the plight of the freedmen. She died in Wayland, Massachusetts, in 1880.

**Questions to Consider.** It was an article of faith for most Americans in the early nineteenth century that women were different from men—that they saw the world differently and expressed themselves differently. Does Lydia Maria Child's *Appeal* seem "feminine" to you? Did she raise points or use arguments that a man might not have? Many Americans of the time thought abolitionists were humorless and self-righteous. Does Child seem to have been humorless? What was her primary method of persuasion? Why did she discuss the slave trade so extensively? What did she mean when she said that efforts to regulate slavery were like efforts to regulate murder?

# That Class of Americans Called Africans (1833)

LYDIA MARIA CHILD

A judicious and benevolent friend lately told me the story of one of her relatives, who married a slave-owner, and removed to his plantation. The lady in question was considered very amiable, and had a serene, affectionate expression of countenance. After several years' residence among her slaves, she visited New England. "Her history was written in her face," said my friend; "its expression had changed into that of a fiend. She brought but few slaves with her; and those few were of course compelled to perform additional labor. One faithful negro-woman nursed the twins of her mistress, and did all the washing, ironing, and scouring. If, after a sleepless night with the restless babes, (driven from the bosom of their own mother,) she

From Lydia Maria Child, *An Appeal in Favor of That Class of Americans Called Africans* (New York, 1833), 28–37, 141–146.

performed her toilsome avocations with diminished activity, her mistress, with her own lady-like hands, applied the cowskin, and the neighborhood resounded with the cries of her victim. The instrument of punishment was actually kept hanging in the entry, to the no small disgust of her New-England visiters. For my part," continued my friend, "I did not try to be polite to her; for I was not hypocrite enough to conceal my indignation."

The following occurred near Natchez, and was told to me by a highly intelligent man, who, being a diplomatist and a courtier, was very likely to make the best of national evils: A planter had occasion to send a female slave some distance on an errand. She did not return so soon as he expected, and he grew angry. At last he gave orders that she should be severely whipped when she came back. When the poor creature arrived, she pleaded for mercy, saying she had been so very ill, that she was obliged to rest in the fields; but she was ordered to receive another dozen lashes, for having had the impudence to speak. She died at the whipping-post; nor did she perish alone—a new-born baby died with her. The gentleman who told me this fact, witnessed the poor creature's funeral. It is true, the master was universally blamed and shunned for the cruel deed; but the laws were powerless.

I shall be told that such examples as these are of rare occurrence; and I have no doubt that instances of excessive severity are far from being common. I believe that a large proportion of masters are as kind to their slaves as they can be, consistently with keeping them in bondage; but it must be allowed that this, to make the best of it, is very stinted kindness. And let it never be forgotten that the negro's fate depends entirely on the character of his master; and it is a mere matter of chance whether he fall into merciful or unmerciful hands; his happiness, nay, his very life, depends on chance. . . .

But it is urged that it is the interest of planters to treat their slaves well. This argument no doubt has some force; and it is the poor negro's only security. But it is likewise the interest of men to treat their cattle kindly; yet we see that passion and short-sighted avarice do overcome the strongest motives of interest. Cattle are beat unmercifully, sometimes unto death; they are ruined by being over-worked; weakened by want of sufficient food; and so forth. Besides, it is sometimes directly *for* the interest of the planter to work his slaves beyond their strength. When there is a sudden rise in the prices of sugar, a certain amount of labor in a given time is of more consequence to the owner of a plantation than the price of several slaves; he can well *afford* to waste a few lives. This is no idle hypothesis—such calculations are gravely and openly made by planters. Hence, it is the slave's prayer that sugars may be cheap. When the negro is old, or feeble from incurable disease, is it his master's *interest* to feed him well, and clothe him comfortably? Certainly not: it then becomes desirable to get rid of the human brute as soon as convenient. It is a common remark, that it is not quite safe, in most cases, for even parents to be entirely dependant on the generosity of their children; and if human nature be such, what has the slave to expect, when he becomes a mere bill of expense? . . .

Among other apologies for slavery, it has been asserted that the Bible does not forbid it. Neither does it forbid the counterfeiting of a bank-bill. It is the *spirit* of the Holy Word, not its particular *expressions,* which must be a rule for our conduct. How can slavery be reconciled with the maxim, "Do unto others, as ye would that others should do unto you"? Does not the command, "Thou shalt not *steal,*" prohibit *kidnapping?* And how does whipping men to death agree with the injunction, "Thou shalt do no *murder*"? Are we not told "to loose the bands of wickedness, to undo the heavy burdens, to let the oppressed go free, and to break every yoke"? It was a Jewish law that he who stole a man, or sold him, or he in whose hands the stolen man was found, should suffer death; and he in whose house a fugitive slave sought an asylum was forbidden to give him up to his master. Modern slavery is so unlike Hebrew servitude, and its regulations are so diametrically opposed to the rules of the Gospel, which came to bring deliverance to the captive, that it is idle to dwell upon this point. . . .

I shall perhaps be asked why I have said so much about the slave-*trade,* since it was long ago abolished in this country. There are several good reasons for it. In the first place, it is a part of the system; for if there were no slaves, there could be no slave-trade; and while there are slaves, the slave-trade *will* continue. In the next place, the trade is still briskly carried on in Africa, and slaves are smuggled into these States through the Spanish colonies. In the third place, a very extensive internal slave-trade is carried on in this country. The breeding of negro-cattle for the foreign markets, (of Louisiana, Georgia, Alabama, Arkansas, and Missouri,) is a very lucrative branch of business. Whole coffles of them, chained and manacled, are driven through our Capital on their way to auction. Foreigners, particularly those who come here with enthusiastic ideas of American freedom, are amazed and disgusted at the sight. A troop of slaves once passed through Washington on the fourth of July, while drums were beating, and standards flying. One of the captive negroes raised his hand, loaded with irons, and waving it toward the starry flag, sung with a smile of bitter irony, "Hail Columbia! *happy* land!". . .

A free man of color is in constant danger of being seized and carried off by these slave-dealers. Mr. Cooper, a Representative in Congress from Delaware, told Dr. Torrey, of Philadelphia, that he was often afraid to send his servants out in the evening, lest they should be encountered by kidnappers. Wherever these notorious slave-jockeys appear in our Southern States, the free people of color hide themselves, as they are obliged to do on the coast of Africa. . . .

Finally, I have described some of the horrors of the slave-trade, because when our constitution was formed, the government pledged itself not to abolish this traffic until 1808. We began our career of freedom by granting a twenty years' lease of iniquity—twenty years of allowed invasion of other men's rights—twenty years of bloodshed, violence, and fraud! And this will be told in our annals—this will be heard of to the end of time!

While the slave-trade was allowed, the South could use it to advance their views in various ways. In their representation to Congress, five slaves counted the same as three freemen; of course, every fresh cargo was not only an increase of property, but an increase of *political power*. Ample time was allowed to lay in a stock of slaves to supply the new slave states and territories that might grow up; and when this was effected, the prohibition of foreign commerce in human flesh, operated as a complete *tariff*, to protect the domestic supply.

Every man who buys a slave promotes this traffic, by raising the value of the article; every man who owns a slave, indirectly countenances it; every man who allows that slavery is a lamentable *necessity*, contributes his share to support it; and he who votes for admitting a slave-holding State into the Union, fearfully augments the amount of this crime. . . .

The abolitionists think it a duty to maintain at all times, and in all places, that slavery *ought* to be abolished, and that it *can* be abolished. When error is so often repeated it becomes very important to repeat the truth; especially as good men are apt to be quiet, and selfish men are prone to be active. They propose no *plan*—they leave that to the wisdom of Legislatures. But they never swerve from the *principle* that slavery is both wicked and unnecessary.—Their object is to turn the public voice against this evil, by a plain exposition of facts.

The Anti-Slavery Society is loudly accused of being seditious, fanatical, and likely to promote insurrections. It seems to be supposed, that they wish to send fire and sword into the South, and encourage the slaves to hunt down their masters. Slave-owners wish to have it viewed in this light, because they know the subject will not bear discussion; and men here, who give the tone to public opinion, have loudly repeated the charge—some from good motives, and some from bad. I once had a very strong prejudice against anti-slavery—(I am ashamed to think *how* strong—for mere prejudice should never be stubborn,) but a candid examination has convinced me, that I was in an error. I made the common mistake of taking things for granted, without stopping to investigate.

Ridicule and reproach has been abundantly heaped upon the laborers in this righteous cause. Power, wealth, talent, pride, and sophistry, are all in arms against them; but God and truth is on their side. The cause of anti-slavery is rapidly gaining ground. Wise heads as well as warm hearts, are joining in its support. In a few years I believe the opinion of New-England will be unanimous in its favor. Maine, which enjoys the enviable distinction of never having had a slave upon her soil, has formed an Anti-Slavery Society composed of her best and most distinguished men. Those who are determined to be on the popular side, should be cautious how they move just now: It is a trying time for such characters, when public opinion is on the verge of a great change.

Men who *think* upon the subject, are fast coming to the conclusion that slavery can never be much ameliorated, while it is allowed to exist. What Mr. Fox said of the *trade* is true of the *system*—"you may as well try to *regulate* murder."

# 28

## THE RIGHTS OF LABOR

American manufacturing experienced dramatic changes after the War of 1812. Before the war, skilled artisans created custom goods from start to finish in their own homes and shops. After the war, as a result of wider demand and improvements in technology, a "factory system" emerged, beginning with the giant New England textile mills, driven by water power, and spreading rapidly to shoe factories and machine shops, driven by steam power, all across the Northeast. Human labor in thrall to mechanization became the foundation of the factory system; large mills and impersonal corporations became its chief features. Consumers benefited from more affordable mass-produced goods. Once-independent artisans, however, slowly but surely fell to the status of wage workers—"hands."

One result of these momentous changes was economic inequality on an unprecedented scale for a nonslave system. By the 1850s, the top 10 percent of the Northern population owned perhaps 60 percent of the national wealth. The labor force, increasingly proletarian (wage-earning), saw its condition deteriorate alarmingly. It was not uncommon for an adult male factory worker to earn a dollar for a fourteen-hour day; women and children sometimes received less. By the 1840s the nation was debating this maldistribution of wealth and income, now painfully noticeable, almost as intensely as it debated slavery, and it was taken to be a threat to democracy as well as the general welfare.

Among the most outspoken participants in that debate were proponents of labor unions. The earliest unions consisted of skilled artisans in a particular craft—carpentry, for example, or barrel making or printing. In the 1820s and 1830s craft unions began to grow and consolidate, first in their respective cities, then nationwide as multicraft workers' alliances. One of the most important of these early unions was the General Trades' Union of New York, which formed the core of the National Trades' Union of the 1830s.

Below are excerpts from a speech by Ely Moore, a New York printer, labor organizer, and Democratic activist, to the first National Trades' Union convention in 1834. Using class conflict rhetoric that foreshadowed Karl Marx's *Communist Manifesto* just fourteen years later, Moore argued that working men were becoming vassals to their employers. He also believed that the unequal distribution of wealth subverted the "natural rights of man" and was hostile to the "spirit and genius" of democracy. Moore's speech, fairly typical of the era, was ultimately fairly moderate in substance. But it still raised the hackles of conservatives, who were as unnerved by his criticism of "undue accumulation" as they were by his cry for workers to unite against the "aristocracy."

Ely Moore was born in New Jersey in 1798, attended public schools, and moved to New York, where he became a printer, land speculator, and politician. He was the first president of the New York General Trades' Union in 1833, edited the *National Trades' Union*, a labor journal, and was head of the National Trades' Union until 1836. That year Moore, a popular orator, was elected to Congress as a Democrat and served until 1839. Thereafter, he held various political patronage positions (posts he received for supporting successful Democratic candidates) in New York City and Kansas, where he moved in 1855. He died in Lecompton, Kansas, in 1861.

**Questions to Consider.** What were the different forces that, in Moore's view, had produced the drift toward "vassalage" and "supremacy"? Why did he think this drift was dangerous? Why did he propose labor unions as a remedy instead of government action? What remedies besides legislation and unionization might he have urged? Why did he spend so much time defending the idea of labor unions? Do you find Moore's arguments about the dangers of inequality and the legitimacy of labor unions persuasive? Would you say that they are less relevant today than in the nineteenth century, or more?

# Address to the General Trades' Union (1833)

### ELY MOORE

We have assembled, on the present occasion, for the purpose of publicly proclaiming the motives which induced us to organize a general union of the various trades and arts in this city and its vicinity, as well as to defend the course and to vindicate the measures we deign to pursue.

From Ely Moore, *Address Before the General Trades' Union of New York City* (New York, 1833), 7–14, 19–20.

This is required of us by a due regard to the opinions of our fellow men. . . .

Wherever man exists, under whatever form of government, or whatever be the structure or organization of society, . . . selfishness will appear, operating either for evil or for good. To curb it sufficiently by legislative enactments is impossible. Much can be done, however, towards restraining it within proper limits by unity of purpose and concert of action on the part of the *producing* classes. To contribute toward the achievement of this great end is one of the objects of the "General Trades' Union." Wealth, we all know, constitutes the aristocracy of this country. Happily no distinctions are known among us save what wealth and worth confer. . . . The greatest danger, therefore, which threatens the stability of our Government and the liberty of the people is an undue accumulation and distribution of wealth. And I do conceive that real danger is to be apprehended from this source, notwithstanding that tendency to distribution which naturally grows out of the character of our statutes of conveyance, of inheritance, and descent of property; but by securing to the producing classes a fair, certain, and equitable compensation for their toil and skill, we insure a more just and equal distribution of wealth than can ever be effected by statutory law.

. . . We ask . . . what better means can be devised for promoting a more equal distribution of wealth than for the producing classes to *claim*, and by virtue of union and concert, *secure their claims* to their respective portions? And why should not those who have the toil have the enjoyment also? Or why should the sweat that flows from the brow of the laborer be converted into a source of revenue for the support of the crafty or indolent?

It has been averred, with great truth, that all governments become cruel and aristocratical in their character and bearing in proportion as one part of the community is elevated and the other depressed, and that misery and degradation to the many is the inevitable result of such a state of society. And we regard it to be equally true that, in proportion as the line of distinction between the employer and employed is *widened,* the condition of the latter inevitably verges toward a state of vassalage, while that of the former as certainly approximates toward supremacy; and that whatever system is calculated to make the many dependent upon or subject to the few not only tends to the subversion of the natural rights of man, but is hostile to the best interests of the community, as well as to the spirit and genius of our Government. Fully persuaded that the foregoing positions are incontrovertible, we, in order to guard against the encroachments of aristocracy, to preserve our natural and political rights, to elevate our moral and intellectual condition, to promote our pecuniary interests, to narrow the line of distinction between the journeyman and employer, to establish the honor and safety of our respective vocations upon a more secure and permanent basis, and to alleviate the distresses of those suffering from want of employment have deemed it expedient to form ourselves into a "General Trades' Union."

It may be asked, how these desirable objects are to be achieved by a general union of trades? How the encroachments of aristocracy, for example, are to be arrested by our plan? We answer, by enabling the producer to enjoy the full benefit of his productions, and thus diffuse the streams of wealth more generally and, consequently, more equally throughout all the ramifications of society. . . .

There are, doubtless, many individuals who are resolved, right or wrong, to misrepresent our principles, impeach our measures, and impugn our motives. Be it so. They can harm us not. . . . We have the consolation of knowing that all good men, all who love their country, and rejoice in the improvement of the condition of their fellow men, will acknowledge the policy of our views and the purity of our motives. . . . And why, let me ask, should the character of our Union be obnoxious to censure? Wherefore is it wrong in principle? Which of its avowed objects reprehensible? What feature of it opposed to the public good? I defy the ingenuity of man to point to a single measure which it recognizes that is wrong in itself or in its tendency. What, is it wrong for men to unite for the purpose of resisting the encroachments of aristocracy? Wrong to restrict the principle of selfishness to its proper and legitimate bounds and objects? Wrong to oppose monopoly and mercenary ambition? Wrong to consult the interests and seek the welfare of the producing classes? Wrong to attempt the elevation of our moral and intellectual standing? Wrong to establish the honor and safety of our respective vocations upon a more secure and permanent basis? I ask—in the name of heaven I ask—can it be wrong for men to attempt the melioration of their condition and the preservation of their natural and political rights?

I am aware that the charge of "illegal combination" is raised against us. The cry is as senseless as 'tis stale and unprofitable. Why, I would inquire, have not journeymen the same right to ask their own price for their own property or services that employers have? or that merchants, physicians, and lawyers have? Is that equal justice which makes it an offense for journeymen to combine for the purpose of maintaining their present prices or raising their wages, while employers may combine with impunity for the purpose of lowering them? I admit that such is the common law. All will agree, however, that it is neither wise, just, nor politic, and that it is directly opposed to the spirit and genius of our free institutions and ought therefore, to be abrogated. . . .

Again, it is alleged that it is setting a dangerous precedent for journeymen to combine for the purpose of coercing a compliance with their terms. It may, indeed, be dangerous to aristocracy, dangerous to monopoly, dangerous to oppression, but not to the general good or the public tranquillity. Internal danger to a state is not to be apprehended from a general effort on the part of the people to improve and exalt their condition, but from an alliance of the crafty, designing, and intriguing few. What! tell us, in this enlightened age, that the welfare of the people will be endangered by a voluntary act of the people themselves? That the people will wantonly seek their own destruction? That the safety of the state will be plotted against by three-fourths of the members comprising the state! O how worthless, how poor and pitiful, are all such arguments and objections! . . .

My object in inviting you to a consideration of this subject at the present time is to impress upon your minds the importance of the situation which you, in reality, ought to occupy in society. This you seem to have lost sight of in a very great degree; and, from some cause or other, have relinquished your claims to that consideration to which, as mechanics and as men, you are entitled. You have, most unfortunately for yourselves and for the respectability of your vocations, become apparently unconscious of your own worth, and been led to regard your callings as humble and inferior, and your stations as too subordinate in life. And why? why is it so? Why should the producer consider himself inferior to the consumer? Or why should the mechanic, who builds a house, consider himself less important than the owner or occupant? It is strange, indeed, and to me perfectly unaccountable that the artificer, who prepares the accommodations, the comforts, and embellishments of life, should consider himself of less consequence than those to whose pleasure and convenience he ministers. . . .

# 29

## PUBLIC VERSUS PRIVATE

The era from the 1830s until the Civil War was marked by intense reform movements, especially in the Northeast. "In the history of the
world," exclaimed Ralph Waldo Emerson, "the doctrine of Reform
had never such a scope as at the present hour." Most reformers were
deeply religious; they took seriously Christianity's emphasis on the
spiritual equality of all human beings and Jesus's special concern for
the lowly and humble. They were also inspired by the Declaration of
Independence, with its insistence on natural rights, and were eager to
make its social and political ideas a reality. Many reformers believed
that human nature was perfectible and that with better social arrangements men and women would be able to live more fully and freely
than they ever had before. During the Age of Reform the antislavery
movement became important. So did the struggles for temperance
(against alcohol abuse), women's rights, more humane prisons and
asylums, and improved conditions for working people.

Civic-minded citizens also turned their attention to education. Believing that the foundation of democracy was an educated citizenry,
they were shocked by the disparity between that ideal and the sorry
state of schooling in most parts of the nation. In most Mid-Atlantic
states only paupers were educated at public expense; in the South,
public schools were almost nonexistent; in the West, the sparse population was simply unable to establish adequate schools. Even in New
England, where a notable educational tradition had evolved from the
Puritan insistence that as many people as possible should be able to
read the Bible, school systems were in disarray from administrative
failure and declining finances.

Observers considered the overcrowded schoolhouse itself a "reproach to human nature." In Connecticut, essayist Bronson Alcott
taught eighty students in one tiny room! Sites were selected with less
regard to comfort "than if the children were animals." Anything would
do, especially if it was "so useless for everything else as to be given
gratis to the district." In Massachusetts, common (public) school "re-
vivalists" went to work to persuade towns and villages to build more
and better schools; to fill them with comfortable desks, blackboards,

books, maps, blocks, and writing materials; to establish standards and train professional (mostly female) teachers; and to make elementary education compulsory.

No one was more devoted to the cause than Horace Mann. A Boston lawyer and politician from Franklin, Massachusetts, Mann had suffered through a miserable childhood and a wretched education. So absorbed did Mann become with expanding and improving the common schools that he stunned his friends by quitting both the law and the Massachusetts Senate to become secretary of the state's fledgling board of education. In that capacity, having little power save moral suasion, Mann brought about a veritable revolution in the state's school system. Largely as a result of his efforts, Massachusetts became a model for common schools across the country.

But there were powerful opposing forces. Prosperous families, in particular, liked to send their children to private schools. One of Mann's greatest challenges was therefore to convince parents to send their children to public schools, as his 1838 *Report on the Common Schools* (excerpted below) makes clear. The report also reflected Mann's view that the common school experience would promote the opportunity, social unity, and compassion that would make students good future citizens: "If we do not prepare children to become good citizens—if we do not . . . enrich their minds with knowledge, imbue their hearts with the love of truth and duty . . . then our republic must go down to destruction."

Mann's devotion to educational reform never faltered. After serving twelve years as secretary of the Massachusetts board of education, he served a term in the U.S. House of Representatives, where he supported efforts to halt the expansion of slavery. In 1853 Mann became the first president of Antioch College in Ohio, where he died in 1859 at the age of sixty-three.

**Questions to Consider.** What, according to Horace Mann, was the main purpose of the common school system? To what extent did Mann's enthusiasm for public schools reflect his view of human nature? Why did some people value private education more than public? What did Mann think would be the social consequences of this preference? What did Mann seem to value most, opportunity for individuals or well-being for the society? Do you find his arguments persuasive? Are they as relevant and persuasive for today as they were for the nineteenth century?

**New England schoolroom, 1857.** Horace Mann's reform efforts succeeded to an astonishing degree in the towns and villages of the Northern states. By modern standards, however, even the new and newly refurbished schools were sometimes stark and gloomy, as this photograph of a girls' class suggests. Even when teachers were better trained and paid, they relied on strict discipline and drill to educate their students. (The Metropolitian Museum of Art, Gift of I. N. Phelps Stokes, Edward S. Hawes, Alice Mary Hawes, Marion Augusta Hawes, 1937)

# Report on the Common Schools (1838)

### HORACE MANN

The object of the common school system of Massachusetts was to give to every child in the Commonwealth a free, straight, solid path-way, by which he could walk directly up from the ignorance of an infant to a knowledge of the primary duties of a man; and could acquire a power and an invincible will to discharge them. Have our children such a way? Are they walking in

From Horace Mann, *First Annual Report of the Board of Education* (Boston, 1838), 47–58.

it? Why do so many, who enter it, falter therein? Are there not many, who miss it altogether? What can be done to reclaim them? What can be done to rescue faculties, powers, divine endowments, graciously designed for individual and social good, from being perverted to individual and social calamity? These are the questions of deep and intense interest, which I have proposed to myself, and upon which I have sought for information and counsel. . . .

An . . . [important] topic . . . is the apathy of the people themselves towards our common schools. The wide usefulness of which this institution is capable is shorn away on both sides, by two causes diametrically opposite. On one side there is a portion of the community who do not attach sufficient value to the system to do the things necessary to its healthful and energetic working. They may say excellent things about it, they may have a conviction of its general utility; but they do not understand, that the wisest conversation not embodied in action, that convictions too gentle and quiet to coerce performance, are little better than worthless. The prosperity of the system always requires some labor. It requires a conciliatory disposition, and oftentimes a little sacrifice of personal preferences. . . .

Through remissness or ignorance on the part of parent and teacher, the minds of children may never be awakened to a consciousness of having, within themselves, blessed treasures of innate and noble faculties, far richer than any outward possessions can be; they may never be supplied with any foretaste of the enduring satisfactions of knowledge; and hence, they may attend school for the allotted period, merely as so many male and female automata, between four and sixteen years of age. As the progenitor of the human race, after being perfectly fashioned in every limb and organ and feature, might have lain till this time, a motionless body in the midst of the beautiful garden of Eden, had not the Creator breathed into him a living soul; so children, without some favoring influences to woo out and cheer their faculties, may remain mere inanimate forms, while surrounded by the paradise of knowledge. It is generally believed, that there is an increasing class of people amongst us, who are losing sight of the necessity of securing ample opportunities for the education of their children. And thus, on one side, the institution of common schools is losing its natural support, if it be not incurring actual opposition.

Opposite to this class, who tolerate, from apathy, a depression in the common schools, there is another class who affix so high a value upon the culture of their children, and understand so well the necessity of a skillful preparation of means for its bestowment, that they turn away from the common schools, in their depressed state, and seek, elsewhere, the helps of a more enlarged and thorough education. Thus the standard, in descending to a point corresponding with the views and wants of one portion of society, falls below the demands and the regards of another. Out of different feelings grow different plans; and while one remains fully content with the common school, the other builds up the private school or the academy.

The education fund is thus divided into two parts. Neither of the halves does a quarter of the good which might be accomplished by a union of the whole. One party pays an adequate price, but has a poor school; the other has a good school, but at more than four-fold cost. Were their funds and their interest combined, the poorer school might be as good as the best; and the dearest almost as low as the cheapest. This last mentioned class embraces a considerable portion, perhaps a majority of the wealthy persons in the state; but it also includes another portion, numerically much greater, who, whether rich or poor, have a true perception of the sources of their children's individual and domestic well-being, and who consider the common necessaries of their life, their food and fuel and clothes, and all their bodily comforts as superfluities, compared with the paramount necessity of a proper mental and moral culture of their offspring.

The maintenance of free schools rests wholly upon the social principle. It is emphatically a case where men, individually powerless, are collectively strong. The population of Massachusetts, being more than *eighty* to the square mile, gives it the power of maintaining common schools. Take the whole range of the western and south-western states, and their population, probably, does not exceed a dozen or fifteen to the square mile. Hence, except in favorable localities, common schools are impossible; as the population upon a territory of convenient size for a district, is too small to sustain a school. Here, nothing is easier. But by dividing our funds, we cast away our natural advantages. We voluntarily reduce ourselves to the feebleness of a state, having but half our density of population.

It is generally supposed, that this severance of interests, and consequent diminution of power, have increased much of late, and are now increasing in an accelerated ratio. This is probable, for it is a self-aggravating evil. Its origin and progress are simple and uniform. Some few persons . . . finding the advantages of the common school inadequate to their wants, unite to establish a private one. They transfer their children from the former to the latter. The heart goes with the treasure. The common school ceases to be visited by those whose children are in the private. Such parents decline serving as committee men. They have now no personal motive to vote for or advocate any increase of the town's annual appropriation for schools; to say nothing of the temptation to discourage such increase in indirect ways, or even to vote directly against it. If, by this means, some of the best scholars happen to be taken from the common school, the standard of that school is lowered. The lower classes in a school have no abstract standard of excellence, and seldom aim at higher attainments than such as they daily witness. All children, like all men, rise easily to the common level. There, the mass stop; strong minds only ascend higher. But raise the standard, and, by a spontaneous movement, the mass will rise again and reach it. Hence the removal of the most forward scholars from a school is not a small misfortune.

Again; the teacher of the common school rarely visits or associates except where the scholars of his own school are the origin of the acquaintance, and the bond of attachment. All this inevitably depresses and degrades the common school. In this depressed and degraded state, another portion of the parents find it, in fitness and adequacy, inferior to their wants; and, as there is now a private school in the neighborhood, the strength of the inducement, and the facility of the transfer, overbalance the objection of increased expense, and the doors of the common school close, at once, upon their children, and upon their interest in its welfare. Thus another blow is dealt; then others escape; action and reaction alternate, until the common school is left to the management of those, who have not the desire or the power either to improve it or to command a better. . . .

The refusal of a town to maintain the free town school drives a portion of its inhabitants to establish the private school or academy. When established, these institutions tend strongly to diminish the annual appropriations of the town; they draw their ablest recruits from the common schools; and, by being able to offer higher compensation, they have a pre-emptive right to the best qualified teachers; while, simultaneously, the district schools are reduced in length, deteriorated in quality, and, to some extent, bereft of talents competent for instruction.

Some objections are urged, on both sides, to a restitution of our system to its original design; but, as they are anti-social in their nature, they must be dissipated by a more enlarged view of the subject. Citizens, living remote from the place, where the town school would probably be kept, allege the difference in the distances of residence, and the consequent inequality of advantages, derivable from it, as arguments against its maintenance. They, therefore, resist its establishment, and thus extinguish all chances of a better education for a vast majority of the children in the town, whatever may be their talents or genius. They debar some, perhaps their own offspring, from the means of reaching a higher sphere of usefulness and honor. They forbid their taking the first steps, which are as necessary as the last, in the ascension to excellence. They surrender every vantage ground to those who can and will, in any event, command the means of a higher education for their children. Because the balance of advantages cannot be mathematically adjusted, as in the nature of things it cannot be, they cast their own shares into the adverse scale; as though it were some compensation, when there is not an absolute equality, to make the inequality absolute. The cost of education is nothing to the rich, while the means of it are every thing to the poor. . . .

On the other hand, the patrons of the private school plead the moral necessity of sustaining it, because, they say, some of the children in the public school are so addicted to profanity or obscenity, so prone to trickishness or to vulgar and mischievous habits, as to render a removal of their own children from such contaminating influences an obligatory precaution. But would such objectors bestow that guardian care, that parental watchfulness upon the common schools, which an institution, so wide and deep-reaching in its influences, demands of all intelligent men, might not these repellent causes be mainly abolished? Reforms ought to be originated and carried forward by the intelligent portion of society; by those who can see most links in the chain of causes and effects; and that intelligence is false to its high trusts, which stands aloof from the labor of enlightening the ignorant and ameliorating the condition of the unfortunate. And what a vision must rise before the minds of all men, endued with the least glimmer of foresight, in the reflection, that, after a few swift years, those children, whose welfare they now discard, and whose associations they deprecate, will constitute more than *five sixths* of the whole body of that community, of which their own children will be only a feeble minority, vulnerable at every point, and utterly incapable of finding a hiding-place for any earthly treasure, where the witness, the juror and the voter cannot reach and annihilate it!

The theory of our laws and institutions undoubtedly is, *first*, that in every district of every town in the Commonwealth, there should be a free district school, sufficiently safe, and sufficiently good, for all the children within its territory, where they may be well instructed in the rudiments of knowledge, formed to propriety of demeanor, and imbued with the principles of duty: and, *secondly*, in regard to every town, having such an increased population as implies the possession of sufficient wealth, that there should be a school of an advanced character, offering an equal welcome to each one of the same children, whom a peculiar destination, or an impelling spirit of genius, shall send to its open doors,—especially to the children of the poor, who cannot incur the expenses of a residence from home in order to attend such a school. It is on this common platform, that a general acquaintanceship should be formed between the children of the same neighborhood. It is here, that the affinities of a common nature should unite them together so as to give the advantages of pre-occupancy and a stable possession to fraternal feelings, against the alienating competitions of subsequent life.

After the state shall have secured to all its children, that basis of knowledge and morality, which is indispensable to its own security; after it shall have supplied them with the instruments of that individual prosperity, whose aggregate will constitute its own social prosperity; then they may be emancipated from its tutelage, each one to go withersoever his well-instructed mind shall determine.

# 30

# INDIVIDUALISM

The "transcendentalists" were a loose group of New England thinkers, writers, and reformers who came to prominence in the 1830s and 1840s. Transcendentalists shared a faith in the spiritual qualities of nature, in the special mission of young people to throw off the "dead hand" of the past, and in the primacy of the free individual over the stifling community. Opposed to slavery, concerned with women's rights and intellectual freedom, they founded journals, organized "utopian" communities, contributed to reform movements. But their bent was individualistic. They were therefore different from reformers such as Horace Mann or Ely Moore, who preached progress through collective action on behalf of institutions that would bring people together instead of drive them apart—public schools, for example, or labor unions. Transcendentalists, by contrast, wanted to "transcend"—rise above, escape from—institutional or social constraints.

Notable transcendentalists included Henry David Thoreau, who lived alone in a cabin at Walden Pond; Bronson Alcott, the father of novelist Louisa May Alcott; and Margaret Fuller, editor and early feminist. But the movement's leading figure was Ralph Waldo Emerson. Indeed, if Jefferson was the prophet of American democracy and Jackson its hero, Ralph Waldo Emerson might have been its high priest. Emerson, a Harvard graduate who abandoned his Unitarian ministry to become "a lay preacher to the world," reflected all the chief points of the transcendentalist credo. In the woods was "perpetual youth" and the true source of "reason and faith." Man should shrug off the "dry bones of the past," walk with his "own feet," work with his "own hands," speak with his "own mind." Audiences recognized immediately that Emerson was preaching a kind of individual "liberation," a message perfectly in tune with the self-conscious democracy of the young republic and its youthful, pushy middle class. Excerpted below is "Self-Reliance," Emerson's single most popular essay. The essay was enormously influential in its day—it helped make Emerson a star and energized countless thousands—and it has been strikingly, powerfully appealing, especially to young people, ever since.

Born in Boston in 1803 to a long line of New England clergymen, Ralph Waldo Emerson graduated from Harvard, taught for a few years, became a Unitarian minister, then gradually, in part through his reading of English and German philosophers, grew skeptical and gave up his Boston pulpit. In 1834 he moved to Concord, Massachusetts, where he published *Nature* (1834), "The American Scholar" (1837), "The Divinity School Address" (1838), and other important works over the next twenty-five years. He also became one of the country's most sought-after lecturers, acclaimed in both the United States and England. Never an avid personal participant in social reform movements, he spent his final years quietly in Concord, where he died in 1882.

**Questions to Consider.** Why did Emerson believe that a man, ceasing to be a boy, was "clapped into jail by his consciousness"? Why did he hold up boys, babes, "even brutes," rather than adults as models? Why did he argue that a true man must be a nonconformist? What specific social groups threatened the nonconformist? Which of these groups posed the greatest threat? What sort of listener would be most likely to respond to the statement, "All history resolves itself very easily into the biography of a few stout and earnest persons"? Why did Emerson say that reliance on property showed a lack of self-reliance? What sort of property should people be most ashamed to have? Were Emerson's views of politics and social reform healthy or unhealthy? Would you say that these views have, as of the late twentieth century, carried the day?

# Self-Reliance (1841)

RALPH WALDO EMERSON

Trust thyself: every heart vibrates to that iron string. Accept the place the divine Providence has found for you; the society of your contemporaries, the connexion of events. Great men have always done so and confided themselves childlike to the genius of their age, betraying their perception that the absolutely trustworthy was seated at their heart, working through their hands, predominating in all their being. And we are now men, and must accept in the highest mind the same transcendent destiny; and not minors and invalids in a protected corner, not cowards fleeing before a revolution, but

From Ralph Waldo Emerson, *Essays and English Traits* (New York, 1909), 47–64.

guides, redeemers, and benefactors, obeying the Almighty effort, and advancing on Chaos and the Dark.

What pretty oracles nature yields us on this text in the face and behavior of children, babes and even brutes. That divided and rebel mind, that distrust of a sentiment because our arithmetic has computed the strength and means opposed to our purpose, these have not. Their mind being whole, their eye is as yet unconquered, and when we look in their faces, we are disconcerted. Infancy conforms to nobody: all conform to it, so that one babe commonly makes four or five out of the adults who prattle and play to it. So God has armed youth and puberty and manhood no less with its own piquancy and charm, and made it enviable and gracious and its claims not to be put by, if it will stand by itself. Do not think the youth has no force because he cannot speak to you and me. Hark! in the next room his voice is sufficiently clear and emphatic. It seems he knows how to speak to his contemporaries. Bashful or bold, then, he will know how to make us seniors very unnecessary.

The nonchalance of boys who are sure of a dinner, and would disdain as much as a lord to do or say aught to conciliate one, is the healthy attitude of human nature. A boy is in the parlour what the pit is in the playhouse; independent, irresponsible, looking out from his corner on such people and facts as pass by, he tries and sentences them on their merits, in the swift summary way of boys, as good, bad, interesting, silly, eloquent, troublesome. He cumbers himself never about consequences, about interests: he gives an independent, genuine verdict. You must court him: he does not court you. But the man is, as it were, clapped into jail by his consciousness. As soon as he has once acted or spoken with eclat, he is a committed person, watched by the sympathy or the hatred of hundreds whose affections must now enter into his account. There is no Lethe for this. Ah, that he could pass again into his neutrality! Who can thus avoid all pledges, and having observed, observe again from the same unaffected, unbiassed, unbribable, unaffrighted innocence, must always be formidable. He would utter opinions on all passing affairs, which being seen to be not private but necessary, would sink like darts into the ear of men, and put them in fear.

These are the voices which we hear in solitude, but they grow faint and inaudible as we enter into the world. Society everywhere is in conspiracy against the manhood of every one of its members. Society is a joint-stock company in which the members agree for the better securing of his bread to each shareholder, to surrender the liberty and culture of the eater. The virtue in most request is conformity. Self-reliance is its aversion. It loves not realities and creators, but names and customs.

Whoso would be a man must be a nonconformist. He who would gather immortal palms must not be hindered by the name of goodness, but must explore if it be goodness. Nothing is at last sacred but the integrity of your own mind. Absolve you to yourself, and you shall have the suffrage of the world. I remember an answer which when quite young I was prompted to make to a valued adviser who was wont to importune me with the dear old doctrines of the church. On my saying, What have I to do with the sacredness of traditions, if I live wholly from within? my friend suggested—"But these impulses may be from below, not from above." I replied, "They do not seem to me to be such; but if I am the Devil's child, I will live then from the Devil." No law can be sacred to me but that of my nature. Good and bad are but names very readily transferable to that or this; the only right is what is after my constitution, the only wrong what is against it. A man is to carry himself in the presence of all opposition as if every thing were titular and ephemeral but he. I am ashamed to think how easily we capitulate to badges and names, to large societies and dead institutions. Every decent and well-spoken individual affects and sways me more than is right. I ought to go upright and vital. . . .

What I must do, is all that concerns me, not what the people think. This rule, equally arduous in actual and in intellectual life, may serve for the whole distinction between greatness and meanness. It is the harder, because you will always find those who think they know what is your duty better than you know it. It is easy in the world to live after the world's opinion; it is easy in solitude to live after our own; but the great man is he who in the midst of the crowd keeps with perfect sweetness the independence of solitude. . . .

For nonconformity the world whips you with its displeasure. And therefore a man must know how to estimate a sour face. The bystanders look askance on him in the public street or in the friend's parlor. If this aversation had its origin in contempt and resistance like his own, he might well go home with a sad countenance; but the sour faces of the multitude, like their sweet faces, have no deep cause, but are put on and off as the wind blows, and a newspaper directs. Yet is the discontent of the multitude more formidable than that of the senate and the college. It is easy enough for a firm man who knows the world to brook the rage of the cultivated classes. Their rage is decorous and prudent, for they are timid as being very vulnerable themselves. But when to their feminine rage the indignation of the people is added, when the ignorant and the poor are aroused, when the unintelligent brute force that lies at the bottom of society is made to growl and mow, it needs the habit of magnanimity and religion to treat it godlike as a trifle of no concernment.

The other terror that scares us from self-trust is our consistency; a reverence for our past act or word, because the eyes of others have no other data for computing our orbit than our past acts, and we are loath to disappoint them.

But why should you keep your head over your shoulder? Why drag about this corpse of your memory, lest you contradict somewhat you have stated in this or that public place? Suppose you should contradict yourself; what then? It seems to be a rule of wisdom never to rely on your memory alone, scarcely even in acts of pure memory, but to bring the past for judgment into the thousand-eyed present, and live ever in a new day. In your metaphysics you have denied personality to the Deity: yet when the devout motions of the soul come, yield to them heart and life, though they should clothe God with shape and color. Leave your theory as Joseph his coat in the hand of the harlot, and flee.

A foolish consistency is the hobgoblin of little minds, adored by little statesmen and philosophers and divines. With consistency a great soul has simply nothing to do. He may as well concern himself with his shadow on the wall. Speak what you think now in hard words, and to-morrow speak what to-morrow thinks in hard words again, though it contradict every thing you said to-day.—'Ah, so you shall be sure to be misunderstood.'—Is it so bad then to be misunderstood? Pythagoras was misunderstood, and Socrates, and Jesus, and Luther, and Copernicus, and Galileo, and Newton, and every pure and wise spirit that ever took flesh. To be great is to be misunderstood. . . .

I hope in these days we have heard the last of conformity and consistency. Let the words be gazetted and ridiculous henceforward. Instead of the gong for dinner, let us hear a whistle from the Spartan fife. Let us never bow and apologize more. A great man is coming to eat at my house. I do not wish to please him: I wish that he should wish to please me. I will stand here for humanity, and though I would make it kind, I would make it true. Let us affront and reprimand the smooth mediocrity and squalid contentment of the times, and hurl in the face of custom, and trade, and office, the fact which is the upshot of all history, that there is a great responsible Thinker and Actor working wherever a man works; that a true man belongs to no other time or place, but is the centre of things. Where he is, there is nature. He measures you, and all men, and all events. Ordinarily every body in society reminds us of somewhat else or of some other person. Character, reality, reminds you of nothing else; it takes place of the whole creation. The man must be so much that he must make all circumstances indifferent. Every true man is a cause, a country, and an age; requires infinite spaces and numbers and time fully to accomplish his design;—and posterity seem to follow his steps as a train of clients. A man Caesar is born, and for ages after, we have a Roman Empire. Christ is born, and millions of minds so grow and cleave to his genius, that he is confounded with virtue and the possible of man. An institution is the lengthened shadow of one man; as, Monachism, of the Hermit Antony; the Reformation, of Luther; Quakerism, of Fox; Methodism, of Wesley; Abolition, of Clarkson. Scipio, Milton called "the height of Rome"; and all history resolves itself very easily into the biography of a few stout and earnest persons.

Let a man then know his worth, and keep things under his feet. Let him not peep or steal, or skulk up and down with the air of a charity-boy, a bastard, or an interloper, in the world which exists for him. But the man in the street finding no worth in himself which corresponds to the force which built a tower or sculptured a marble god, feels poor when he looks on these.

To him a palace, a statue, or a costly book have an alien and forbidding air, much like a gay equipage, and seem to say like that, "Who are you, sir?" Yet they all are his, suitors for his notice, petitioners to his faculties that they will come out and take possession. The picture waits for my verdict: it is not to command me, but I am to settle its claims to praise. That popular fable of the sot who was picked up dead drunk in the street, carried to the duke's house, washed and dressed and laid in the duke's bed, and, on his waking, treated with all obsequious ceremony like the duke, and assured that he had been insane, owes its popularity to the fact, that it symbolizes so well the state of man, who is in the world a sort of sot, but now and then wakes up, exercises his reason, and finds himself a true prince. . . .

The magnetism which all original action exerts is explained when we inquire the reason of self-trust. Who is the Trustee? What is the aboriginal Self on which a universal reliance may be grounded? What is the nature and power of that science-baffling star, without parallax, without calculable elements, which shoots a ray of beauty even into trivial and impure actions, if the least mark of independence appear? The inquiry leads us to that source, at once the essence of genius, of virtue, and of life, which we call Spontaneity or Instinct. We denote this primary wisdom as Intuition, whilst all later teachings are tuitions. In that deep force, the last fact behind which analysis cannot go, all things find their common origin. For the sense of being which in calm hours rises, we know not how, in the soul, is not diverse from things, from space, from light, from time, from man, but one with them, and proceeds obviously from the same source whence their life and being also proceed. We first share the life by which things exist, and afterwards see them as appearances in nature, and forget that we have shared their cause. Here is the fountain of action and of thought. Here are the lungs of that inspiration which giveth man wisdom, and which cannot be denied without impiety and atheism. We lie in the lap of immense intelligence, which makes us receivers of its truth and organs of its activity. When we discern justice, when we discern truth, we do nothing of ourselves, but allow a passage to its beams. If we ask whence this comes, if we seek to pry into the soul that causes, all philosophy is at fault. Its presence or its absence is all we can affirm. . . .

The relations of the soul to the divine spirit are so pure that it is profane to seek to interpose helps. It must be that when God speaketh, he should communicate not one thing, but all things; should fill the world with his voice; should scatter forth light, nature, time, souls, from the centre of the present thought; and new date and new create the whole. Whenever a mind is simple, and receives a divine wisdom, old things pass away,—means, teachers, texts, temples fall; it lives now and absorbs past and future into the present hour. All things are made sacred by relation to it,—one as much as another. All things are dissolved to their centre by their cause, and in the universal miracle petty and particular miracles disappear. If, therefore, a man claims to know and speak of God, and carries you backward to the phraseology of some old mouldered nation in another country, in another world, believe him not. Is the acorn better than the oak which is its fulness and completion? Is the parent better than the child into whom he has cast his ripened being? Whence then this worship of the past? The centuries are conspirators against the sanity and authority of the soul. Time and space are but physiological colors which the eye makes, but the soul is light; where it is, is day; where it was, is night; and history is an impertinence and an injury, if it be anything more than a cheerful apologue or parable of my being and becoming.

Man is timid and apologetic; he is no longer upright; he dares not say 'I think,' 'I am,' but quotes some saint or sage. He is ashamed before the blade of grass or the blowing rose. These roses under my window make no reference to former roses or to better ones; they are for what they are; they exist with God to-day. There is no time to them. There is simply the rose; it is perfect in every moment of its existence. Before a leaf-bud has burst, its whole life acts; in the full-blown flower, there is no more; in the leafless root, there is no less. Its nature is satisfied, and it satisfies nature, in all moments alike. But man postpones or remembers; he does not live in the present, but with reverted eye laments the past, or, heedless of the riches that surround him, stands on tiptoe to foresee the future. He cannot be happy and strong until he too lives with nature in the present. . . .

Society is a wave. The wave moves onward, but the water of which it is composed, does not. The same particle does not rise from the valley to the ridge. Its unity is only phenomenal. The persons who make up a nation to-day, next year die, and their experience with them.

And so the reliance on Property, including the reliance on governments which protect it, is the want of self-reliance. Men have looked away from themselves and at things so long, that they have come to esteem the religious, learned, and civil institutions, as guards of property, and they deprecate assaults on these, because they feel them to be assaults on property. They measure their esteem of each other, by what each has, and not by what each is. But a cultivated man becomes ashamed of his property, out of new respect for his nature. Especially he hates what he has, if he see that it is accidental,—came to him by inheritance, or gift, or crime; then he feels that it is not having; it does not belong to him, has no root in him, and merely lies there, because no revolution or no robber takes it away. But that which a man is, does always by necessity acquire, and what the man acquires is living property, which does not wait the beck of rulers, or mobs, or revolutions, or fire, or storm, or bankruptcies, but perpetually renews itself wherever the man breathes. "Thy lot or portion of life," said the Caliph Ali, "is seeking after thee; therefore be at rest from seeking after it." Our dependence on these foreign goods leads us to our slavish respect for numbers. The political parties meet in numerous conventions; the greater the concourse, and with each new uproar of announcement, The delegation from Essex! The Democrats from New Hampshire! The Whigs of Maine! the young patriot feels himself stronger than before by a new thousand of eyes and arms. In like manner the reformers summon conventions, and vote and resolve in multitude. Not so, O friends! will the God deign to enter and inhabit you, but by a method precisely the reverse. It is only as a man puts off all foreign support, and stands alone, that I see him to be strong and to prevail.

# 31

## WOMEN'S FREEDOM

In March 1776, when the Continental Congress in Philadelphia was beginning to contemplate independence from Britain, Abigail Adams wrote her husband, John, from Braintree, Massachusetts: "I long to hear that you have declared an independency. And, by the way," she added, "in the new code of laws which I suppose it will be necessary for you to make, I desire you would remember the ladies and be more generous and favorable to them than your ancestors. Do not put unlimited power into the hands of the husbands. Remember, all men would be tyrants if they could. If particular care and attention is not paid to the ladies, we are determined to foment a rebellion, and will not hold ourselves bound by any laws in which we have no voice or representation. That your sex are naturally tyrannical is a truth so thoroughly established as to admit of no dispute. . . ." Adams wrote back good-humoredly. "We are obliged to go fairly and softly," he told his wife, "and, in practice, you know we are the subjects. We have only the name of masters, and rather than give this up, which would completely subject us to the despotism of the petticoat, I hope General Washington and all our brave heroes would fight. . . ."[1]

Adams wasn't being accurate. American men had more than "the name of masters." The status of women in Adams's day and for many years afterward was distinctly inferior. Sir William Blackstone, the great eighteenth-century British legal authority, set the standard for the American view. "The husband and wife are one," he proclaimed, "and that one is the husband." Women were regarded as the wards of their husbands, were barred from professions like the law, medicine, and the ministry, and had few opportunities for higher education. According to a little verse composed in 1844:

> The father gives his kind command
> The mother joins, approves,
> And children all attentive stand,
> Then each, obedient, moves.

1. Charles Francis Adams, ed., *Familiar Letters of John Adams and His Wife During the Revolution* (New York, 1876), 149–150, 155.

Abigail Adams wasn't the only woman to chafe at the situation. In 1832 Lydia Maria Child published a two-volume *History of the Condition of Woman in All Ages,* deploring woman's subservience, and in 1843 Margaret Fuller published a long essay, later expanded and published as *Woman in the Nineteenth Century,* in which she declared: "What woman needs is not as a woman to act or rule, but as a nature to grow, as an intellect to discern, as a soul to live freely and unimpeded, to unfold such powers as were given her when we left our common home."

Born near Boston in 1810 to parents who emphasized intellectual development, Margaret Fuller became one of the most learned Americans of her time despite the fact that academies and colleges did not then admit women. Fuller taught school in the Boston area, wrote for literary journals, and conducted highly popular public "conversations" on the education of women while still in her twenties. In 1840 she became an editor of the *Dial.* In 1844 she took a position as a literary columnist at the *New York Tribune,* and she soon earned the reputation as a leading American critic. After the publication of *Woman in the Nineteenth Century* in 1843 and *Papers on Literature and Art* in 1846, Fuller sailed for Europe, where she married Angelo Ossoli, an Italian revolutionary. In July 1850, the ship on which she and her husband and child were returning to the United States foundered off the coast of Long Island, drowning all passengers.

**Questions to Consider.** What aspect of women's position most distressed Margaret Fuller? How specifically did she expect that position to be changed? Did she believe men *could* not speak effectively on behalf of women, or that they *would* not? What audience does she seem to have been addressing in this passage? How important was religion in her argument? Was this statement conservative or radical in its implications? Would Fuller have endorsed the Seneca Falls Declaration of 1848?

# Woman in the Nineteenth Century (1845)

MARGARET FULLER

The gain of creation consists always in the growth of individual minds, which live and aspire as flowers bloom and birds sing in the midst of morasses; and in the continual development of that thought, the thought of

From S. Margaret Fuller, *Woman in the Nineteenth Century* (Greeley & McElrath, New York, 1845), 14–15, 23–28, 52.

human destiny, which is given to eternity adequately to express, and which ages of failure only seemingly impede.

Knowing that there exists in the minds of men a tone of feeling toward women as toward slaves, such as is expressed in the common phrase, "Tell that to women and children"; that the infinite soul can only work through them in already ascertained limits; that the gift of reason, Man's highest prerogative, is allotted to them in much lower degree; that they must be kept from mischief and melancholy by being constantly engaged in active labor, which is to be furnished and directed by those better able to think, &c., &c.—we need not multiply instances without recalling words which imply, whether in jest or earnest, these views or views like these—knowing this, can we wonder that many reformers think that measures are not likely to be taken in behalf of women, unless their wishes could be publicly represented by women?

"That can never be necessary," cry the other side. "All men are privately influenced by women; each has his wife, sister, or female friends, and is too much biased by these relations to fail of representing their interests; and if this is not enough, let them propose and enforce their wishes with the pen. The beauty of home would be destroyed, the delicacy of the sex be violated, the dignity of halls of legislation degraded by an attempt to introduce them there. Such duties are inconsistent with those of a mother"; and then we have ludicrous pictures of ladies in hysterics at the polls, and senate chambers filled with cradles.

But if in reply we admit as truth that Woman seems destined by nature rather for the inner circle, we must add that the arrangements of civilized life have not been as yet such as to secure it to her. Her circle, if the duller, is not the quieter. If kept from "excitement," she is not from drudgery. Not only the Indian squaw carries the burdens of the camp, but the favorites of Louis XIV accompany him in his journeys, and the washerwoman stands at her tub and carries home her work at all seasons and in all states of health. Those who think the physical circumstances of Woman would make a part in the affairs of national government unsuitable are by no means those who think it impossible for Negresses to endure field work even during pregnancy, or for seamstresses to go through their killing labors. . . .

While we hear from men who owe to their wives not only all that is comfortable or graceful but all that is wise in the arrangement of their lives the frequent remark, "You cannot reason with a woman"—when not one man in the million, shall I say? no, not in the hundred million, can rise above the belief that Woman was made *for Man*—when such traits as these are daily forced upon the attention, can we feel that Man will always do justice to the interests of Woman? Can we think that he takes a sufficiently discerning and religious view of her office and destiny *ever* to do her justice, except when prompted by sentiment? . . . The lover, the poet, the artist are likely to view her nobly. The father and the philosopher have some chance of liberality; the man of the world, the legislator for expediency none.

Under these circumstances, without attaching importance in themselves to the changes demanded by the champions of Woman, we hail them as signs of the times. We would have every arbitrary barrier thrown down. We would have every path laid open to Woman as freely as to Man. Were this done and a slight temporary fermentation allowed to subside, we should see crystallizations more pure and of more various beauty. We believe the divine energy would pervade nature to a degree unknown in the history of former ages, and that no discordant collision but a ravishing harmony of the spheres would ensue.

Yet then and only then will mankind be ripe for this, when inward and outward freedom for Woman as much as for Man shall be acknowledged as a *right*, not yielded as a concession. As the friend of the Negro assumes that one man cannot by right hold another in bondage, so should the friend of Woman assume that Man cannot by right lay even well-meant restrictions on Woman. If the Negro be a soul, if the woman be a soul, appareled in flesh, to one Master only are they accountable. There is but one law for souls, and if there is to be an interpreter of it, he must come not as man or son of man, but as son of God.

Were thought and feeling once so far elevated that Man should esteem himself the brother and friend, but nowise the lord and tutor, of Woman— were he really bound with her in equal worship—arrangements as to function and employment would be of no consequence. What Woman needs is not as a woman to act or rule, but as a nature to grow, as an intellect to discern, as a soul to live freely and unimpeded to unfold such powers as were given her when we left our common home. If fewer talents were given her, yet if allowed the free and full employment of these, so that she may render back to the giver his own with usury, she will not complain; nay, I dare to say she will bless and rejoice in her earthly birthplace, her earthly lot. . . .

It is not the transient breath of poetic incense that women want; each can receive that from a lover. It is not lifelong sway; it needs but to become a coquette, a shrew, or a good cook to be sure of that. It is not money nor notoriety nor the badges of authority which men have appropriated to themselves. If demands made in their behalf lay stress on any of these particulars, those who make them have not searched deeply into the need. The want is for that which at once includes these and precludes them; which would not be forbidden power, lest there be temptation to steal and misuse it; which would not have the mind perverted by flattery from a worthiness of esteem; it is for that which is the birthright of every being capable of receiving it—the freedom, the religious, the intelligent freedom of the universe to use its means, to learn its secret as far as Nature has enabled them, with God alone for their guide and their judge.

# 32

## WOMEN'S RIGHTS

In the first part of the nineteenth century, women in increasing numbers began asking for equality before the law and asserting their right to be educated, enter the professions, and participate in public affairs along with men. Some women became active in reform, participating in the temperance movement, the fight against slavery, and the crusade for world peace. But even as reformers they were required to take a subordinate position. When a woman tried to speak at a temperance convention in New York she was shouted down. One man yelled, "Shame on the woman, shame on the woman!" And when several women attended the World Anti-Slavery Convention in London in 1840, men refused to seat them as delegates and made them sit in a curtained enclosure out of the public view. Two delegates— Lucretia Mott and Elizabeth Cady Stanton—began talking of holding a convention to battle for their own rights.

In July 1848 the first organized meeting for women's rights ever held met in Seneca Falls, New York, attended by two hundred delegates, including thirty-two men. Stanton drew up the Declaration of Sentiments, using the Declaration of Independence as a model. She also drafted a series of resolutions that were adopted by the convention. Only one of her demands ran into trouble: the right to vote. Woman suffrage still seemed so outlandish that it took the eloquence of Frederick Douglass, a black abolitionist and journalist, to persuade the delegates to adopt it by a small majority. Many people were shocked by the Seneca Falls convention. They denounced the "Reign of Petticoats" and warned against the "Insurrection among Women." But many distinguished Americans—including Ralph Waldo Emerson, John Greenleaf Whittier, and William Lloyd Garrison—supported the movement.

Elizabeth Cady Stanton, who drafted the Seneca Falls Declaration, was born in Johnstown, New York, in 1815. She attended Emma Willard's seminary in Troy, and while studying law with her father, became aware of the injustices suffered by women from American legal practices. When she married the abolitionist lawyer Henry B. Stanton in 1840, she insisted that the word *obey* be omitted from the ceremony. At an antislavery convention that she attended with her husband the same year, she got to know Lucretia Mott, and the two of them began working together for women's rights. Following the Seneca Falls Conference, Stanton joined Mott (and later Susan B. Anthony) in sponsoring conventions, writing articles, delivering lectures, and appearing before legislative bodies on behalf of the cause. Despite Stanton's grace and charm, she was considered a dangerous radical for espousing woman suffrage and easier divorce laws for women. During the Civil War she helped organize the Women's Loyal National League and urged emancipation. After the war she resumed her work for woman suffrage, became president of the National Woman Suffrage Association, lectured on family life, wrote for *Revolution*, a women's rights weekly, and contributed to the three-volume *History of Woman Suffrage*, published in the 1880s. One of the most distinguished feminist leaders in the country, she died in New York City in 1902.

**Questions to Consider.** Many years passed before the women's rights movement in America began achieving some of its objectives. But the Seneca Falls convention marks the formal beginning of the organized movement to advance women's position, so it merits careful study. Do you think there were any advantages in using the Declaration of Independence as a model for the Declaration of Sentiments? Does the Seneca Falls Declaration emphasize legal, economic, or political rights? Were any rights overlooked? Some of those who signed the declaration withdrew their names when the suffrage resolution met with ridicule. Why do you suppose this happened? How radical do the Seneca Falls demands seem today? Which demands have been met by legislation since 1848?

# The Seneca Falls Declaration of 1848

ELIZABETH CADY STANTON

When, in the course of human events, it becomes necessary for one portion of the family of man to assume among the people of the earth a position different from that which they have hitherto occupied, but one to which the laws of nature and of nature's God entitle them, a decent respect to the opin-

From Susan B. Anthony, Elizabeth Cady Stanton, and Matilda Joslyn Gage, eds., *History of Woman Suffrage* (3 v., Susan B. Anthony, Elizabeth Cady Stanton, and Matilda Joslyn Gage, Rochester, N.Y., 1889), I: 75–80.

**Elizabeth Cady Stanton with two of her children about the time of the Seneca Falls Convention of 1848.** (Rhoda Barney Jenkins)

ions of mankind requires that they should declare the causes that impel them to such a course.

We hold these truths to be self-evident: that all men and women are created equal; that they are endowed by their Creator with certain inalienable rights; that among these are life, liberty, and the pursuit of happiness; that to secure these rights governments are instituted, deriving their just powers from the consent of the governed. . . . But when a long train of abuses and usurpations, pursuing invariably the same object evinces a design to reduce them under absolute despotism, it is their duty to throw off such government, and to provide new guards for their future security. Such has been the patient sufferance of the women under this government, and such is now the necessity which constrains them to demand the equal station to which they are entitled.

The history of mankind is a history of repeated injuries and usurpations on the part of man toward woman, having in direct object the establishment of an absolute tyranny over her. To prove this, let facts be submitted to a candid world.

He has never permitted her to exercise her inalienable right to the elective franchise.

He has compelled her to submit to laws, in the formation of which she had no voice.

He has withheld from her rights which are given to the most ignorant and degraded men—both natives and foreigners.

Having deprived her of this first right of a citizen, the elective franchise, thereby leaving her without representation in the halls of legislation, he has opposed her on all sides.

He has made her, if married, in the eye of the law, civilly dead.

He has taken from her all right in property, even to the wages she earns.

He has made her, morally, an irresponsible being, as she can commit many crimes with impunity, provided they be done in the presence of her husband. In the covenant of marriage, she is compelled to promise obedience to her husband, he becoming, to all intents and purposes, her master—the law giving him power to deprive her of her liberty, and to administer chastisement.

He has so framed the laws of divorce, as to what shall be the proper causes, and in case of separation, to whom the guardianship of the children shall be given, as to be wholly regardless of the happiness of women—the law, in all cases, going upon a false supposition of the supremacy of man, and giving all power into his hands.

After depriving her of all rights as a married woman, if single, and the owner of property, he has taxed her to support a government which recognizes her only when her property can be made profitable to it.

He has monopolized nearly all the profitable employments, and from those she is permitted to follow, she receives but a scanty remuneration. He closes against her all the avenues to wealth and distinction which he considers most honorable to himself. As a teacher of theology, medicine, or law, she is not known.

He has denied her the facilities for obtaining a thorough education, all colleges being closed against her.

He allows her in Church, as well as State, but a subordinate position, claiming Apostolic authority for her exclusion from the ministry, and, with some exceptions, from any public participation in the affairs of the Church.

He has created a false public sentiment by giving to the world a different code of morals for men and women, by which moral delinquencies which exclude women from society, are not only tolerated, but deemed of little account in man.

He has usurped the prerogative of Jehovah himself, claiming it as his right to assign for her a sphere of action, when that belongs to her conscience and to her God.

He has endeavored, in every way that he could, to destroy her confidence in her own powers, to lessen her self-respect, and to make her willing to lead a dependent and abject life.

Now, in view of this entire disfranchisement of one-half the people of this country, their social and religious degradation—in view of the unjust laws above mentioned, and because women do not feel themselves aggrieved, oppressed, and fraudulently deprived of their most sacred rights, we insist that they have immediate admission to all the rights and privileges which belong to them as citizens of the United States.

In entering upon the great work before us, we anticipate no small amount of misconception, misrepresentation, and ridicule; but we shall use every instrumentality within our power to effect our object. We shall employ agents, circulate tracts, petition the State and National legislatures, and endeavor to enlist the pulpit and the press in our behalf. We hope this Convention will be followed by a series of Conventions embracing every part of the country.

## Resolutions

WHEREAS, The great precept of nature is conceded to be, that "man shall pursue his own true and substantial happiness." Blackstone in his Commentaries remarks, that this law of Nature being coequal with mankind, and dictated by God himself, is of course superior in obligation to any other. It is binding over all the globe, in all countries and at all times; no human laws are of any validity if contrary to this, . . . therefore,

*Resolved,* That such laws as conflict, in any way, with the true and substantial happiness of woman, are contrary to the great precept of nature and of no validity, for this is "superior in obligation to any other."

*Resolved,* That all laws which prevent woman from occupying such a station in society as her conscience shall dictate, or which place her in a position inferior to that of man, are contrary to the great precept of nature, and therefore of no force or authority.

*Resolved,* That woman is man's equal—was intended to be so by the Creator, and the highest good of the race demands that she should be recognized as such.

*Resolved,* That the women of this country ought to be enlightened in regard to the laws under which they live, that they may no longer publish their degradation by declaring themselves satisfied with their present position, nor their ignorance, by asserting that they have all the rights they want.

*Resolved,* That inasmuch as man, while claiming for himself intellectual superiority, does accord to woman moral superiority, it is pre-eminently his duty to encourage her to speak and teach, as she has an opportunity, in all religious assemblies.

*Resolved,* That the same amount of virtue, delicacy, and refinement of behavior that is required of woman in the social state, should also be required of man, and the same transgressions should be visited with equal severity on both man and woman.

*Resolved,* That the objection of indelicacy and impropriety, which is so often brought against woman when she addresses a public audience, comes with a very ill-grace from those who encourage, by their attendance, her appearance on the stage, in the concert, or in feats of the circus.

*Resolved,* That woman has too long rested satisfied in the circumscribed limits which corrupt customs and a perverted application of the Scriptures have marked out for her, and that it is time she should move in the enlarged sphere which her great Creator has assigned her.

*Resolved,* That it is the duty of the women of this country to secure to themselves their sacred right to the elective franchise.

*Resolved,* That the equality of human rights results necessarily from the fact of the identity of the race in capabilities and responsibilities.

*Resolved, therefore,* That, being invested by the Creator with the same capabilities, and the same consciousness of responsibility for their exercise, it is demonstrably the right and duty of woman, equally with man, to promote every righteous cause by every righteous means; and especially in regard to the great subjects of morals and religion, it is self-evidently her right to participate with her brother in teaching them, both in private and in public, by writing and by speaking, by any instrumentalities proper to be used, and in any assemblies proper to be held; and this being a self-evident truth growing out of the divinely implanted principles of human nature, any custom or authority adverse to it, whether modern or wearing the hoary sanction of antiquity, is to be regarded as a self-evident falsehood, and at war with mankind.

# 33

## THE ANTISLAVERY IMPULSE

Women played a major role in the antislavery struggle. They helped sensitize the Protestant churches to the evils of slavery and organized petition drives urging Congress to abolish the slave trade. At a time when the male-dominant mainstream culture of the United States was intolerant of women who commented on political issues, many women wrote and spoke out against slavery. No woman was more important in this struggle than Harriet Beecher Stowe, whose novel *Uncle Tom's Cabin* (excerpted below) made the nation feel "what an accursed thing slavery is." Some readers believed the novel moved the nation closer to civil war—a view apparently shared by Abraham Lincoln, who remarked on meeting Stowe, "So this is the little lady who made this big war."

*Uncle Tom's Cabin* may not have "caused" the Civil War. But by 1852, when the book was published, the nation was enveloped in an atmosphere charged with sectional suspicion and hatred. The Compromise of 1850, an effort to cobble North and South together, was unraveling because Northerners, many of whom were set aflame by the novel, resisted the Fugitive Slave Law. In 1854 bitter fighting between proslavery and antislavery forces broke out in "Bleeding Kansas." In 1856 Preston Brooks, a representative from South Carolina, brutally beat Charles Sumner, an antislavery senator from Massachusetts, as he sat at his desk in the Senate chamber. For Northerners, the episode was a symbol of Southern bestiality. For Southerners, Brooks was a hero.

As these events inflamed sectional feelings, *Uncle Tom's Cabin* engaged readers to an extraordinary degree. It was so sensational and moving a tale about life under slavery that it became a testament of Northern abolitionists and compelled readers who had never given slavery much thought to feel somehow responsible for its horrors. In the South, which instantly denounced the novel, it was actually dangerous to possess a copy. Sales were so great that Stowe's Boston publisher could not find enough paper to meet the demand. Thousands of Americans also attended stage versions. Perhaps no other novel in history has matched the influence of *Uncle Tom's Cabin*, which brought the author international acclaim and made her a much sought-after lecturer.

Harriet Beecher Stowe was born in Connecticut in 1811. The daughter of Lyman Beecher, a famous Calvinist minister, in 1832 she went to Cincinnati with her father, who became president of Lane Theological Seminary. She married a Lane professor in 1836, began to write magazine stories, and after moving to Maine in 1850, where her husband taught and preached, began work on a novel, *Uncle Tom's Cabin*, based on what she learned of the South while living in Ohio, just across the river from the slave plantations of Kentucky. In answer to questions about the novel's immense power, Stowe was fond of saying that God wrote it, that she was simply the instrument of His will and not its true author. Biographers have used this to argue her modesty. But Stowe was the daughter of a Calvinist and so was ready to see God's hand in every event. She continued to write for the next twenty years, producing a steady stream of excellent novels, stories, and articles about slavery and life in old New England. She died in Hartford in 1896.

**Questions to Consider.** Why was Eliza, the slave, attempting to escape? What emotion was Harriet Beecher Stowe counting on to engage her readers? How did Eliza manage to avoid detection? Would a typical slave have been able to do this? In what ways was Eliza not typical? Why was Sam, another slave, in the slave-catching party? What point was Stowe making in having Sam help Eliza escape capture by the trick of losing his hat? What was on the other side of the river? By what device did Stowe try to enlist the sympathies of male as well as female readers?

# Uncle Tom's Cabin (1851)

HARRIET BEECHER STOWE

It is impossible to conceive of a human creature more wholly desolate and forlorn than Eliza [a slave], when she turned her footsteps from Uncle Tom's cabin [on a Kentucky plantation].

Her husband's suffering and dangers, and the danger of her child, all blended in her mind, with a confused and stunning sense of the risk she was running, in leaving the only home she had ever known, and cutting loose

From Harriet Beecher Stowe, *Uncle Tom's Cabin*, chapter 7, "The Mother's Struggle," (New York, 1852), 60–74.

from the protection of a friend whom she loved and revered. Then there was the parting from every familiar object,—the place where she had grown up, the trees under which she had played, the groves where she had walked many an evening in happier days, by the side of her young husband,—everything, as it lay in the clear, frosty starlight, seemed to speak reproachfully to her, and ask her whither she could go from a home like that?

But stronger than all was maternal love, wrought into a paroxysm of frenzy by the near approach of a fearful danger. Her boy was old enough to have walked by her side, and, in an indifferent case, she would only have led him by the hand; but now the bare thought of putting him out of her arms made her shudder, and she strained him to her bosom with a convulsive grasp, as she went rapidly forward.

The frosty ground creaked beneath her feet, and she trembled at the sound; every quaking leaf and fluttering shadow sent the blood backward to her heart, and quickened her footsteps. She wondered within herself at the strength that seemed to be come upon her; for she felt the weight of her boy as if it had been a feather, and every flutter of fear seemed to increase the supernatural power that bore her on, while from her pale lips burst forth, in frequent ejaculations, the prayer to a Friend above,—"Lord, help! Lord, save me!"

If it were *your* Harry, mother, or your Willie, that were going to be torn from you by a brutal trader, to-morrow morning,—if you had seen the man, and heard that the papers were signed and delivered, and you had only from twelve o'clock till morning to make good your escape,—how fast could *you* walk? How many miles could you make in those few brief hours, with the darling at your bosom,—the little sleepy head on your shoulder,—the small, soft arms trustingly holding on to your neck?

For the child slept. At first, the novelty and alarm kept him waking; but his mother so hurriedly repressed every breath or sound, and so assured him that if he were only still she would certainly save him, that he clung quietly round her neck, only asking, as he found himself sinking to sleep,—

"Mother, I don't need to keep awake, do I?"

"No, my darling; sleep, if you want to."

"But, mother, if I do get asleep, you won't let him get me?"

"No! so may God help me!" said his mother, with a paler cheek and a brighter light in her large, dark eyes.

"You 're *sure,* an't you, mother?"

"Yes, *sure!*" said the mother, in a voice that startled herself; for it seemed to her to come from a spirit within, that was no part of her; and the boy dropped his little weary head on her shoulder and was soon asleep. How the touch of those warm arms, and gentle breathings that came in her neck, seemed to add fire and spirit to her movements. It seemed to her as if strength poured into her in electric streams, from every gentle touch and movement of the sleeping, confiding child. Sublime is the dominion of the mind over the body, that, for a time, can make flesh and nerve impregnable, and string the sinews like steel, so that the weak become so mighty.

**Eliza, the runaway slave, crossing the Ohio River with her baby to freedom, from the frontispiece of an 1853 collection of scenes for children drawn from Harriet Beecher Stowe's *Uncle Tom's Cabin.*** Eliza and her baby had light complexions in the book—in contrast, for example, to the dark-skinned field hands in the plantation view at the top of the page. Eliza's skin color enabled her to "pass" at times for a European American and thus facilitated her escape to the free state of Ohio. (New York Historical Society)

The boundaries of the farm, the grove, the wood-lot, passed by her dizzily, as she walked on; and still she went, leaving one familiar object after another, slacking not, pausing not, till reddening daylight found her many a long mile from all traces of any familiar objects upon the open highway.

She had often been, with her mistress, to visit some connections, in the little village of T———, not far from the Ohio River, and knew the road well. To go thither, to escape across the Ohio River, were the first hurried outlines of her plan of escape; beyond that, she could only hope in God.

When horses and vehicles began to move along the highway, with that alert perception peculiar to a state of excitement, and which seems to be a sort of inspiration, she became aware that her headlong pace and distracted air might bring on her remark and suspicion. She therefore put the boy on the ground, and, adjusting her dress and bonnet, she walked on at as rapid a pace as she thought consistent with the preservation of appearances. In her little bundle she had provided a store of cakes and apples, which she used as expedients for quickening the speed of the child, rolling the apple some yards before them, when the boy would run with all his might after it; and this ruse, often repeated, carried them over many a half-mile.

After a while, they came to a thick patch of woodland, through which murmured a clear brook. As the child complained of hunger and thirst, she climbed over the fence with him; and, sitting down behind a large rock which concealed them from the road, she gave him a breakfast out of her little package. The boy wondered and grieved that she could not eat; and when, putting his arms round her neck, he tried to wedge some of his cake into her mouth, it seemed to her that the rising in her throat would choke her.

"No, no, Harry darling! mother can't eat till you are safe! We must go on,—on,—till we come to the river!" And she hurried again into the road, and again constrained herself to walk regularly and composedly forward.

She was many miles past any neighborhood where she was personally known. If she should chance to meet any who knew her, she reflected that the well-known kindness of the family would be of itself a blind to suspicion, as making it an unlikely supposition that she could be a fugitive. As she was also so white as not to be known as of colored lineage, without a critical survey, and her child was white also, it was much easier for her to pass on unsuspected.

On this presumption, she stopped at noon at a neat farmhouse, to rest herself, and buy some dinner for her child and self; for, as the danger decreased with the distance, the supernatural tension of the nervous system lessened, and she found herself both weary and hungry.

The good woman, kindly and gossiping, seemed rather pleased than otherwise with having somebody come in to talk with; and accepted, without examination, Eliza's statement, that she "was going on a little piece, to spend a week with her friends,"—all which she hoped in her heart might prove strictly true.

An hour before sunset, she entered the village of T———, by the Ohio River, weary and footsore, but still strong in heart. Her first glance was at the river, which lay, like Jordan, between her and the Canaan of liberty on the other side.

It was now early spring, and the river was swollen and turbulent; great cakes of floating ice were swinging heavily to and fro in the turbid waters. Owing to the peculiar form of the shore on the Kentucky side, the land bending far out into the water, the ice had been lodged and detained in great quantities, and the narrow channel which swept round the bend was full of ice, piled one cake over another, thus forming a temporary barrier to the descending ice, which lodged, and formed a great, undulating raft, filling up the whole river, and extending almost to the Kentucky shore.

Eliza stood, for a moment, contemplating this unfavorable aspect of things, which she saw at once must prevent the usual ferry-boat from running, and then turned into a small public house on the bank, to make a few inquiries.

The hostess, who was busy in various fizzing and stewing operations over the fire, preparatory to the evening meal, stopped, with a fork in her hand, as Eliza's sweet and plaintive voice arrested her.

"What is it?" she said.

"Is n't there any ferry or boat, that takes people over to B———, now?" she said.

"No, indeed!" said the woman; "the boats has stopped running."

Eliza's look of dismay and disappointment struck the woman, and she said, inquiringly,—

"May be you're wanting to get over?—anybody sick? Ye seem mighty anxious?"

"I 've got a child that 's very dangerous," said Eliza. "I never heard of it till last night, and I 've walked quite a piece to-day, in hopes to get to the ferry."

"Well, now, that 's onlucky," said the woman, whose motherly sympathies were much aroused; "I 'm re'lly consarned for ye. Solomon!" she called, from the window, towards a small back building. A man, in leather apron and very dirty hands, appeared at the door.

"I say, Sol," said the woman, "is that ar man going to tote them bar'ls over to-night?"

"He said he should try, if 't was any way prudent," said the man.

"There 's a man a piece down here, that 's going over with some truck this evening, if he durs' to; he 'll be in here to supper to-night, so you 'd better set down and wait. That 's a sweet little fellow," added the woman, offering him a cake.

But the child, wholly exhausted, cried with weariness.

"Poor fellow! he is n't used to walking, and I 've hurried him on so," said Eliza.

"Well, take him into this room," said the woman, opening into a small bedroom, where stood a comfortable bed. Eliza laid the weary boy upon it, and held his hands in hers till he was fast asleep. For her there was no rest. As a fire in her bones, the thought of the pursuer urged her on; and she gazed with longing eyes on the sullen, surging waters that lay between her and liberty. . . .

In consequence of all the various delays, it was about three quarters of an hour after Eliza had laid her child to sleep in the village tavern that the [slave-chasing] party came riding into the same place. Eliza was standing by the window, looking out in another direction, when Sam's [a slave from Eliza's plantation and a friend] quick eye caught a glimpse of her. Haley and Andy were two yards behind. At this crisis, Sam contrived to have his hat blown off, and uttered a loud and characteristic ejaculation, which startled her at once; she drew suddenly back; the whole train swept by the window, round to the front door.

A thousand lives seemed to be concentrated in that one moment to Eliza. Her room opened by a side door to the river. She caught her child, and sprang down the steps towards it. The trader caught a full glimpse of her, just as she was disappearing down the bank, and throwing himself from his horse, and calling loudly on Sam and Andy, he was after her like a hound after a deer. In that dizzy moment her feet to her scarce seemed to touch the ground, and a moment brought her to the water's edge. Right on behind her they came; and, nerved with strength such as God gives only to the desperate, with one wild cry and flying leap, she vaulted sheer over the turbid current by the shore, on to the raft of ice beyond. It was a desperate leap,—impossible to anything but madness and despair; and Haley, Sam, and Andy instinctively cried out, and lifted up their hands, as she did it.

The huge green fragment of ice on which she alighted pitched and creaked as her weight came on it, but she stayed there not a moment. With wild cries and desperate energy she leaped to another and still another cake;—stumbling,—leaping,—slipping,—springing upwards again! Her shoes are gone,—her stockings cut from her feet,—while blood marked every step; but she saw nothing, felt nothing, till dimly, as in a dream, she saw the Ohio side, and a man helping her up the bank.

"Yer a brave gal, now, whoever ye ar!" said the man, with an oath.

Eliza recognized the voice and face of a man who owned a farm not far from her old home.

"Oh, Mr. Symmes!—save me,—do save me,—do hide me!" said Eliza.

"Why, what 's this?" said the man. "Why, if 't an't Shelby's gal!"

"My child!—this boy!—he 'd sold him! There is his Mas'r," said she, pointing to the Kentucky shore. "Oh, Mr. Symmes, you 've got a little boy!"

"So I have," said the man, as he roughly, but kindly, drew her up the steep bank. "Besides, you 're a right brave gal. I like grit, wherever I see it."

When they had gained the top of the bank, the man paused. "I 'd be glad to do something for ye," said he; "but then there 's nowhar I could take ye. The best I can do is to tell ye to go *thar*," said he, pointing to a large white house which stood by itself, off the main street of the village. "Go thar; they 're kind folks. Thar 's no kind o' danger but they 'll help you,—they 're up to all that sort o' thing."

"The Lord bless you!" said Eliza earnestly.

"No 'casion, no 'casion in the world," said the man. "What I 've done 's of no 'count."

"And oh, surely, sir, you won't tell any one!"

"Go to thunder, gal! What do you take a feller for? In course not," said the man. "Come, now, go along like a likely, sensible gal, as you are. You 've arnt your liberty, and you shall have it, for all me."

# ★ 34 ★

## RACE, SLAVERY, AND THE CONSTITUTION

The spread of slavery during the early nineteenth century divided the nation and so fanned the flames of sectionalism that the United States was able to remain united only by careful political compromise between North and South. The Missouri Compromise of 1820 admitted Maine, a free state, and Missouri, a slave state, to the Union about the same time, thus preserving the balance between the two sections; it also barred slavery from all territories north of a line (36°30′N) drawn westward from Missouri's southern border. The Compromise of 1850 admitted California as a free state but organized New Mexico and Utah on the principle of popular sovereignty, with slavery left to the inhabitants' decision.

In 1854 Congress violated the Missouri Compromise line. By the Kansas-Nebraska Act of that year, sponsored by Illinois Senator Stephen A. Douglas, who wanted settlers to decide whether or not to have slavery, territory north of 36°30′N was opened to slavery on a "local option" basis. The result was a bloody conflict in Kansas between free-soil settlers opposed to slavery there and those favoring slavery. In 1857, moreover, Chief Justice Roger B. Taney's opinion in the *Dred Scott* case placed the Supreme Court squarely behind the institution of slavery. (A Missouri slave, Dred Scott, had sued his master for freedom, basing his case on the fact that they had lived for a time in free territory.) Speaking for the majority of the justices, Taney announced that blacks could not be American citizens and that Congress could not prohibit slavery even in territories under its direct jurisdiction. The *Dred Scott* decision made all previous compromises over slavery unconstitutional. It also exacerbated sectional tensions. Proslavery Southerners were anxious to extend slavery into new areas; antislavery Northerners were just as determined to do all they could to prevent the further expansion of human bondage despite the Court's ruling. Even Northerners who were not abolitionists opposed Taney's decision. They did not like the idea of Southerners bringing their slaves into the federal territories.

Roger Taney was born in 1777 in Maryland, where he practiced law for a time and then entered politics. An early supporter of Andrew Jackson, he became attorney general in 1831 and helped draft Jackson's message to Congress in 1832 vetoing the recharter bill for the Bank of the United States. In 1836 Jackson made Taney chief justice of the Supreme Court. Taney's major opinion before *Dred Scott* was an antimonopoly decision in the *Charles River Bridge* case in 1837. After the *Dred Scott* decision, Taney's prestige declined rapidly, and it all but disappeared after the Republican victory in 1860. He died in Washington four years later.

Scott himself became free because when his master died, the widow married an abolitionist who arranged for Scott's freedom. Scott became a hotel porter in St. Louis and died there of tuberculosis a year after the Supreme Court decision.

**Questions to Consider.** The *Dred Scott* decision purports to cite historical facts as well as advance opinions about those facts. How accurate is Taney's statement that American blacks had never possessed any of the rights and privileges the U.S. Constitution confers on citizens? Why did he make a careful distinction between the rights of citizenship that a state may confer and the rights conferred by the federal Constitution? Do you think Taney's position on the right of states "to confer on whomever it pleased the character of citizen" had implications that he did not intend? Note that Taney insisted that Dred Scott, not being a citizen, was "not entitled to sue in the courts." If he believed this, why did he agree to rule on the case at all? Was he correct in saying that when the nation was founded "no one thought of disputing" the idea that "the negro might justly and lawfully be reduced to slavery"? Do you think his reference to the constitutional provision permitting the slave trade until 1808 strengthened his arguments? Note that in order to find the Missouri Compromise unconstitutional, Taney maintained that the clause in the Constitution giving Congress power to regulate the federal territories applied only to territories belonging to the United States at the time the Constitution was adopted. Do you think he made a convincing case for this assertion? Would Taney's insistence that Congress cannot prohibit slavery in the federal territories logically apply to whites as well as blacks?

# *Dred Scott* v. *Sanford* (1857)

ROGER B. TANEY

The question is simply this: Can a negro, whose ancestors were imported into this country, and sold as slaves, become a member of the political com-

From 19 *Howard* 393 (1857).

munity formed and brought into existence by the Constitution of the United States, and as such become entitled to all the rights, and privileges, and immunities, guaranteed by that instrument to the citizen? One of which rights is the privilege of suing in a court of the United States in the cases specified in the Constitution.

It will be observed, that the plea applies to that class of persons only whose ancestors were negroes of the African race, and imported into this country, and sold and held as slaves. The only matter in issue before the court, therefore, is, whether the descendants of such slaves, when they shall be emancipated, or who are born of parents who had become free before their birth, are citizens of a State, in the sense in which the word citizen is used in the Constitution of the United States. And this being the only matter in dispute on the pleadings, the court must be understood as speaking in this opinion of that class only, that is of persons who are the descendants of Africans who were imported into this country and sold as slaves. . . .

We proceed to examine the case as presented by the pleadings.

The words "people of the United States" and "citizens" are synonymous terms, and mean the same thing. They both describe the political body who, according to our republican institutions, form the sovereignty, and who hold the power and conduct the government through their representatives. They are what we familiarly call the "sovereign people," and every citizen is one of this people, and a constituent member of this sovereignty. The question before us is, whether the class of persons described in the plea in abatement compose a portion of this people, and are constituent members of this sovereignty? We think they are not, and that they are not included, and were not intended to be included, under the word "citizens" in the Constitution, and can, therefore, claim none of the rights and privileges which that instrument provides for and secures to citizens of the United States. On the contrary, they were at that time considered as a subordinate and inferior class of beings, who had been subjugated by the dominant race, and whether emancipated or not, yet remained subject to their authority, and had no rights or privileges but such as those who held the power and the government might choose to grant them. . . .

In discussing this question, we must not confound the rights of citizenship which a state may confer within its own limits, and the rights of citizenship as a member of the Union. It does not by any means follow, because he has all the rights and privileges of a citizen of a State, that he must be a citizen of the United States. He may have all of the rights and privileges of a State, and yet not be entitled to the rights and privileges of a citizen in any other State. For, previous to the adoption of the Constitution of the United States, every State had the undoubted right to confer on whomsoever it pleased the character of a citizen, and to endow him with all its rights. But this character, of course, was confined to the boundaries of the State, and gave him no rights or privileges in other States beyond those secured to him by the laws of nations and the comity [mutual jurisdiction] of States. Nor have the several States surrendered the power of conferring these rights and privileges by adopting the Constitution of the United States. Each State may still confer them upon an alien, or any one it thinks proper, or upon any class or description of persons; yet he would not be a citizen in the sense in which that word is used in the Constitution of the United States, nor entitled to sue as such in one of its courts, nor to the privileges and immunities of a citizen in the other States. The rights which he would acquire would be restricted to the State which gave them. . . .

The question then arises, whether the provisions of the Constitution, in relation to the personal rights and privileges to which the citizen of a State should be entitled, embraced the negro African race, at that time in this country, or who might afterwards be imported, who had then or should afterwards be made free in any State; and to put it in the power of a single State to make him a citizen of the United States, and endue him with the full rights of citizenship in every other State without their consent. Does the Constitution of the United States act upon him whenever he shall be made free under the laws of a State, and raised there to the rank of a citizen, and immediately clothe him with all the privileges of a citizen in every other State, and in its own courts?

The court think the affirmative of these propositions cannot be maintained. And if it cannot, the plaintiff in error could not be a citizen of the State of Missouri, within the meaning of the Constitution of the United States, and, consequently, was not entitled to sue in its courts. . . .

It is difficult at this day to realize the state of public opinion in relation to that unfortunate race, which prevailed in the civilized and enlightened portions of the world at the time of the Declaration of Independence, and when the Constitution of the United States was framed and adopted. . . .

They had for more than a century before been regarded as beings of an inferior order; and altogether unfit to associate with the white race, either in social or political relations; and so far inferior that they had no rights which the white man was bound to respect; and that the negro might justly and lawfully be reduced to slavery for his benefit. . . . This opinion was at that time fixed and universal in the civilized portion of the white race. It was regarded as an axiom in morals as well as in politics, which no one thought of disputing, or supposed to be open to dispute; and men in every grade and position in society daily and habitually acted upon it in their private pursuits, as well as in matters of public concern, without doubting for a moment the correctness of this opinion. . . .

But there are two clauses in the Constitution which point directly and specifically to the negro race as a separate class of persons, and show clearly that they were not regarded as a portion of the people or citizens of the Government then formed.

One of these clauses reserves to each of the thirteen States the right to import slaves until the year 1808, if he thinks it proper. And the importation which it thus sanctions was unquestionably of persons of the race of which we are speaking, as the traffic in slaves in the United States had always been confined to them. And by the other provision the States pledge themselves to each other to maintain the right of property of the master, by delivering up to him any slave who may have escaped from his service, and be found within their respective territories. . . . And these two provisions show, conclusively, that neither the description of persons therein referred to, nor their descendants, were embraced in any of the other provisions of the Constitution; for certainly these two clauses were not intended to confer on them or their posterity the blessings of liberty, or any of the personal rights so carefully provided for the citizen. . . .

Indeed, when we look to the condition of this race in the several States at the time, it is impossible to believe that these rights and privileges were intended to be extended to them. . . .

The Act of Congress, upon which the plaintiff relies, declares that slavery and involuntary servitude, except as a punishment for crime, shall be forever prohibited in all that part of the territory ceded by France, under the name of Louisiana, which lies north of thirty-six degrees thirty minutes north latitude, and not included within the limits of Missouri. And the difficulty which meets us at the threshold of this part of the inquiry is, whether Congress was authorized to pass this law under any of the powers granted to it by the Constitution; for if the authority is not given by that instrument, it is the duty of this court to declare it void and inoperative, and incapable of conferring freedom upon any one who is held as a slave under the laws of any one of the States.

The counsel for the plaintiff has laid much stress upon that article in the Constitution which confers on Congress the power "to dispose of and make all needful rules and regulations respecting the territory or other property belonging to the United States," but, in the judgment of the court, that provision has no bearing on the present controversy, and the power there given, whatever it may be, is confined, and was intended to be confined, to the territory which at that time belonged to, or was claimed by, the United States, and was within their boundaries as settled by the treaty with Great Britain, and can have no influence upon a territory afterwards acquired from a foreign Government. It was a special provision for a known and particular territory, and to meet a present emergency, and nothing more. . . .

If this clause is construed to extend to territory acquired by the present Government from a foreign nation, outside of the limits of any charter from the British Government to a colony, it would be difficult to say, why it was deemed necessary to give the Government the power to sell any vacant lands belonging to the sovereignty which might be found within it; and if this was necessary, why the grant of this power should precede the power to legislate over it and establish a Government there; and still more difficult to say, why it was deemed necessary so specially and particularly to grant the power to make needful rules and regulations in relation to any personal or movable property it might acquire there. For the words, *other property* necessarily, by every known rule of interpretation, must mean property of a different description from territory or land. And the difficulty would perhaps be insurmountable in endeavoring to account for the last member of the sentence, which provides that "nothing in this Constitution shall be so construed as to prejudice any claims of the United States or any particular State," or to say how any particular State could have claims in or to a territory ceded by a foreign Government, or to account for associating this provision with the preceding provisions of the clause, with which it would appear to have no connection. . . .

The rights of private property have been guarded. . . . Thus the rights of property are united with the rights of person, and placed on the same ground by the fifth amendment to the Constitution. . . . An Act of Congress which deprives a person of the United States of his liberty or property merely because he came himself or brought his property into a particular Territory of the United States, and who had committed no offense against the laws, could hardly be dignified with the name of due process of law. . . .

It seems, however, to be supposed, that there is a difference between property in a slave and other property, and that different rules may be applied to it in expounding the Constitution of the United States. And the laws and usages of nations, and the writings of eminent jurists upon the relation of master and slave and their mutual rights and duties, and the powers which governments may exercise over it, have been dwelt upon in the argument.

But . . . if the Constitution recognizes the right of property of the master in a slave, and makes no distinction between that description of property and other property owned by a citizen, no tribunal, acting under the authority of the United States, whether it be legislative, executive, or judicial, has a right to draw such a distinction, or deny to it the benefit of the provisions and guarantees which have been provided for the protection of private property against the encroachments of the Government.

Now . . . the right of property in a slave is distinctly and expressly affirmed in the Constitution. The right to traffic in it, like an ordinary article of merchandise and property, was guaranteed to the citizens of the United States, in every State that might desire it, for twenty years. And the Government in express terms is pledged to protect it in all future time, if the slave escapes from his owner. . . . And no word can be found in the Constitution which gives Congress a greater power over slave property, or which entitles property of that kind to less protection than property of any other description. The only power conferred is the power coupled with the duty of guarding and protecting the owner in his rights.

Upon these considerations, it is the opinion of the court that the Act of Congress which prohibited a citizen from holding and owning property of this kind in the territory of the United States north of the line therein mentioned, is not warranted by the Constitution, and is therefore void; and that neither Dred Scott himself, nor any of his family, were made free by being carried into this territory; even if they had been carried there by the owner, with the intention of becoming a permanent resident.

# 35

## LIBERTY AND UNION

The great vehicle for antislavery politics was the Republican party. Founded in Ripon, Wisconsin, in 1854, the new party rapidly absorbed members of earlier, smaller antislavery organizations by pledging itself to oppose the further extension of slavery in the United States. In the election of 1856, the Republicans showed amazing strength: their candidate, John C. Frémont, won 1,339,932 popular and 114 electoral votes to Democratic candidate James Buchanan's 1,832,955 popular and 174 electoral votes. During the next four years the party broadened its appeal to attract industrialists and workers as well as farmers, professional people, and religious leaders who were opposed to slavery. It also developed able party leaders and made impressive gains at the state and congressional levels.

The Republican party's 1860 platform not only upheld the Union and reiterated its stand against the extension of slavery but also contained a number of economic planks that would appeal to industrialists in the Northeast and farmers in the West. It favored a protective tariff, the building of a transcontinental railroad, and a homestead act giving free land to settlers. Adopted in Chicago in May 1860, the platform conformed closely to the views of such moderates as William H. Seward and Horace Greeley of New York, Benjamin F. Wade and Salmon P. Chase of Ohio, and its standard-bearer, Abraham Lincoln of Illinois. Only when leading abolitionists threatened to walk out of the convention did Republican leaders incorporate a reaffirmation of the Declaration of Independence into their platform. But though the Republicans took a moderate position in their platform, the victory of Lincoln in the 1860 election triggered secession and civil war.

**Questions to Consider.** To what did the Republican platform refer when it announced that events of the past four years had established the necessity of organizing a new party? Do you agree with the statement that the principles of the Declaration of Independence are "essential to the preservation of our Republican institutions"? Do you agree with the assertion that "threats of Disunion" are equivalent to "an avowal of contemplated treason"? In denouncing "the lawless invasion by armed force of the soil of any State or Territory," what did the platform makers have in mind? What did the platform say about Kansas and the *Dred Scott* decision? What dominated the platform, the slavery issue or economic issues? On balance, to whom was the platform supposed to appeal?

# The Republican Party Platform of 1860

*Resolved,* That we, the delegated representatives of the Republican electors of the United States, in Convention assembled, in discharge of the duty we owe to our constituents and our country, unite in the following declarations:

1. That the history of the nation, during the last four years, has fully established the propriety and necessity of the organization and perpetuation of the Republican party, and that the causes which called it into existence are permanent in their nature, and now, more than ever before, demand its peaceful and constitutional triumph.

2. That the maintenance of the principles promulgated in the Declaration of Independence and embodied in the Federal Constitution, "That all men are created equal; that they are endowed by their Creator with certain inalienable rights; that among these are life, liberty and the pursuit of happiness; that, to secure these rights, governments are instituted among men, deriving their just powers from the consent of the governed," is essential to the preservation of our Republican institutions, and that the Federal Constitution, the Rights of the States, and the Union of the States, must and shall be preserved.

3. That to the Union of the States this nation owes its unprecedented increase in population, its surprising development of material resources, its rapid augmentation of wealth, its happiness at home and its honor abroad; and we hold in abhorrence all schemes for Disunion, come from whatever source they may; And we congratulate the country that no Republican member of Congress has uttered or countenanced the threats of Disunion so often made by Democratic members, without rebuke and with applause from their political associates; and we denounce those threats of Disunion, in case of a popular overthrow of their ascendancy, as denying the vital principles of a free government, and as an avowal of contemplated treason, which it is the imperative duty of an indignant People sternly to rebuke and forever silence.

4. That the maintenance inviolate of the rights of the States, and especially the right of each State to order and control its own domestic institu-

From Francis Curtis, *The Republican Party* (2 v., G. P. Putnam's Sons, New York, 1904), I: 355–358.

tions according to its own judgment exclusively, is essential to that balance of powers on which the perfection and endurance of our political fabric depends; and we denounce the lawless invasion by armed forces of the soil of any State or Territory, no matter under what pretext, as among the gravest of crimes.

5. That the present Democratic Administration has far exceeded our worst apprehensions, in its measureless subserviency to the exactions of a sectional interest, as especially evinced in its desperate exertions to force the infamous Lecompton constitution[1] upon the protesting people of Kansas; in construing the personal relation between master and servant to involve an unqualified property in persons; in its attempted enforcement, everywhere, on land and sea, through the intervention of Congress and of the Federal Courts of the extreme pretensions of a purely local interest; and in its general and unvarying abuse of the power intrusted to it by a confiding people. . . .

7. That the new dogma that the Constitution, of its own force, carries Slavery into any or all of the Territories of the United States, is a dangerous political heresy, at variance with the explicit provisions of that instrument itself, with contemporaneous exposition, and with legislative and judicial precedent; is revolutionary in its tendency, and subversive of the peace and harmony of the country.

8. That the normal condition of all the territory of the United States is that of freedom; That as our Republican fathers, when they had abolished slavery in all our national territory, ordained that "no person should be deprived of life, liberty, or property, without due process of law," it becomes our duty, by legislation, whenever such legislation is necessary, to maintain this provision of the Constitution against all attempts to violate it; and we deny the authority of Congress, of a territorial legislature, or of any individuals, to give legal existence to Slavery in any Territory of the United States.

9. That we brand the recent re-opening of the African slave-trade, under the cover of our national flag, aided by perversions of judicial power, as a crime against humanity and a burning shame to our country and age; and we call upon Congress to take prompt and efficient measures for the total and final suppression of that execrable traffic.

10. That in the recent vetoes, by their Federal Governors, of the acts of the Legislatures of Kansas and Nebraska, prohibiting Slavery in those territories, we find a practical illustration of the boasted Democratic principle of Non-Intervention and Popular Sovereignty embodied in the Kansas-Nebraska bill, and a demonstration of the deception and fraud involved therein.

---

1. **Lecompton constitution:** A proslavery constitution adopted by a proslavery legislature in 1857 and not submitted to a popular vote.—*Eds.*

11. That Kansas should, of right, be immediately admitted as a State under the Constitution recently formed and adopted by her people, and accepted by the House of Representatives.

12. That, while providing revenue for the support of the General Government by duties upon imports, sound policy requires such an adjustment of these imposts as to encourage the development of the industrial interests of the whole country; and we commend that policy of national exchanges which secures to the working men liberal wages, to agriculture remunerating prices, to mechanics and manufacturers an adequate reward for their skill, labor and enterprise, and to the nation commercial prosperity and independence.

13. That we protest against any sale or alienation to others of the Public Lands held by actual settlers, and against any view of the Homestead policy which regards the settlers as paupers or supplicants for public bounty; and we demand the passage by Congress of the complete and satisfactory Homestead measure which has already passed the House.

14. That the Republican Party is opposed to any change in our Naturalization Laws or any State legislation by which the rights of our citizenship hitherto accorded to immigrants from foreign lands shall be abridged or impaired; and in favor of giving a full and efficient protection to the rights of all classes of citizens, whether native or naturalized, both at home and abroad.

15. That appropriations by Congress for River and Harbor improvements of a National character, required for the accommodation and security of an existing commerce, are authorized by the Constitution, and justified by the obligations of Government to protect the lives and property of its citizens.

16. That a Railroad to the Pacific Ocean is imperatively demanded by the interests of the whole country; that the Federal Government ought to render immediate and efficient aid in its construction; and that, as preliminary thereto, a daily Overland Mail should be promptly established.

**The bombardment of Fort Sumter, May 4, 1861.** The people of Charleston watched the bombing of Fort Sumter from the rooftops of their homes. (The New York Historical Society)

CHAPTER FIVE

# Rebels, Yankees, and Freedmen

# 36

## FLIGHT FROM UNION

The election of 1860 centered on slavery and the Union. The Republicans ran Abraham Lincoln for president on a platform opposing the further extension of slavery. The Democrats split over the issue. The Northern Democrats ran Illinois Senator Stephen A. Douglas on a platform calling for "popular sovereignty," that is, the right of people in the federal territories to decide for themselves whether they wanted slavery. The Southern Democrats ran Kentucky's John C. Breckenridge on a frankly proslavery platform demanding federal protection of slavery in the territories. A fourth party, the Constitutional Union party, which ran John Bell of Tennessee, tried to play down the slavery issue by emphasizing the preservation of the Union. This division of Lincoln's opponents made his victory an almost foregone conclusion. Though Lincoln did not win the majority of popular votes cast in the election, he won more popular votes than any of his three opponents and he also took the majority of electoral votes. But he received not one electoral vote in the South.

Even before Lincoln's election, Mississippi had contemplated withdrawing from the Union if the Republicans won. When Lincoln did win, Governor John J. Pettus issued a proclamation denouncing the "Black Republicans," held a conference with the state's congressional delegation, including Jefferson Davis, and recommended a state convention to take action on secession. Late in November 1860, the Mississippi legislature met in Jackson, received the governor's recommendation, and passed a bill providing for elections the following month for a convention to meet on January 7 "to consider the then existing relations between the government of the United States and the government and people of the State of Mississippi." It also passed a series of resolutions outlining the reasons for adopting secession as "the proper remedy" for the state's grievances.

On December 20, South Carolina seceded from the Union. Shortly afterward ten other states followed its lead: Mississippi, Florida, Alabama, Georgia, Louisiana, Texas, Virginia, Arkansas, Tennessee, and North Carolina. In February 1861, delegates from the seceding states met in Montgomery, Alabama, to adopt a constitution for the Confederate States of America. They chose Mississippi's Jefferson Davis as president. On April 12, the Civil War began.

**Questions to Consider.** The Mississippi resolutions contained a succinct summary of the outlook of Southern secessionists. To what extent did they depend on John C. Calhoun's "compact" theory of the Union? Were the resolutions correct in stating that the Northern states had "assumed a revolutionary position" toward the Southern states? Was the charge that the Northern states had violated the Constitution in their behavior toward the South valid? Was it accurate to say that Northerners sought an abolitionist amendment to the Constitution? To what "incendiary publications" do the resolutions refer? What "hostile invasion of a Southern State" did the drafters of the resolutions have in mind? Do you see any similarities between the arguments advanced here and those appearing in the Declaration of Independence?

# Mississippi Resolutions on Secession (1860)

*Whereas,* The Constitutional Union was formed by the several States in their separate sovereign capacity for the purpose of mutual advantage and protection;

That the several States are distinct sovereignties, whose supremacy is limited so far only as the same has been delegated by voluntary compact to a Federal Government, and when it fails to accomplish the ends for which it was established, the parties to the compact have the right to resume, each State for itself, such delegated powers;

That the institution of slavery existed prior to the formation of the Federal Constitution, and is recognized by its letter, and all efforts to impair its value or lessen its duration by Congress, or any of the free States, is a violation of the compact of Union and is destructive of the ends for which it was ordained, but in defiance of the principles of the Union thus established, the people of the Northern States have assumed a revolutionary position towards the Southern States;

That they have set at defiance that provision of the Constitution which was intended to secure domestic tranquillity among the States and promote their general welfare, namely: "No person held to service or labor in one State, under the laws thereof, escaping into another, shall, in consequence of any law or regulation therein, be discharged from such service or labor, but shall be delivered up on claim of the party to whom such service or labor may be due;"

That they have by voluntary associations, individual agencies and State legislation interfered with slavery as it prevails in the slave-holding States;

Reprinted by permission of Louisiana State University Press from *Mississippi in the Confederacy,* edited by John K. Bettersworth, copyright © 1961, pp. 22–24.

**Private Tresvant ("Tris") Childers, Confederate States of America, displaying his rebel spirit for the camera.** Childers was born on an Alabama plantation in 1835, enlisted in an artillery regiment in 1862, and fought in Florida, Tennessee, and Alabama before surrendering on May 4, 1865. Some years after the war he moved to Arkansas to farm, although he was unable to purchase his modest holdings outright until 1910. (Private Collection)

That they have enticed our slaves from us, and by State intervention obstructed and prevented their rendition under the fugitive slave law;

That they continue their system of agitation obviously for the purpose of encouraging other slaves to escape from service, to weaken the institution in the slave-holding States by rendering the holding of such property insecure, and as a consequence its ultimate abolition certain;

That they claim the right and demand its execution by Congress to exclude slavery from the Territories, but claim the right of protection for every species of property owned by themselves;

That they declare in every manner in which public opinion is expressed their unalterable determination to exclude from admittance into the Union any new State that tolerates slavery in its Constitution, and thereby force Congress to a condemnation of that species of property;

That they thus seek by an increase of abolition States "to acquire two-thirds of both houses" for the purpose of preparing an amendment to the Constitution of the United States, abolishing slavery in the States, and so continue the agitation that the proposed amendment shall be ratified by the Legislatures of three-fourths of the States;

That they have in violation of the comity of all civilized nations, and in violation of the comity established by the Constitution of the United States, insulted and outraged our citizens when travelling among them for pleasure, health or business, by taking their servants and liberating the same, under the forms of State laws, and subjecting their owners to degrading and ignominious punishment;

That to encourage the stealing of our property they have put at defiance that provision of the Constitution which declares that fugitives from justice (escaping) into another State, on demand of the Executive authority of that State from which he fled, shall be delivered up;

That they have sought to create domestic discord in the Southern States by incendiary publications;

That they encouraged a hostile invasion of a Southern State to excite insurrection, murder and rapine;

That they have deprived Southern citizens of their property and continue an unfriendly agitation of their domestic institutions, claiming for themselves perfect immunity from external interference with their domestic policy. . . .

That they have elected a majority of Electors for President and Vice-President on the ground that there exists an irreconcilable conflict between the two sections of the Confederacy in reference to their respective systems of labor and in pursuance of their hostility to us and our institutions, thus declaring to the civilized world that the powers of this Government are to be used for the dishonor and overthrow of the Southern Section of this great Confederacy. Therefore,

*Be it resolved by the Legislature of the State of Mississippi,* That in the opinion of those who now constitute the said Legislature, the secession of each aggrieved State is the proper remedy for these injuries.

# 37

## UNION INVIOLATE

Fifteen states had significant slave populations when Abraham Lincoln was elected president of the United States on November 6, 1860. One of these, South Carolina, seceded from the Union in late December; others appeared ready to follow early in the new year. To forestall this mass exit, various last-minute compromise proposals emerged in Congress, including the so-called Crittenden Plan. This plan called for two constitutional amendments, the first guaranteeing slavery forever in the states where it already existed, and the second dividing the territories between slavery and freedom. President-elect Lincoln had no objection to the first proposed amendment, but he was unalterably opposed to the second, which would have nullified the free-soil plank of the Republican Party. A territorial division, Lincoln wrote, would only encourage planter expansionism and thus "put us again on the highroad to a slave empire," and on this point "I am inflexible."

Taking this as their cue, five more states—Georgia, Florida, Alabama, Mississippi, and Louisiana—seceded in January 1861. Texas followed on February 1. Seven states were therefore already gone, at least by their own declaration, as Lincoln prepared to deliver his inaugural address on March 4. The stakes were enormously high. Eight slave states, all in the strategically significant upper South, still remained in the Union. Should war begin, their allegiance would be invaluable and the inaugural address could help achieve that. Moreover, in the event of war, the North would have to unite behind the goals of the new president and his party. The address could articulate those unifying goals.

Lincoln believed his first inaugural address could be the most important speech of his life. Like most American politicians, he was a lawyer by trade, and the numerous legalistic formulations of the speech perhaps reflect this background. But the crisis Lincoln faced was fundamentally a constitutional—that is, a legalistic—crisis: Could a nation permit secessionist activity and remain a nation? What compromise with basic principles was possible before constitutional rights were destroyed? Because these were questions partly of constitutional law, Lincoln addressed them partly in legal language. But, as always in his great speeches, he also relied on common sense, common sentiments of patriotism, and, particularly in his conclusion, common familiarity with the cadences of the single most popular work in nineteenth-century America—the King James Bible.

Born to a frontier farming family in Kentucky in 1809, Abraham Lincoln grew up in Indiana and Illinois. As a young man he worked as a farmer, rail-splitter, boatsman, and storekeeper before turning to law and politics. He was enormously successful as a lawyer and served several years in the Illinois legislature and one term in the House of Representatives. Largely a self-educated man, Lincoln read and reread such books as the Bible, Aesop's fables, the works of Shakespeare, and the poems of Robert Burns. He also developed great skill as a writer. In 1858, his debates with Stephen Douglas over slavery brought him national prominence and helped him win the Republican nomination for president in 1860. Although he made restoration of the Union his primary objective during the Civil War, in time he also made it clear that, eventually, it must be a Union without slavery. On April 14, 1865, while attending a performance at Ford's Theatre in Washington, he was shot by actor John Wilkes Booth, a Confederate sympathizer. Lincoln died the next morning.

**Questions to Consider.** In what ways did Lincoln try to reassure Southerners about his intentions? Could he have said more without compromising his principles? What *was* his basic operating principle in this crisis? What did Lincoln see as the "only substantial dispute" between North and South, and why did he think secession would only make this dispute worse? Was he right in thinking that "deliberate" would be better than "hurried"? To what impulse was Lincoln trying to appeal when he referred to "the better angels of our nature"?

# First Inaugural Address (1861)

ABRAHAM LINCOLN

I consider that in view of the Constitution and the laws, the Union is unbroken, and to the extent of my ability I shall take care, as the Constitution itself expressly enjoins me, that the laws of the Union be faithfully executed in all the States. Doing this I deem to be only a simple duty on my part, and

From James D. Richardson, ed., *A Compilation of the Messages and Papers of the Presidents* (Government Printing Office, Washington, D.C., 1897–1907) VI: 6–12.

**The inauguration of Abraham Lincoln, March 1861, from a late-nineteenth-century rendering.** Like all presidents, Lincoln prepared this speech with great care. Like Daniel Webster, Henry Clay, and other great political speakers of the nineteenth century, he also prepared every other public address with care, working and reworking them to get them exactly right. This was partly because Lincoln, like his contemporaries, expected his speeches to appear in print. It was also because to do less—to speak without preparation, extemporaneously, off the cuff—would seem disrespectful to the audience, and no politician, preacher, or popular lecturer could afford to appear disrespectful. (Culver Pictures)

I shall perform it so far as practicable unless my rightful masters, the American people, shall withhold the requisite means or in some authoritative manner direct the contrary. I trust this will not be regarded as a menace, but only as the declared purpose of the Union that it *will* constitutionally defend and maintain itself.

In doing this there needs to be no bloodshed or violence, and there shall be none unless it be forced upon the national authority. The power confided to me will be used to hold, occupy, and possess the property and places belonging to the Government and to collect the duties and imposts; but beyond what may be necessary for these objects, there will be no invasion, no using of force against or among the people anywhere. . . .

Plainly the central idea of secession is the essence of anarchy. A majority held in restraint by constitutional checks and limitations, and always changing easily with deliberate changes of popular opinions and sentiments, is the only true sovereign of a free people. Whoever rejects it does of necessity fly to anarchy or to despotism. Unanimity is impossible. The rule of a minority, as a permanent arrangement, is wholly inadmissible; so that, rejecting the majority principle, anarchy or despotism in some form is all that is left. . . .

One section of our country believes slavery is *right* and ought to be extended, while the other believes it is *wrong* and ought not to be extended. This is the only substantial dispute. The fugitive-slave clause of the Constitution and the law for the suppression of the foreign slave trade are each as well enforced, perhaps, as any law can ever be in a community where the moral sense of the people imperfectly supports the law itself. The great body of the people abide by the dry legal obligation in both cases, and a few break over in each. This, I think, can not be perfectly cured, and it would be worse in both cases *after* the separation of the sections than before. The foreign slave trade, now imperfectly suppressed, would be ultimately revived without restriction in one section, while fugitive slaves, now only partially surrendered, would not be surrendered at all by the other.

Physically speaking, we can not separate. We can not remove our respective sections from each other nor build an impassable wall between them. A husband and wife may be divorced and go out of the presence and beyond the reach of each other, but the different parts of our country can not do this. They can not but remain face to face, and intercourse, either amicable or hostile, must continue between them. Is it possible, then, to make that intercourse more advantageous or more satisfactory *after* separation than *before?* Can aliens make treaties easier than friends can make laws? Can treaties be more faithfully enforced between aliens than laws can among friends? Suppose you go to war, you can not fight always; and when, after much loss on both sides and no gain on either, you cease fighting, the identical old questions, as to terms of intercourse, are again upon you. . . .

My countrymen, one and all, think calmly and *well* upon this whole subject. Nothing valuable can be lost by taking time. If there be an object to *hurry* any of you in hot haste to a step which you would never take *deliber-*

*ately*, that object will be frustrated by taking time; but no good object can be frustrated by it. Such of you as are now dissatisfied still have the old Constitution unimpaired, and, on the sensitive point, the laws of your own framing under it; while the new Administration will have no immediate power, if it would, to change either. If it were admitted that you who are dissatisfied hold the right side in the dispute, there still is no single good reason for precipitate action. Intelligence, patriotism, Christianity, and a firm reliance on Him who has never yet forsaken this favored land are still competent to adjust in the best way all our present difficulty.

In *your* hands, my dissatisfied fellow-countrymen, and not in *mine*, is the momentous issue of civil war. The Government will not assail *you*. You can have no conflict without being yourselves the aggressors. *You* have no oath registered in heaven to destroy the Government, while *I* shall have the most solemn one to "preserve, protect, and defend it."

I am loath to close. We are not enemies, but friends. We must not be enemies. Though passion may have strained it must not break our bonds of affection. The mystic chords of memory, stretching from every battlefield and patriot grave to every living heart and hearthstone all over this broad land, will yet swell the chorus of the Union, when again touched, as surely they will be, by the better angels of our nature.

# 38

## A Declaration of Freedom

From the outset, the abolitionists urged Abraham Lincoln to make freeing the slaves the major objective of the war. But Lincoln declared: "My paramount object in this struggle is to save the Union." The Republican platform had promised to check the extension of slavery, but it also pledged not to interfere with slavery where it legally existed. Four border slave states—Maryland, Kentucky, Missouri, and Delaware—had remained in the Union, and Lincoln was afraid that an abolitionist policy would drive them into the Confederacy, with disastrous results for the Union cause. He was not convinced at first, moreover, that the majority of Northerners favored abolition.

As the Civil War progressed, Northern public opinion moved slowly in the direction of emancipation. At the same time it was becoming clear that a Union victory would mean the end of slavery. Whenever Union troops occupied any part of the Confederacy, the slaves promptly left the plantations and became camp followers of the Northern armies. Union generals began asking what policy to adopt toward slavery in the occupied parts of the South. In addition, the European public was becoming critical of the North for its failure to emancipate the slaves. Lincoln finally decided that the time had come to take action.

At a secret cabinet meeting on July 22, 1862, Lincoln presented a proclamation abolishing slavery, on which he had been working nearly a month. Secretary of State William H. Seward urged him not to issue it until after a Union victory. Then, on September 17, came the battle of Antietam, at which the Union armies of General George M. McClellan halted the advance of General Robert E. Lee's troops. On September 22, Lincoln officially proclaimed emancipation. In his capacity as commander in chief he announced that, "on the 1st day of January, A.D. 1863, all persons held as slaves within any State or designated part of a State the people whereof shall then be in rebellion against the United States shall be then, thenceforward, and forever free."

The Emancipation Proclamation did not immediately end slavery. It did not apply to the border states because they were not in rebellion. Nor did it apply to those parts of the Confederacy then held by Union troops. Nevertheless, in all Confederate territories subsequently occupied by Northern troops, the slaves became free by the terms of Lincoln's proclamation. Furthermore, the proclamation led to the voluntary freeing of slaves in many places where it did not apply; Missouri and Maryland freed their slaves in 1863 and 1864. But it was the Thirteenth Amendment that ended slavery everywhere in the United States for all time. Introduced in Congress in December 1863 and adopted with Lincoln's energetic support in January 1865, it became part of the Constitution the following December when the necessary three-fourths of the states had ratified it.

**Questions to Consider.** The Emancipation Proclamation has been called as prosaic as a bill of lading. Do you think this is a fair appraisal? Do you think a statement more like the preamble to the Declaration of Independence would have been better? Why do you think Lincoln, a great prose master, avoided exalted language in writing the proclamation? On what constitutional powers as president did he depend in announcing his policy? In what ways does the proclamation demonstrate that Lincoln was a practical man? Reactions to the proclamation were varied. The London *Spectator* made fun of it. "The principle," sneered the editor, "is not that a human being cannot justly own another, but that he cannot own him unless he is loyal to the United States." Was the editor's comment justified? Not everyone agreed with the *Spectator.* Many abolitionists and most Southern blacks hailed the proclamation as a giant step on the road to freedom. Were they correct?

# The Emancipation Proclamation (1863)

ABRAHAM LINCOLN

Whereas on the 22d day of September, A.D. 1862, a proclamation was issued by the President of the United States, containing among other things, the following, to wit:

"That on the 1st day of January, A.D. 1863, all persons held as slaves within any State or designated part of a State the people whereof shall then be in rebellion against the United States shall be then, thenceforward, and forever free; and the executive government of the United States, including

From John Nicolay and John Hay, eds., *Complete Works of Abraham Lincoln* (12 v., Lincoln Memorial University, n.p., 1894), VIII: 161–164.

the military and naval authority thereof, will recognize and maintain the freedom of such persons and will do no act or acts to repress such persons, or any of them, in any efforts they may make for their actual freedom.

"That the executive will on the 1st day of January aforesaid, by proclamation, designate the States and parts of States, if any, in which the people thereof, respectively, shall then be in rebellion against the United States; and the fact that any State or the people thereof shall on that day be in good faith represented in the Congress of the United States by members chosen thereto at elections wherein a majority of the qualified voters of such States shall have participated shall, in the absence of strong countervailing testimony, be deemed conclusive evidence that such State and the people thereof are not then in rebellion against the United States."

Now, therefore, I, Abraham Lincoln, President of the United States, by virtue of the power in me vested as Commander-in-Chief of the Army and Navy of the United States in time of actual armed rebellion against the authority and government of the United States, and as a fit and necessary war measure for suppressing said rebellion, do, on this 1st day of January, A.D. 1863, and in accordance with my purpose so to do, publicly proclaimed for the full period of one hundred days from the first day above mentioned, order and designate as the States and parts of States wherein the people thereof, respectively, are this day in rebellion against the United States the following, to wit:

Arkansas, Texas, Louisiana (except the parishes of St. Bernard, Plaquemines, Jefferson, St. John, St. Charles, St. James, Ascension, Assumption, Terrebonne, Lafourche, St. Mary, St. Martin, and Orleans, including the city of New Orleans), Mississippi, Alabama, Florida, Georgia, South Carolina, North Carolina, and Virginia (except the forty-eight counties designated as West Virginia, and also the counties of Berkeley, Accomac, Northhampton, Elizabeth City, York, Princess Anne, and Norfolk, including the cities of Norfolk and Portsmouth), and which excepted parts are for the present left precisely as if this proclamation were not issued.

And by virtue of the power and for the purpose aforesaid, I do order and declare that all persons held as slaves within said designated States and parts of States are, and henceforward shall be, free; and that the Executive Government of the United States, including the military and naval authorities thereof, will recognize and maintain the freedom of said persons.

And I hereby enjoin upon the people so declared to be free to abstain from all violence, unless in necessary self-defense; and I recommend to them that, in all cases when allowed, they labor faithfully for reasonable wages.

And I further declare and make known that such persons of suitable condition will be received into the armed service of the United States to garrison forts, positions, stations, and other places, and to man vessels of all sorts in said service.

And upon this act, sincerely believed to be an act of justice, warranted by the Constitution upon military necessity, I invoke the considerate judgment of mankind and the gracious favor of Almighty God.

# 39

## PEOPLE'S GOVERNMENT

Late in June 1863, General Robert E. Lee crossed the Potomac River and moved his Confederate army rapidly through Maryland into Pennsylvania. On July 1 his troops met the Union army, commanded by General George G. Meade, at Gettysburg, Pennsylvania. After three days of fierce fighting, with thousands of casualties, Lee's greatly weakened army began to retreat. Lincoln was disappointed that Lee's army was able to escape, but he realized that the Confederates had suffered a decisive defeat. "I am very grateful to Meade," he said, "for the great service he did at Gettysburg." The Gettysburg battle marked the peak of the Confederate effort. Never again were the Confederates able to invade the North, and they never came close to winning the war after that time.

Four months after the bloody encounter—on November 19, 1863—when a national cemetery was dedicated on the Gettysburg battlefield, Lincoln delivered perhaps his most famous address. Edward Everett, famed for his oratory, spoke first, talking for almost two hours. Lincoln's address lasted only a couple of minutes. Afterward, it is said, Everett took Lincoln's hand and told him, "My speech will soon be forgotten; yours never will be. How gladly I would exchange my hundred pages for your twenty lines!" Everett was right. His own speech was soon forgotten, whereas Lincoln's brief address came to be regarded as one of the most powerful statements of the democratic outlook ever made.

**Questions to Consider.** Why was Everett so impressed with Lincoln's address? Lincoln once said that his basic political ideas came from the Declaration of Independence. Do you think this influence appears in the Gettysburg Address? What in Lincoln's opinion was the basic meaning of the Civil War? To what extent was style, as well as substance, important in the address Lincoln wrote for the Gettysburg dedication?

# The Gettysburg Address (1863)

ABRAHAM LINCOLN

Fourscore and seven years ago our fathers brought forth on this continent a new nation, conceived in liberty, and dedicated to the proposition that all men are created equal.

Now we are engaged in a great civil war, testing whether that nation, or any nation so conceived and so dedicated, can long endure. We are met on a great battle-field of that war. We have come to dedicate a portion of that field as a final resting-place for those who here gave their lives that that nation might live. It is altogether fitting and proper that we should do this.

But, in a larger sense, we cannot dedicate—we cannot consecrate—we cannot hallow—this ground. The brave men, living and dead, who struggled here, have consecrated it far above our poor power to add or detract. The world will little note nor long remember what we say here, but it can never forget what they did here. It is for us, the living, rather, to be dedicated here to the unfinished work which they who fought here have thus far so nobly advanced. It is rather for us to be here dedicated to the great task remaining before us—that from these honored dead we take increased devotion to that cause for which they gave the last full measure of devotion; that we here highly resolve that these dead shall not have died in vain; that this nation, under God, shall have a new birth of freedom; and that government of the people, by the people, for the people, shall not perish from the earth.

From John Nicolay and John Hay, eds., *Complete Works of Abraham Lincoln* (12 v., Lincoln Memorial University, n.p., 1894), IX: 209–210.

# 40

## THE FACE OF WAR

Northerners believed the war that broke out with the Southern bombardment of Fort Sumter in April 1861 would be over in months. But the Confederate army, led by officers whose military prowess far exceeded that of the Union command, proved to be a wily and formidable adversary, and to the dismay of President Lincoln, in the early years of the war—until the Battle of Gettysburg in 1863—decisive victory eluded the Union.

In 1864 Lincoln placed the strong-willed Ulysses S. Grant at the head of all Union forces. Late that same year, as Grant advanced toward Richmond with the Army of the Potomac, the forty-four-year-old General William Tecumseh Sherman drove the western army through three hundred miles of Georgia, cutting a thirty- to sixty-mile wide path of destruction from Atlanta to the sea. To avoid extended supply lines, he ordered his soldiers—nearly 60,000 men—to "forage liberally on the country" for provisions, supplies, pack animals, and wagons. His commanders were to "enforce a devastation more or less relentless" wherever there was resistance of any kind. Demolitions engineers tore up railroad tracks, heated them, and hung them from trees, and wherever it was "necessary," troops put houses, mills, cotton gins, plantations, and entire towns to the torch. Sherman was determined not only to destroy the South's capacity to wage war, but to break its will to resist.

It was as a result of such thinking that he burned Atlanta. In September the mayor of Atlanta had petitioned Sherman to reconsider his order that Atlanta be evacuated because of the "extraordinary hardship" and "inconvenience" it would entail:

How is it possible for the . . . women and children to find any shelter? And how can they live through the winter in the woods [with] no shelter or subsistence. . . . You know the woe, the horrors, and the suffering, cannot be described by words; imagination can only conceive of it, and we ask you to take these things into consideration. . . . What has this helpless people done, that they should be driven from their homes, to wander strangers and outcasts, and exiles, and to subsist on charity?

As the first document shows, Sherman did not revoke his order. After the evacuation was complete, he ordered the city destroyed.

Yet Sherman was not a brutal man. In 1879, eleven years before his death, he addressed the graduating class of a military academy:

I am tired and sick of war. Its glory is all moonshine. It is only those who have neither fired a shot nor heard the shrieks and groans of the wounded who cry aloud for blood, more vengeance, more desolation. War is hell.

Perhaps as well as any soldier of his generation, Sherman understood the nature of modern warfare and refused to be sentimental about it. Georgia reeled from the destruction he had brought upon it, but his scorched-earth policies worked. So awful, however, was the devastation of his "March to the Sea" that the physical and psychological wounds inflicted on the South took generations to heal.

The destruction is vividly described by Eliza Andrews in *The War-Time Diary of a Georgia Girl,* a portion of which is reproduced in the second document. In 1864 Andrews was twenty-four and living at a relative's plantation in southwest Georgia, where her father had sent her for safety. Observing the terrible effects of Sherman's march, she recorded how she felt about the destruction, the collapse of the Confederacy, and the impact of the war on women. "The exigencies of the times did away with many conventions," Andrews observed, and her diary provides insights into the plight of Southern women during the war and Reconstruction.

Her own life exemplified how the war had indeed wiped out "many conventions." Having lost her father's substantial estate (Garnett Andrews, although a Unionist, had owned two hundred slaves), she was forced to rely on her own resources to survive, and did so by teaching and by writing novels, serial fiction for periodicals, books on botany, and articles on socialism. In 1931 Andrews died in Rome, Georgia, at the age of ninety. Convinced that for the North the Civil War had been not a moral crusade but a fight to promote the interests of capitalism, she went to her grave a Marxist.

**Questions to Consider.** How persuasive do you find Sherman's reasoning in his message to the Atlantans? Would his arguments justify the unlimited destruction of hostile cities? In contrast to the North, where during the war women had opportunities to work in the Sanitary Commission or the Nursing Corps, in the Confederacy there were no government-sponsored wartime organizations that employed women. They had to cope on their own. Do you think Eliza Andrews's response might have been typical? What was the specific nature of the destruction she witnessed?

# Message to the Atlanta City Council (1864)

WILLIAM TECUMSEH SHERMAN

Gentlemen: I have your letter of the 11th, in the nature of a petition to revoke my orders removing all the inhabitants from Atlanta. I have read it carefully, and give full credit to your statements of the distress that will be occasioned, and yet shall not revoke my orders, because they were not designed to meet the humanities of the case, but to prepare for the future struggles in which millions of good people outside of Atlanta have a deep interest. We must have peace, not only at Atlanta, but in all America. To secure this, we must stop the war that now desolates our once happy and favored country. To stop war, we must defeat the rebel armies which are arrayed against the laws and Constitution that all must respect and obey. To defeat those armies, we must prepare the way to reach them in their recesses, provided with the arms and instruments which enable us to accomplish our purpose. Now, I know the vindictive nature of our enemy, that we may have many years of military operations from this quarter; and, therefore, deem it wise and prudent to prepare in time. The use of Atlanta for warlike purposes is inconsistent with its character as a home for families. There will be no manufactures, commerce, or agriculture here, for the maintenance of families, and sooner or later want will compel the inhabitants to go. Why not go now, when all the arrangements are completed for the transfer, instead of waiting till the plunging shot of contending armies will renew the scenes of the past month? Of course, I do not apprehend any such thing at this moment, but you do not suppose this army will be here until the war is over. I cannot discuss this subject with you fairly, because I cannot impart to you what we propose to do, but I assert that our military plans make it necessary for the inhabitants to go away, and I can only renew my offer of services to make their exodus in any direction as easy and comfortable as possible.

You cannot qualify war in harsher terms than I will. War is cruelty, and you cannot refine it; and those who brought war into our country deserve all the curses and maledictions a people can pour out. I know I had no hand in making this war, and I know I will make more sacrifices to-day than any of you to secure peace. But you cannot have peace and a division of our country. If the United States submits to a division now, it will not stop, but will go on until we reap the fate of Mexico, which is eternal war. The United States does and must assert its authority, wherever it once had power; for, if it relaxes one bit to pressure, it is gone, and I believe that such is the national feeling. This feeling assumes various shapes, but always comes back to that

From William T. Sherman, *Memoirs of General William T. Sherman* (Appleton, New York, 1875).

**A devastated land.** In this painting by David English Henderson, a Virginia family returns to a home shattered by the bloody battle of Fredericksburg. Significantly, no men of military age remain. (Gettysburg National Military Park)

of Union. Once admit the Union, once more acknowledge the authority of the national Government, and, instead of devoting your houses and streets and roads to the dread uses of war, I and this army become at once your protectors and supporters, shielding you from danger, let it come from what quarter it may. I know that a few individuals cannot resist a torrent of error and passion, such as swept the South into rebellion, but you can point out, so that we may know those who desire a government, and those who insist on war and its desolation.

You might as well appeal against the thunder-storm as against these terrible hardships of war. They are inevitable, and the only way the people of Atlanta can hope once more to live in peace and quiet at home, is to stop the war, which can only be done by admitting that it began in error and is perpetuated in pride.

We don't want your Negroes, or your horses, or your houses, or your lands, or any thing you have, but we do want and will have a just obedience to the laws of the United States. That we will have, and if it involves the destruction of your improvements, we cannot help it.

You have heretofore read public sentiment in your newspapers, that live by falsehood and excitement; and the quicker you seek for truth in other quarters, the better. I repeat then that, by the original compact of government, the United States had certain rights in Georgia, which have never been relinquished and never will be; that the South began war by seizing forts, arsenals, mints, custom-houses, etc., etc., long before Mr. Lincoln was installed, and before the South had one jot or tittle of provocation. I myself have seen in Missouri, Kentucky, Tennessee, and Mississippi, hundreds and thousands of women and children fleeing from your armies and desperadoes, hungry and with bleeding feet. In Memphis, Vicksburg, and Mississippi, we fed thousands upon thousands of the families of rebel soldiers left on our hands, and whom we could not see starve. Now that war comes home to you, you feel very different. You deprecate its horrors, but did not feel them when you sent car-loads of soldiers and ammunition, and moulded shells and shot, to carry war into Kentucky and Tennessee, to desolate the homes of hundreds and thousands of good people who only asked to live in peace at their old homes, and under the Government of their inheritance. But these comparisons are idle. I want peace, and believe it can only be reached through union and war, and I will ever conduct war with a view to perfect an early success.

But, my dear sirs, when peace does come, you may call on me for any thing. Then will I share with you the last cracker, and watch with you to shield your homes and families against danger from every quarter.

Now you must go, and take with you the old and feeble, feed and nurse them, and build for them, in more quiet places, proper habitations to shield them against the weather until the mad passions of men cool down, and allow the Union and peace once more to settle over your old homes at Atlanta.

# Diary of a Georgia Girl (1864)

ELIZA ANDREWS

December 24, 1864.—About three miles from Sparta we struck the "burnt country," as it is well named by the natives, and then I could better understand the wrath and desperation of these poor people. I almost felt as if I should like to hang a Yankee myself. There was hardly a fence left standing all the way from Sparta to Gordon. The fields were trampled down and the road was lined with carcasses of horses, hogs, and cattle that the invaders, unable either to consume or to carry away with them, had wantonly shot down, to starve out the people and prevent them from making their crops.

From Eliza Andrews, *The War-Time Diary of a Georgia Girl* (Appleton, New York, 1908).

The stench in some places was unbearable; every few hundred yards we had to hold our noses or stop them with the cologne Mrs. Elzey had given us, and it proved a great boon. The dwellings that were standing all showed signs of pillage, and on every plantation we saw the charred remains of the ginhouse and packing screw, while here and there lone chimney stacks, "Sherman's sentinels," told of homes laid in ashes. The infamous wretches! I couldn't wonder now that these poor people should want to put a rope round the neck of every red-handed "devil of them" they could lay their hands on. Hayricks and fodder stacks were demolished, corncribs were empty, and every bale of cotton that could be found was burnt by the savages. I saw no grain of any sort except little patches they had spilled when feeding their horses and which there was not even a chicken left in the country to eat. A bag of oats might have lain anywhere along the road without danger from the beasts of the field, though I cannot say it would have been safe from the assaults of hungry man.

Crowds of soldiers were tramping over the road in both directions; it was like traveling through the streets of a populous town all day. They were mostly on foot, and I saw numbers seated on the roadside greedily eating raw turnips, meat skins, parched corn—anything they could find, even picking up the loose grains that Sherman's horses had left. I felt tempted to stop and empty the contents of our provision baskets into their laps, but the dreadful accounts that were given of the state of the country before us made prudence get the better of our generosity.

Before crossing the Oconee at Milledgeville we ascended an immense hill, from which there was a fine view of the town, with Governor Brown's fortifications in the foreground and the river rolling at our feet. The Yankees had burnt the bridge; so we had to cross on a ferry. There was a long train of vehicles ahead of us, and it was nearly an hour before our turn came; so we had ample time to look about us. On our left was a field where thirty thousand Yankees had camped hardly three weeks before. It was strewn with the debris they had left behind, and the poor people of the neighborhood were wandering over it, seeking for anything they could find to eat, even picking up grains of corn that were scattered around where the Yankees had fed their horses. We were told that a great many valuables were found there at first, plunder that the invaders had left behind, but the place had been picked over so often by this time that little now remained except tufts of loose cotton, piles of half-rotted grain, and the carcasses of slaughtered animals, which raised a horrible stench. Some men were plowing in one part of the field, making ready for next year's crop.

# 41

## BINDING WOUNDS

In June 1864, when the Republicans nominated Abraham Lincoln for a second term, the end of the war seemed as far away as ever. Northerners were shocked at the heavy casualties reported from battlefields in Virginia, and criticism of the administration had become so harsh that in mid-August Lincoln was convinced he would not be reelected. The Radical Republicans, who spoke for the antislavery faction of the party, condemned him as "politically, militarily, and financially a failure" and for a time backed John C. Frémont for the presidency. The Northern Democrats nominated General George B. McClellan, a former federal commander, and adopted a platform calling for the immediate cessation of hostilities and the restoration of the Union by a negotiated peace. Lincoln was so sure McClellan would defeat him that he wrote a secret memorandum explaining how he would cooperate with the new president after the election in order to save the Union.

But a series of federal victories—the closing of Mobile Bay, the capture of Atlanta, and the routing of Southern forces in the Shenandoah Valley—led public opinion to swing back rapidly to Lincoln. Republican newspapers began ridiculing the "war-is-a-failure" platform of the Democrats, and Frémont decided to drop out of the campaign. Lincoln's prediction that he would not be reelected proved wrong. On election day he won a plurality of nearly half a million votes and carried every state in the Union except Kentucky, Delaware, and New Jersey.

In his second inaugural address on March 4, 1865, Lincoln singled out slavery as the cause of the Civil War and stated that its eradication was inevitable. He expressed hope for a speedy end to the conflict, called for "malice toward none" and "charity for all," and looked forward to the day when Americans would achieve a "just and lasting peace" among themselves and with all nations. On April 9, Lee surrendered to Grant at Appomattox; two days later Lincoln made his last public address, outlining his reconstruction policy. He had never considered the South to be outside of the Union and hoped for a speedy reconciliation. On April 14, at his last cabinet meeting, he urged the cabinet members to put aside all thoughts of hatred and revenge. That evening he was shot.

**Questions to Consider.** Lincoln's second inaugural address is commonly regarded as one of the greatest addresses ever made by an American president. Why do you think this is so? What did he regard as the basic issue of the Civil War? What irony did he see in the attitude of the contestants? What use of the Bible did he make? Do you think this was likely to appeal to Americans in 1865?

# Second Inaugural Address (1865)

### ABRAHAM LINCOLN

FELLOW-COUNTRYMEN:—At this second appearing to take the oath of the presidential office there is less occasion for an extended address than there was at the first. Then a statement somewhat in detail of a course to be pursued seemed fitting and proper. Now, at the expiration of four years, during which public declarations have been constantly called forth on every point and phase of the great contest which still absorbs the attention and engrosses the energies of the nation, little that is new could be presented. The progress of our arms, upon which all else chiefly depends, is as well known to the public as to myself, and it is, I trust, reasonably satisfactory and encouraging to all. With high hope for the future, no prediction in regard to it is ventured.

On the occasion corresponding to this four years ago all thoughts were anxiously directed to an impending civil war. All dreaded it, all sought to avert it. While the inaugural address was being delivered from this place, devoted altogether to *saving* the Union without war, insurgent agents were in the city seeking to *destroy* it without war—seeking to dissolve the Union and divide effects by negotiation. Both parties deprecated war, but one of them would *make* war rather than let the nation survive, and the other would *accept* war rather than let it perish, and the war came.

One eighth of the whole population was colored slaves, not distributed generally over the Union, but localized in the southern part of it. These slaves constituted a peculiar and powerful interest. All knew that this interest was somehow the cause of the war. To strengthen, perpetuate, and extend this interest was the object for which the insurgents would rend the Union even by war, while the Government claimed no right to do more than

From James D. Richardson, ed., *A Compilation of the Messages and Papers of the Presidents* (Government Printing Office, Washington, D.C., 1897–1907), VIII: 3477–3478.

to restrict the territorial enlargement of it. Neither party expected for the war the magnitude nor the duration which it has already attained. Neither anticipated that the *cause* of the conflict might cease with or even before the conflict itself should cease. Each looked for an easier triumph, and a result less fundamental and astounding. Both read the same Bible and pray to the same God, and each invokes His aid against the other. It may seem strange that any men should dare to ask a just God's assistance in wringing their bread from the sweat of other men's faces, but let us judge not, that we be not judged. The prayers of both could not be answered. That of neither has been answered fully. The Almighty has His own purposes. "Woe unto the world because of offenses; for it must needs be that offenses come, but woe to that man by whom the offense cometh." If we shall suppose that American slavery is one of those offenses which, in the providence of God, must needs come, but which, having continued through His appointed time, He now wills to remove, and that He gives to both North and South this terrible war as the woe due to those by whom the offense came, shall we discern therein any departure from those divine attributes which the believers in a living God always ascribe to Him? Fondly do we hope, fervently do we pray, that this mighty scourge of war may speedily pass away. Yet, if God wills that it continue until all the wealth piled by the bondsman's two hundred and fifty years of unrequited toil shall be sunk, and until every drop of blood drawn with the lash shall be paid by another drawn with the sword, as was said three thousand years ago, so still it must be said, "The judgments of the Lord are true and righteous altogether."

With malice toward none, with charity for all, with firmness in the right as God gives us to see the right, let us strive on to finish the work we are in, to bind up the nation's wounds, to care for him who shall have borne the battle and for his widow and his orphan, to do all which may achieve and cherish a just and lasting peace among ourselves and with all nations.

# 42

## KLANSMEN OF THE CAROLINAS

Reconstruction developed in a series of moves and countermoves. In a white Southern backlash to Union victory and emancipation came the "black codes" for coercing black laborers and President Andrew Johnson's pardon of Confederate landowners. Then in a Northern backlash to these codes and pardons came the Civil Rights bills, the sweeping Reconstruction Acts of 1867, and the Fourteenth and Fifteenth Amendments, all designed to guarantee black political rights. White Southerners reacted to these impositions in turn with secret night-time terrorist or "night rider" organizations designed to shatter Republican political power. Congress tried to protect Republican voters and the freedmen with the Force Acts of 1870 allowing the use of the army to prevent physical assaults, but Northern willingness to commit troops and resources to the struggle was waning. By the mid-1870s only three states remained in Republican hands, and within three years racist Democrats controlled these, too. The night riders had turned the tide.

Although numerous secret societies for whites appeared in the Reconstruction South—including the Order of the White Camelia (Louisiana), the Pale Faces (Tennessee), the White Brotherhood (North Carolina), and the Invisible Circle (South Carolina)—the largest and most influential society, and the one that spawned these imitators, was the Ku Klux Klan, the so-called Invisible Empire. The Klan began in Tennessee in 1866 as a young men's social club with secret costumes and rituals similar to those of the Masons, the Odd-Fellows, and other popular societies. In 1867, however, following passage of the Reconstruction Acts, anti-Republican racists began to see the usefulness of such a spookily secret order, and the Klan was reorganized to provide for "dens," "provinces" (counties), and "realms" (states), all under the authority of a "Grand Wizard," who in 1867 was believed to have been Nathan B. Forrest, a former slave trader and Confederate general.

The Klan structure was probably never fully established because of the disorganized conditions of the postwar South. Other societies with different names emerged, and the Reconstruction-era "Ku-Klux" may have disbanded as a formal entity in the early 1870s. But it clearly survived in spirit and in loosely formed groups, continuing to terrorize Republicans and their allies among the newly enfranchised freedmen into the 1870s and sowing fear among the black families who composed, after all, the labor force on which the white planters still depended. The excerpt reprinted below includes congressional testimony by David Schenck, a member of the North Carolina Klan seeking to portray it in the best possible light, followed by testimony from Elias Hill, a South Carolina black man victimized by a local "den" of the Klan. Schenck and Hill were testifying before a joint Senate-House committee concerned with antiblack terrorism.

**Questions to Consider.** The oath taken by David Schenck emphasizes the Klan's religious, constitutional, and benevolent qualities, whereas Elias Hill's story reveals its terrorist features. Are there elements in the Klan oath that seem to hint at or justify the use of violence? Why does the oath contain the phrases "original purity," "pecuniary embarrassments," and "traitor's doom"? What "secrets of this order" could deserve death? Klansmen later claimed that because they could terrorize the superstitious freedmen simply by using masks, odd voices, and ghostly sheets, no real violence was necessary. Opponents have claimed, on the other hand, that Klansmen were basically sadists acting out sexual phobias and deep paranoia. What light does Elias Hill's testimony shed on these conflicting claims? What position did Hill hold in the black community? Did the Klansmen seem to be assaulting him because of his condition or because of his position in the black community? Why did they ask Hill to pray for them? Would it be fair or accurate to call the Ku Klux Klan a terrorist organization that succeeded?

# Report of the Joint Committee on Reconstruction (1872)

A select committee of the Senate, upon the 10th of March, 1871, made a report of the result of their investigation into the security of person and property in the State of North Carolina. . . . A sub-committee of their number proceeded to the State of South Carolina, and examined witnesses in that State until July 29. . . .

David Schenck, esq., a member of the bar of Lincoln County, North Carolina . . . was initiated in October, 1868, as a member of the Invisible Em-

From *Report of the Joint Select Committee to Inquire into the Condition of Affairs in the Late Insurrectionary States* (Government Printing Office, Washington, D.C., 1872), 25–27, 44–47.

**A North Carolina Ku Klux Klan meeting to plan the murder of a black Republican, from an 1871 engraving in a New York publication.** Although the artist imagined the scene, he managed to convey both the bizarre and spooky garb of the Klan members and the defenselessness and terror of the lone kneeling freedman. The Klan victimized not only former slaves suspected of supporting the Republican party but also freedmen who managed to obtain land or learn to read and write. (Library of Congress)

pire. . . . In his own words: "We were in favor of constitutional liberty as handed down to us by our forefathers. I think the idea incorporated was that we were opposed to the [fourteenth and fifteenth] amendments to the Constitution. I desire to explain in regard to that that it was not to be—at least, I did not intend by that that it should be—forcible resistance, but a political principle."

The oath itself is as follows:

I, (name,) before the great immaculate Judge of heaven and earth, and upon the Holy Evangelist of Almighty God, do, of my own free will and accord, subscribe to the following sacred, binding obligation:

I. I am on the side of justice and humanity and constitutional liberty, as bequeathed to us by our forefathers in its original purity.

II. I reject and oppose the principles of the radical [Republican] party.

III. I pledge aid to a brother of the Ku-Klux Klan in sickness, distress, or pecuniary embarrassments. Females, friends, widows, and their households shall be the special objects of my care and protection.

IV. Should I ever divulge, or cause to be divulged, any of the secrets of this order, or any of the foregoing obligations, I must meet with the fearful punishment of death and traitor's doom, which is death, death, death, at the hands of the brethren. . . .

Elias Hill of York County, South Carolina, is a remarkable character. He is crippled in both legs and arms, which are shriveled by rheumatism; he cannot walk, cannot help himself . . .; was in early life a slave, whose freedom was purchased by his father. . . . He learned his letters and to read by calling the school children into the cabin as they passed, and also learned to write. He became a Baptist preacher, and after the war engaged in teaching colored children, and conducted the business correspondence of many of his colored neighbors. . . . We put the story of his wrongs in his own language:

"On the night of the 5th of May, after I had heard a great deal of what they had done in that neighborhood, they came . . . to my brother's door, which is in the same yard, and broke open the door and attacked his wife, and I heard her screaming and mourning. I could not understand what they said, for they were talking in an outlandish and unnatural tone, which I had heard they generally used at a negro's house. They said, 'Where's Elias?' She said, 'He doesn't stay here; yon is his house.' I had heard them strike her five or six licks. Someone then hit my door. . . .

"They carried me into the yard between the houses, my brother's and mine, and put me on the ground. . . . 'Who did that burning? Who burned our houses?' I told them it was not me. I could not burn houses. Then they hit me with their fists, and said I did it, I ordered it. They went on asking me didn't I tell the black men to ravish all the white women. No, I answered them. They struck me again. . . . 'Haven't you been preaching and praying about the Ku-Klux? Haven't you been preaching political sermons? Doesn't a [Republican Party newspaper] come to your house? Haven't you written letters?' Generally one asked me all the questions, but the rest were squatting over me—some six men I counted as I lay there. . . . I told them if they would take me back into the house, and lay me in the bed, which was close adjoining my books and papers, I would try and get it. They said I would never go back to that bed, for they were going to kill me. . . . They caught my leg and pulled me over the yard, and then left me there, knowing I could not walk nor crawl. . . .

"After they had stayed in the house for a considerable time, they came back to where I lay and asked if I wasn't afraid at all. They pointed pistols at me all around my head once or twice, as if they were going to shoot me. . . . One caught me by the leg and hurt me, for my leg for forty years has been drawn each year, more and more, and I made moan when it hurt so. One said, 'G–d d—n it, hush!' He had a horsewhip, [and] I reckon he struck me eight cuts right on the hip bone; it was almost the only place he could hit my body, my legs are so short. They all had disguises. . . . One of them then took a strap, and buckled it around my neck and said, 'Let's take him to the river and drown him.' . . .

"Then they said, 'Look here! Will you put a card in the paper to re-nounce all republicanism? Will you quit preaching?' I told them I did not know. I said that to save my life. . . . They said if I did not they would come back the next week and kill me. [After more licks with the strap] one of them went into the house where my brother and sister-and-law lived, and brought her to pick me up. As she stooped down to pick me up one of them struck her, and as she was carrying me into the house another struck her with a strap. . . . They said, 'Don't you pray against Ku-Klux, but pray that God may forgive Ku-Klux. Pray that God may bless and save us.' I was so chilled with cold lying out of doors so long and in such pain I could not speak to pray, but I tried to, and they said that would do very well, and all went out of the house. . . ."

Satisfied that he could no longer live in that community, Hill wrote to make inquiry about the means of going to Liberia. Hearing this, many of his neighbors desired to go also. . . . Others are still hoping for relief, through the means of this sub-committee.

# 43

## A KIND OF UNITY

Despite Congress's seizure of control over Reconstruction policy and Ulysses S. Grant's defeat of Andrew Johnson for the presidency in 1868, Radical Reconstruction—the garrisoning of the South, the disfranchisement of former rebels, and the control of Southern state governments by Republican votes—did not last long in most places. During President Grant's first term of office, the white-dominated Democratic Party gained control of North Carolina, Tennessee, and Virginia, the three ex-Confederate states with the lowest percentage of black population. During Grant's second term, Democrats seized control of Alabama, Arkansas, Georgia, Mississippi, and Texas. That left Republican governments (and federal troops) in Florida, Louisiana, and South Carolina, three states with large black populations.

Those states mattered greatly in national politics. During the election of 1876 both parties resorted to fraud. Two sets of electoral returns came in from the three states, and it was necessary for Congress to set up an electoral commission to decide whether Rutherford B. Hayes, the Republican candidate, or Samuel J. Tilden, the Democratic standard bearer, had won. By a strict party vote of 8 to 7, the commission awarded all 20 disputed electoral votes to the Republicans. Hayes became president, with 185 votes to Tilden's 184. In the end, Southern Democrats reached a compromise with Northern Republicans. The Democrats agreed to accept the commission's decision and the Republicans promised to withdraw the remaining federal troops from the South. In April 1877, the last federal soldiers left the South. Solid Democratic control—and stepped-up measures to disfranchise black voters—quickly followed.

Although political maneuvering was important in finally killing Republican Reconstruction, the underlying reason it died was simply that Northerners were losing the will to suppress an increasingly violent white South. The nation's approaching centennial celebration in 1876 triggered an especially strong outpouring of sentiment in favor of improving sectional feelings by withdrawing the troops, even if withdrawal meant the resurgence of the Democratic Party. That, in turn, would permit an overdue rebonding of the century-old republic.

The following unsigned editorial ran in the August 1875 issue of *Scribner's Monthly*, an influential, generally Republican, New York magazine. It expressed, with unusual eloquence, this emotional yearning for peace.

**Questions to Consider.** What was the occasion of the *Scribner's* editorial? Was this a natural time to consider troop withdrawals? What, in the view of the editor, was the major accomplishment of the Civil War? What specific political theory had been tested and defeated? When addressing the "men of the South," was the editor speaking to all Southern men? What did the phrase "brotherly sympathy" mean? Was it naive or was it realistic for the writer to think that the upcoming centennial could "heal all the old wounds" and "reconcile all the old differences"? Would Abraham Lincoln have agreed with the spirit of this editorial?

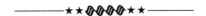

# What the Centennial Ought to Accomplish (1875)

### SCRIBNER'S MONTHLY

We are to have grand doings next year. There is to be an Exposition. There are to be speeches, and songs, and processions, and elaborate ceremonies and general rejoicings. Cannon are to be fired, flags are to be floated, and the eagle is expected to scream while he dips the tip of either pinion in the Atlantic and the Pacific, and sprinkles the land with a new baptism of freedom. The national oratory will exhaust the figures of speech in patriotic glorification, while the effete civilizations of the Old World, and the despots of the East, tottering upon their tumbling thrones, will rub their eyes and sleepily inquire, "What's the row?" The Centennial is expected to celebrate in a fitting way—somewhat dimly apprehended, it is true—the birth of a nation.

Well, the object is a good one. When the old colonies declared themselves free, they took a grand step in the march of progress; but now, before we begin our celebration of this event, would it not be well for us to inquire whether we have a nation? In a large number of the States of this country there exists not only a belief that the United States do not constitute a nation, but a theory of State rights which forbids that they ever shall become one. We hear about the perturbed condition of the Southern mind. We hear it said that multitudes there are just as disloyal as they were during the civil war. This, we believe, we are justified in denying. Before the war they had a theory of State rights. They fought to establish that theory, and they now speak

From *Scribner's Monthly* 10 (August 1875), 509–510.

**Miss Liberty's torch.** A display at the great 1876 Centennial Exposition, Philadelphia. (Samuel Castner Collection/Free Library of Philadelphia)

of the result as "the lost cause." They are not actively in rebellion, and they do not propose to be. They do not hope for the re-establishment of slavery. They fought bravely and well to establish their theory, but the majority was against them; and if the result of the war emphasized any fact, it was that *en masse* the people of the United States constitute a nation—indivisible in constituents, in interest, in destiny. The result of the war was without significance, if it did not mean that the United States constitute a nation which cannot be divided; which will not permit itself to be divided; which is integral, indissoluble, indestructible. We do not care what theories of State rights are entertained outside of this. State rights, in all the States, should be jealously guarded, and, by all legitimate means, defended. New York should be as jealous of her State prerogatives as South Carolina or Louisiana; but this theory which makes of the Union a rope of sand, and of the States a collection of petty nationalities that can at liberty drop the bands which hold them together, is forever exploded. It has been tested at the point of the bayonet. It went down in blood, and went down for all time. Its adherents may mourn over the fact, as we can never cease to mourn over the events which accompanied it, over the sad, incalculable cost to them and to those who opposed them. The great point with them is to recognize the fact that, for richer or poorer, in sickness and health, until death do us part, these United States constitute a nation; that we are to live, grow, prosper, and suffer together, united by bands that cannot be sundered.

Unless this fact is fully recognized throughout the Union, our Centennial will be but a hollow mockery. If we are to celebrate anything worth celebrating, it is the birth of a nation. If we are to celebrate anything worth celebrating, it should be by the whole heart and united voice of the nation. If we can make the Centennial an occasion for emphasizing the great lesson of the war, and universally assenting to the results of the war, it will, indeed, be worth all the money expended upon and the time devoted to it. If around the old Altars of Liberty we cannot rejoin our hands in brotherly affection and national loyalty, let us spike the cannon that will only proclaim our weakness, put our flags at half-mast, smother our eagles, eat our ashes, and wait for our American aloe to give us a better blossoming.

A few weeks ago, Mr. Jefferson Davis, the ex-President of the Confederacy, was reported to have exhorted an audience to which he was speaking to be as loyal to the old flag of the Union now as they were during the Mexican War. If the South could know what music there was in these words to Northern ears—how grateful we were to their old chief for them—it would appreciate the strength of our longing for a complete restoration of the national feeling that existed when Northern and Southern blood mingled in common sacrifice on Mexican soil. This national feeling, this national pride, this brotherly sympathy *must be restored;* and accursed be any Northern or Southern man, whether in power or out of power, whether politician, theorizer, carpet-bagger, president-maker or plunderer, who puts obstacles in the way of such a restoration. Men of the South, we want you. Men of the South, we long for the restoration of your peace and your prosperity. We would see your cities thriving, your homes happy, your plantations teeming with plenteous harvests, your schools overflowing, your wisest statesmen leading you, and all causes and all memories of discord wiped out forever. You do not believe this? Then you do not know the heart of the North. Have you cause of complaint against the politicians? Alas! so have we. Help us, as

loving and loyal American citizens, to make our politicians better. Only remember and believe that there is nothing that the North wants so much to-
day, as your recognition of the fact that the old relations between you and
us are forever restored—that your hope, your pride, your policy, and your
destiny are one with ours. Our children will grow up to despise our child-
ishness, if we cannot do away with our personal hates so far, that in the
cause of an established nationality we may join hands under the old flag.

To bring about this reunion of the two sections of the country in the old
fellowship, should be the leading object of the approaching Centennial. A
celebration of the national birth, begun, carried on, and finished by a section, would be a mockery and a shame. The nations of the world might well
point at it the finger of scorn. The money expended upon it were better sunk
in the sea, or devoted to repairing the waste places of the war. Men of the
South, it is for you to say whether your magnanimity is equal to your
valor—whether you are as reasonable as you are brave, and whether, like
your old chief, you accept that definite and irreversible result of the war
which makes you and yours forever members of the great American nation
with us. Let us see to it, North and South, that the Centennial heals all the
old wounds, reconciles all the old differences, and furnishes the occasion for
such a reunion of the great American nationality, as shall make our celebration an expression of fraternal good-will among all sections and all States,
and a corner-stone over which shall be reared a new temple to national freedom, concord, peace, and prosperity.

# 44

## AFTERMATH

Fredrick Douglass regarded the Declaration of Independence as a "watchword of freedom." But he was tempted to turn it to the wall, he said, because its human rights principles were so shamelessly violated. A former slave himself, Douglass knew what he was talking about. Douglass thought that enslaving blacks fettered whites as well and that the United States would never be truly free until it ended chattel slavery. During the Civil War, he had several conversations with Lincoln, urging him to make emancipation his major aim. He also put unremitting pressure on the Union army to accept black volunteers, and after resistance to admitting blacks into the army gave way, he toured the country encouraging blacks to enlist and imploring the government to treat black and white soldiers equally in matters of pay and promotion.

Douglass had great hopes for his fellow blacks after the Civil War. He demanded they be given full rights—political, legal, educational, and economic—as citizens. He also wanted to see the wall of separation between the races crumble and see "the colored people of this country, enjoying the same freedom [as whites], voting at the same ballot-box, using the same cartridge-box, going to the same schools, attending the same churches, travelling in the same street cars, in the same railroad cars, on the same steam-boats, proud of the same country, fighting the same war, and enjoying the same peace and all its advantages." He regarded the Republican party as the "party of progress, justice and freedom" and at election time took to the stump and rallied black votes for the party. He was rewarded for these services by appointment as marshal of the District of Columbia in 1877, as recorder of deeds for the District in 1881, and as minister to Haiti in 1889. But he was also asked by Republican leaders to keep a low profile, was omitted from White House guest lists, and was excluded from presidential receptions even though one duty of the District marshal was to introduce the guests at White House state occasions.

Douglass was puzzled and then upset by the increasing indifference of Republican leaders to conditions among blacks after the Civil War. In 1883 he attended a convention of blacks in Louisville, Kentucky, which met to discuss their plight and reaffirm their demand for full civil rights. In his keynote address, which is reprinted here, Douglass vividly portrayed the discrimination and persecution his people encountered, but he continued to believe that "prejudice, with all its malign accomplishments, may yet be removed by peaceful means."

Born into slavery in Maryland in 1817, Frederick Augustus Washington Bailey learned to read and write despite efforts to keep him illiterate. In 1838 he managed to escape to freedom and adopted the name Frederick Douglass. Shortly afterward he became associated with William Lloyd Garrison and developed into such an articulate spokesman for the antislavery cause that people doubted he had ever been a slave. In 1845 he published his *Narrative of the Life of Frederick Douglass, an American Slave,* naming names, places, dates, and precise events to convince people he had been born in bondage. Douglass continued to be an articulate spokesman for the black cause throughout his life. Shortly before his death in 1895 a college student asked him what a young black could do to help the cause. "Agitate! Agitate! Agitate!" Douglass is supposed to have told him.

**Questions to Consider.** In the following address Douglass was speaking to a convention of blacks in Louisville, but his appeal was primarily to American whites. How did he try to convince them that blacks deserved the same rights and opportunities as all Americans? How powerful did he think the color line was? What outrages against his people did he report? What was his attitude toward the Republican party, which he had so faithfully served? Were the grievances he cited largely economic or were they social and political in nature?

# Address to the Louisville Convention (1883)

### FREDERICK DOUGLASS

Born on American soil in common with yourselves, deriving our bodies and our minds from its dust, centuries having passed away since our ancestors were torn from the shores of Africa, we, like yourselves, hold ourselves to be in every sense Americans, and that we may, therefore, venture to speak to you in a tone not lower than that which becomes earnest men and American citizens. Having watered your soil with our tears, enriched it with our blood, performed its roughest labor in time of peace, defended it against en-

From Philip Foner, ed., *The Life and Writings of Frederick Douglass* (4 v., International Publishers, New York, 1955), IV: 373–392. Reprinted by permission.

**Frederick Douglass.** Douglass's greatest work came before and during the Civil War. One of the most eloquent and magnetic of all the abolitionist leaders, he contributed enormously to the antislavery cause. During the Civil War he pressed hard for the enlistment of blacks to fight in the Union armies on an equal footing with whites. After the war he continued his efforts for civil rights, including black suffrage. For his services to the Republican party he received appointments as secretary to the Santo Domingo commission, marshal and recorder deeps for the District of Columbia, and U.S. minister to Haiti. (National Portrait Gallery, Smithsonian Institution/Washington, D.C.)

emies in time of war, and at all times been loyal and true to its best interests, we deem it no arrogance or presumption to manifest now a common concern with you for its welfare, prosperity, honor and glory. . . .

It is our lot to live among a people whose laws, traditions, and prejudices have been against us for centuries, and from these they are not yet free. To assume that they are free from these evils simply because they have changed their laws is to assume what is utterly unreasonable and contrary to facts. Large bodies move slowly. Individuals may be converted on the instant and change their whole course of life. Nations never. Time and events are required for the conversion of nations. Not even the character of a great political organization can be changed by a new platform. It will be the same old snake though in a new skin. Though we have had war, reconstruction and abolition as a nation, we still linger in the shadow and blight of an extinct institution. Though the colored man is no longer subject to be bought and sold, he is still surrounded by an adverse sentiment which fetters all his movements. In his downward course he meets with no resistance, but his course upward is resented and resisted at every step of his progress. If he comes in ignorance, rags, and wretchedness, he conforms to the popular belief of his character, and in that character he is welcome. But if he shall come as a gentleman, a scholar, and a statesman, he is hailed as a contradiction to the national faith concerning his race, and his coming is resented as impudence. In the one case he may provoke contempt and derision, but in the other he is an affront to pride, and provokes malice. Let him do what he will, there is at present, therefore, no escape for him. The color line meets him everywhere, and in a measure shuts him out from all respectable and profitable trades and callings. In spite of all your religion and laws he is a rejected man.

He is rejected by trade unions, of every trade, and refused work while he lives, and burial when he dies, and yet he is asked to forget his color, and forget that which everybody else remembers. If he offers himself to a builder as a mechanic, to a client as a lawyer, to a patient as a physician, to a college as a professor, to a firm as a clerk, to a Government Department as an agent, or an officer, he is sternly met on the color line, and his claim to consideration in some way is disputed on the ground of color.

Not even our churches, whose members profess to follow the despised Nazarene, whose home, when on earth, was among the lowly and despised, have yet conquered this feeling of color madness, and what is true of our churches is also true of our courts of law. Neither is free from this all-pervading atmosphere of color hate. The one describes the Deity as impartial, no respecter of persons, and the other the Goddess of Justice as blindfolded, with sword by her side and scales in her hand held evenly between high and low, rich and low, white and black, but both are the images of American imagination, rather than American practices.

Taking advantage of the general disposition in this country to impute crime to color, white men *color* their faces to commit crime and wash off the hated color to escape punishment. In many places where the commission of crime is alleged against one of our color, the ordinary processes of law are set aside as too slow for the impetuous justice of the infuriated populace. They take the law into their own bloody hands and proceed to whip, stab, shoot, hang, or burn the alleged culprit, without the intervention of courts, counsel, judges, juries, or witnesses. In such cases it is not the business of the accusers to prove guilt, but it is for the accused to prove his innocence, a thing hard for him to do in these infernal Lynch courts. A man accused, surprised, frightened, and captured by a motley crowd, dragged with a rope about his neck in midnight-darkness to the nearest tree, and told in the coarsest terms of profanity to prepare for death, would be more than human if he did not, in his terror-stricken appearance, more confirm suspicion of guilt than the contrary. Worse still, in the presence of such hell-black outrages, the pulpit is usually dumb, and the press in the neighborhood is silent or openly takes side with the mob. There are occasional cases in which white men are lynched, but one sparrow does not make a summer. Every one knows that what is called Lynch law is peculiarly the law for colored people and for nobody else. If there were no other grievance than this horrible and barbarous Lynch law custom, we should be justified in assembling, as we have now done, to expose and denounce it. But this is not all. Even now, after twenty years of so-called emancipation, we are subject to lawless raids of midnight riders, who, with blackened faces, invade our homes and perpetrate the foulest of crimes upon us and our families. This condition of things is too flagrant and notorious to require specifications or proof. Thus in all the relations of life and death we are met by the color line.

While we recognize the color line as a hurtful force, a mountain barrier to our progress, wounding our bleeding feet with its flinty rocks at every step, we do not despair. We are a hopeful people. This convention is a proof of our faith in you, in reason, in truth and justice—our belief that prejudice, with all its malign accomplishments, may yet be removed by peaceful means; that, assisted by time and events and the growing enlightenment of both races, the color line will ultimately become harmless. When this shall come it will then only be used, as it should be, to distinguish one variety of the human family from another. It will cease to have any civil, political, or moral significance, and colored conventions will then be dispensed with as anachronisms, wholly out of place, but not till then. Do not marvel that we are discouraged. The faith within us has a rational basis, and is confirmed by facts. When we consider how deep-seated this feeling against us is; the long centuries it has been forming; the forces of avarice which have been marshaled to sustain it; how the language and literature of the country have been pervaded with it; how the church, the press, the play-house, and other influences of the country have been arrayed in its support, the progress toward its extinction must be considered vast and wonderful. . . .

We do not believe, as we are often told, that the Negro is the ugly child of the national family, and the more he is kept out of sight the better it will be for him. You know that liberty given is never so precious as liberty sought for and fought for. The man outraged is the man to make the outcry. Depend upon it, men will not care much for a people who do not care for themselves. Our meeting here was opposed by some of our members, because it would disturb the peace of the Republican party. The suggestion came from coward lips and misapprehended the character of that party. If the Republican party cannot stand a demand for justice and fair play, it ought to go down. We were men before that party was born, and our manhood is more sacred than any party can be. Parties were made for men, not men for parties.

The colored people of the South are the laboring people of the South. The labor of a country is the source of its wealth; without the colored laborer to-day the South would be a howling wilderness, given up to bats, owls, wolves, and bears. He was the source of its wealth before the war, and has been the source of its prosperity since the war. He almost alone is visible in her fields, with implements of toil in his hands, and laboriously using them to-day.

Let us look candidly at the matter. While we see and hear that the South is more prosperous than it ever was before and rapidly recovering from the waste of war, while we read that it raises more cotton, sugar, rice, tobacco, corn, and other valuable products than it ever produced before, how happens it, we sternly ask, that the houses of its laborers are miserable huts, that their clothes are rags, and their food the coarsest and scantiest? How happens it that the land-owner is becoming richer and the laborer poorer?

The implication is irresistible—that where the landlord is prosperous the laborer ought to share his prosperity, and whenever and wherever we find this is not the case there is manifestly wrong somewhere. . . .

Flagrant as have been the outrages committed upon colored citizens in respect to their civil rights, more flagrant, shocking, and scandalous still have been the outrages committed upon our political rights by means of bull-dozing and Kukluxing, Mississippi plans, fraudulent courts, tissue ballots, and the like devices. Three States in which the colored people outnumber the white population are without colored representation and their political voice suppressed. The colored citizens in those States are virtually disfranchised, the Constitution held in utter contempt and its provisions nullified. This has been done in the face of the Republican party and successive Republican administrations. . . .

This is no question of party. It is a question of law and government. It is a question whether men shall be protected by law, or be left to the mercy of cyclones of anarchy and bloodshed. It is whether the Government or the mob shall rule this land; whether the promises solemnly made to us in the constitution be manfully kept or meanly and flagrantly broken. Upon this vital point we ask the whole people of the United States to take notice that whatever of political power we have shall be exerted for no man of any party who will not, in advance of election, promise to use every power given him by the Government, State or National, to make the black man's path to the ballot-box as straight, smooth and safe as that of any other American citizen. . . .

We hold it to be self-evident that no class or color should be the exclusive rulers of this country. If there is such a ruling class, there must of course be a subject class, and when this condition is once established this Government of the people, by the people, and for the people, will have perished from the earth.